Why economists disagree

Why economists disagree:
the political economy of economics

Ken Cole
John Cameron
Chris Edwards

Longman London and New York

Longman Group UK Limited
Longman House
Burnt Mill, Harlow, Essex CM20 2JE, England
and Associated Companies throughout the world

*Published in the United States of America
by Longman Inc., New York*

© Longman Group Limited 1983

First published 1983
Third impression 1987

British Library Cataloguing in Publication Data

Cole, Ken
  Why economists disagree: the political economy
  of economics.
  1. Economics-History
  I. Title II. Cameron, John III. Edwards, Chris
  330.1   HB75

ISBN 0-582-29546-7

Library of Congress Cataloguing in Publication Data

Cole, Ken.
  Why economists disagree.

  Bibliography: p. 290
  Includes index.
  1. Economics. 2. Economics-History.
  I. Cameron, John, 1937-   . II. Edwards, Chris.
  III. Title.
  HB171.5.C799   330   81-20908
  ISBN 0-582-29546-7   AACR2

Produced by Longman Group (FE) Ltd
Printed in Hong Kong

Contents

Contents

Preface

From our own initial experience of being taught economics and later of teaching and practising economics ourselves, we came to the conclusion that existing frameworks for the understanding of economic theory and therefore existing means of presentation for teaching purposes (both textbooks and course structure) were inadequate. This led to the development of a new teaching structure for the Principles of Economics course in the School of Development Studies at the University of East Anglia, and subsequently to this book. The presentation of the ideas in this book has already been tried out a number of times and, although there have been teething problems in the development of the course, the results have only served to confirm our faith in the structure as a whole. In particular, economics is not presented as a unified science with a set of fundamental principles. Indeed, three essentially opposed theoretical perspectives are examined, which cannot be synthesised into any single school of thought. Each perspective has to be understood and presented in its own terms as a logical system and it is precisely those chapters in which their specific logic is made explicit which are perhaps the most difficult. The development of economics over time is seen as the outcome of battles between schools of thought to provide acceptable explanations and answer criticism over current issues. Such battles are strongly related to conflicts in the sphere of politics and, as such, economic theory cannot be divorced from political practice. The basic divisions constituting economic theory between various schools of thought are outlined in Chapter 1.

Not only do the ideas themselves reflect our teaching experience but also their form of presentation. Each section of each chapter, except in the case of Chapter 10, is summarised in the form of a 'flow diagram' (summaries). This idea comes from the excellent book by Tony Buzan (1974), called *Use Your Head*. The summaries are intended to show the point of an argument and its main direction by relating concepts to each other *spatially*. When arguments are written down, because of the form of the medium, an argument has to be presented linearly and yet there may be two or more parallel points in the argument. The 'flow diagram' method allows such complex arguments to be presented and has proved useful for teaching and we hope will be as practical in showing the arguments in each chapter. The reason no summaries have been provided for Chapter 10 is that we want the political arguments there to stand on their own without being forced into our logical framework. The arguments involve current political debates and we want readers to make up their own minds on where they stand. For the reader who has persevered with the book this far, the *logic* of the argument should be quite clear, a logic whose intelligibility should be enhanced by the summaries in the earlier chapters. But a word of warning. The summaries are not meant to be self-explanatory and must be understood in conjunction with the text. Indeed, readers may well wish to construct their own summaries and there is no reason why their particular diagrams should be the same as ours. Each summary reflects the particular thought patterns of the reader/writer and her/his previous knowledge and therefore may gloss over or completely exclude some points and emphasise others.

At the end of each chapter we have also given a guide to further reading, except again in the case of Chapter 10. These are not meant to be exhaustive bibliographies but are intended merely to indicate particular references that we have found useful, useless or even worse than useless. The notes on further reading are likely to be especially useful for the chapters which the reader might find more difficult, namely Chapters 3, 5, 6 and 8. The reader is advised not to linger and labour over these chapters, but to read the whole book through once and then to return to these if he or she feels so inclined.

Whenever a book is written by a number of people, it is sometimes of interest to readers to know how the task was undertaken and shared. Despite the three-fold division in the book we are in fact of roughly the same economic and political persuasion. The divisions in the book between three schools were the product of a common dedication to the rigorous pursuit of logic. The early development of the three arguments belongs more or less equally to all three authors with many hours spent especially by Ken Cole and Chris Edwards, checking and tightening the logical links and reading the writings of many economists in the original (or as close to the original as possible) to see how their arguments related to our own. Turning these arguments into a book required steady commitment and the labour of writing.

The commitment throughout and much of the earlier writing came from Ken Cole. Indeed there was a time when it seemed he would write the book on his own. A terrible accident almost cost Ken his life in early 1980, but he fought his way back to work sufficiently by March 1981 to write the final chapter. In this very important human sense, that chapter is the most important in the book. During Ken's illness, the major role in writing the final version of the book was taken over by John Cameron. But, in general, we are happy to take joint credit and blame for the whole book.

Preface

Lastly we would like to thank all those who made the writing of this book possible, especially our loved ones who have had to put up with our being alternatively distraught over some fine point of economic theory and elated over resolving some apparent contradiction. Also all the economics students in the School of Development Studies who have put up with us trying out our ideas on them and our colleagues at the University of East Anglia, Norwich, England and elsewhere who took the effort to comment on our proposals and drafts of particular chapters. Any shortcomings are naturally our responsibility.

Ken Cole, John Cameron and Chris Edwards

Chapter 1

Towards a political economy of economics

1.1 What is economics?

Many people call themselves 'economists' today and thus apparently accept some shared identity. Government departments, large industrial corporations, banks and stockbrokers, trade unions and international organisations all employ at least one person who when asked, 'What do you do?' will reply, perhaps slightly nervously, 'Well, actually I'm the economist', as if this badge of office were so self-explanatory that conversation can now move on to more controversial issues, like which team will top the league (be it baseball, football or ice hockey) this season. However, if the questioner presses the point, then soon this unsuspecting innocent will be buried in a pile of words none of which seem to have the same meanings as they do in common usage. And if this earnest inquirer is masochistic enough to engage another of these self-identified 'economists' in the same conversation, then it is quite possible that these same words will be used, not only in a way different from normal usage, but also in a different context from the first 'economist'.

This can be illustrated by a number of quotes on growth and inflation from 'economists' who have taken special efforts in our own time to make their ideas accessible to a wider audience.

On the analysis of growth:

... a proper analysis of longterm trends in other countries that are sufficiently similar in organisation and orientation for comparison should reveal a variety of growth experience and of feasible institutional changes which may be borrowed with some assurance of their tested contribution (Kuznets 1965: 326).

Differences in investment ratios were found to be inadequate to account for observed differences in growth rates; in any case, the investment differences seemed at least as likely to be a *consequence* as a *cause* of growth... There have been fast-growing economies in both the capitalist and the communist world; and even among Western countries there has been almost no systematic relation between growth rates and degrees of intervention (Brittan 1975: 95, emphasis in the original).

Social productivity is increased continuously by mechanisation and the

division and reorganisation of labour, not in order to satisfy the needs of the
producers, but in order to increase the proportion of the social product
which accrues to capital...(Arrighi 1978: 3).

These quotes may be mystifying in precise content to anybody
totally unacquainted with economics, but a degree of disagreement is
obvious. While Kuznets, Nobel Prize winner for economics, argues for
institutional changes in the economy to promote economic growth,
Samuel Brittan, Principal Economic Commentator for the *Financial
Times* and former Economic Adviser at the Department of Economic
Affairs, sees no systematic relation between growth and investment nor
any case on grounds of growth for intervention in the economy. And
finally, Giovanni Arrighi, a well-known writer on the left of the political
spectrum argues that even where there is growth, its stimulus comes
from capitalists hoping to increase their profits rather than to meet the
needs of the community at large.

On the analysis of inflation we have:

Governments have not produced high inflation as a deliberate announced
policy but as a consequence of other policies – in particular, policies of full
employment and welfare state policies raising government spending
(Friedman 1977: 25).

Private capital, then, faced with a declining profitability [N B: due to
competition between capitalists] attempts to acquire the profits required for
further accumulation by increasing prices.... The increase in the money
supply through the extension of credit and state loans, is the
guarantee...that...commodities will be sold at those prices (Bullock and
Yaffe 1975: 32).

In the absence of deliberate policy and deliberate agreement, which is
likely only through government intervention, there is no determinate
solution. The political atmosphere, the social environment and institutional
factors will mainly determine the rate of the absolute increase in wages and
prices.... It is trade union action which, through wage induced price
movements, has created the basic problem (Balogh 1970: 32).

Thus, while Milton Friedman, another Nobel Prize winner, attributes inflation to government expenditure, Bullock and Yaffe, activists
within the political left in Britain, identify declining profitability
through capitalist competition as the prime cause, and Thomas Balogh,
former Economic adviser to the Cabinet in Britain in the 1960s, blames
militant trade unionism.

Similarly, divergent quotes could be produced for any issue of economic policy. Such disagreements involve questions of definition (what
is inflation?), problems of imputing causality (what *determines* the rise
in prices?), problems of priority (is price stability the *most important*
objective?), and closely related problems of how to test competing
theories (if one economist asserts that wage rises cause prices to rise
and another that price rises lead to higher wages, how can you *judge*
between the explanations?)

The apparent inability of economists to agree on anything has brought the subject into disrepute. Never happier than when gathered together in some educational fortress, preferably with a bar which never closes, these men – women economists still being relatively rare – lurk under the cover of conferences with comforting titles, like 'Conference of the Association of University Teachers of Economics' and the more pithy, less comfortable, 'Conference of Socialist Economists'. Perhaps the kindest act would be to leave these people alone and let them continue their pratices, whose ineffectiveness is universally acknowledged outside the 'ivory towers' of educational institutions. Unfortunately, this option is blocked by their insistence on seeking converts by advertising in the wider society. But unfortunately the advertising violates any Trades Descriptions Act by lulling would-be economists into a false sense of security, since the subject is presented as if there are no *real* differences between the practitioners. To illustrate this point we look at the two introductory textbooks which have dominated the field over the past fifteen years to see how they face the two issues we raised earlier, namely growth and inflation.

First, a quote from Lipsey:

Certain theories have been put forward. One is that periods of very high demand and mild inflationary pressures are beneficial to growth. It is argued that such periods provide the businessman with both the incentive to invest and the funds (which can be withheld out of profits) with which to finance the investment. Another theory says that periods of moderate excess capacity, with an absence of inflationary pressures, are most conducive to growth. The argument here is that when there is some unemployment in the economy, resources for new investment will be readily available, and that innovations in terms of new products or cost reductions in old ones provide the only possible promise of large profits. As yet we really do not know enough to choose between them. (Lipsey 1971: 705).

– and another from Samuelson:

Is there a tendency for price levels to rise even when a sizeable and undesirable level of unemployment persists? If there is such a modern tendency, then policy decision becomes hard and compromises for growth. 'Growth is a prerequisite for reasonable price stability.' 'New mechanisms for an incomes policy must coordinate free collective bargaining.' 'Some price creep may at times be the necessary compromise that must be made in the interest of growth and tolerably high employment.' These are varying views among which citizens and statesmen must today choose. (Samuelson 1967: 77).

So the student after reading 1500 pages of these two texts finds that all the analysis has produced is statements which are either ambiguous or non-committal. But all around the student, people, including those who call themselves economists, are firmly taking positions which show both direction and commitment. At the end of a year or more

3

of studying economics, students cannot be blamed for thinking that they have learned nothing about, and cannot relate to, the rough and tumble of the world outside. Thus, economics can easily seem irrelevant, arbitrary, boring and confusing.

Of course, one possible response is to say that nobody expects to learn a difficult subject in a year, but unless the student is treated with respect at the start, then there is a strong incentive to discontinue the study of the subject or not to treat it seriously. Students know that economists disagree, they see incoming governments bring in their 'own' economic advisers, and in most universities and colleges there are obvious disagreements between teachers, not just on detail but on fundamental principles. And yet texts they are faced with blandly assure them that in many cases of disagreement 'further research could lead to a consensus of option' (Lipsey 1971: 722) and

> The reader who has persisted this far now has a general knowledge of the economic analysis that is used all over the world *sic* – in the United States, Britain, Western Europe, Latin America, Africa and Asia. The tools of economic analysis, developed and tested over more than a century, are turning out to have an applicability beyond the range of economics narrowly defined. In the hands of scholars like Michigan's Kenneth Boulding, they are applied to the pressing problem of conflict resolution and struggle; in countless departments of operations research, and in the Pentagon military establishment itself, they are being used to increase the efficiency of executive decision making. Like a gun, which can be used to defend a home or bully a harmless stranger, these tools have an efficiency whose final contribution to welfare must depend on how they are used and by whom. They also have a certain austere aesthetic grace. (Samuelson 1967: 798).

In contrast, our approach in this book takes both the disagreements among economists and the students' experience of such discord seriously. There are no efforts to paper over cracks here by concealing conflict. Neither do we wish to set up any case as simply a target to be knocked down. In this book, fights over policy are shown to have roots in deep conflicts over the very nature of human activity and, perhaps, over the very nature of science. These conflicts do not merely divide economists, they also run right through contemporary societies. And, as we shall see, the sphere of knowledge we call economics has been peculiarly, but not uniquely, split.

1.2 Defunct economists and practical men

But what, then, is economics? Economics is essentially concerned with *valuation* in its widest sense. Although some economists claim only to present politicians with objective evaluations of the likely outcome of policies, in practice they have found it impossible to stand back from pronouncing on the way to achieve improved states of society. In order to communicate to the politician, the economist must adopt the same basic assumptions about the nature of social activity. For example, the analysis of the 1979 UK budget by some leading economic forecasters predicted that the impact of the budget in the coming year would be increased unemployment, higher inflation, lower economic growth and a rise in an already substantial balance of payments surplus, compared with the outcome if the government had done nothing. But these economists now found themselves in the wilderness, no longer connected with policy decisions, because their whole concept of valuing the state of society by such indicators was called into question by the incoming government, backed by other economists. Essentially, the issue centres on the definition of, and road to, economic welfare. Is the economic welfare of society a *technical* problem, to be measured by technical indicators of economic performance and to be improved by government intervention in society, removing obstacles (both technical and social) to further economic growth (see our earlier quote from Kuznets)? Or is economic welfare, like obscenity, in the eye of the beholder, and crucially dependent upon *individual taste* and, therefore, to be achieved not by state intervention, but by extending the opportunities for free individual choice (see our earlier quote from Brittan)?

Whether or not the economic models of the above-mentioned forecasters are fundamentally wrong is not the essence of our argument. What is most in question are the principles of valuation that give these particular calculations any great significance. And so economists are forced to choose whether to go into the wilderness with principled politicians of similar conviction when power is lost, or stay close to the seat of decision-making by adopting the values of the new incumbent. 'Multi-principled' people may well exist, but history suggests that the distinction between the 'multi-principled', the confused and the unprincipled is difficult to discern. In trying to serve all masters, the economist is likely to achieve the confidence of none; in serving one master, the economist may fail over long periods to achieve any influence or effectiveness in policy-making. Keynes, whose own experience of moving from influence to wilderness and back to influence again gave him good reason to reflect on the relationship between economics and power, wrote at the end of his major work: 'Practical men, who believe themselves to be quite exempt from any intellectual influences are usually the slaves of some defunct economist.' (Keynes 1973: 383). Whilst this thought is comforting to economists out of favour, more worrying, but probably more accurate, is an amended version along the lines: 'Defunct economists are usually slaving to bring themselves to the attention of practical men.'

All the efforts of economists to pass themselves off as a profession standing above the political fray, capable of passing disinterested judgement on the petty disagreements of politicians, have foundered on internal dissension, not on external criticism. In economics, dog does eat dog, but not indiscriminately. There is pack loyalty between dogs

5

of similar breed. Our investigations over the last five years have identified three breeds which form a basis for successful in-breeding, but have never given rise to healthy cross-breeds. In our view, the only link between these three pure breeds of economists is their concern with valuation.

The particular perspective that the economist brings to the understanding of human activity, is a judgement of its worth. This judgement may be only qualitative (e.g. that job is socially unproductive) or relative (e.g. my fee is £50 for that service). Bound up with any judgement of worth is a theory of *how* value comes into existence, i.e. what is the *cause* of value? Armed with such a theory it is possible to *describe* what is happening in society, and to relate events to each other in a causal sequence. This done, the economist implicitly or explicitly prescribes what should be done in order to achieve a worthier state of society. But if the theory should only describe some part of social experience without deriving obvious policy prescriptions, it will be rejected by those who believe in our power to change the world for the better and, therefore, consider themselves *activists*. On the other hand, if policies suggesting a desirable future are not linked to an analysis of the present, the crock of gold will be considered to be unobtainable, and the theory will lose the support of those who consider themselves *realists*. And finally, the links from description to prescription imply the application of reason. We can only agree on action if the outcome of activity is clear. Reason implies an agreed set of rules about the nature of the links and economists have emphasised the rules of logic. Without clear links of reason, the theory runs the risk of inconsistency, thus losing its appeal to those who consider themselves *rationalists*.

A theory which offends realists, rationalists and/or activists is unlikely to gain wide support. All three of our schools of economic thought, however, do meet these criteria for survival. Each point to an area of experience as matching its description, carefully displays the logic of its arguments, and arrives at appropriate policy conclusions.

1.3 The nature of the disagreement

In the past, judgements of valuation and worth were not the prerogative of people called economists, but belonged to other people, often calling themselves bishops and kings. Theology has always concerned itself with value and worth, as has the study of the exercise of law. For economists to gain predominance required a change in society which came with the development of exchange through relatively anonymous markets. The market grants the experience of not being directly governed by representatives of either gods or kings. The extension of markets into more and more areas of life was thus a revolutionary, and in many ways liberating, experience for the mass of people and a threat to vested interests. The expression of this experience in the realm of ideas was a shift towards justifying the valuation of activities produced by markets in the form of prices. But, since those who have the privilege of time to write down ideas are often closest to old vested interests, the intellectual support of the market as an independent source of value was slow in developing.

In Chapter 2 we look at two English writers in the sixteenth and seventeenth centuries, Thomas More and Thomas Hobbes, whose arguments over the moral and political basis of valuation in relationship to the market represent this trend. We then consider mercantilism, the first school of *economic* thought to have a significant influence over state policy, before considering the reaction to mercantilism by vested interests in France in the form of physiocracy. Chapter 2 then moves on to the thought of Adam Smith in the eighteenth century, who raised value as revealed in the market place to a dominant position. Thus Chapter 2 shows how economic theory never completely displaced values in the pew (i.e. moral judgements), but rather raised market valuation to prominence. Thus, the position of economists as arbiters on valuation has never been without challenge from outside and, even though in this book we are concerned with debates between economists, the moral and political spheres of valuation are always implicit. Words like 'liberty', 'dignity', 'alienation', 'authority' and 'control' are inextricably linked in the minds of economists with the central concern with valuation as revealed in the market.

The subjective preference theory of value

Adam Smith identified the market as the arena in which prices appear as the form in which valuations are expressed. But he failed to provide an unambiguous explanation of the origin of value and the determination of prices, even though he generally approved of the free reign of market forces. The missing links between the identification of the market as the primary focus of attention and the justification of free exchange as the means to prosperity have been developed by a series of writers stretching from Smith's time to our own. The common basis of their thinking we have termed the subjective preference theory of value, which is analysed in Chapters 3 and 4. Their starting point is *the individual endowed with tastes and talents and who calculates actions so as to maximise personal welfare or utility*. The individual's tastes define preferences between alternative consumption patterns including leisure. The individual's talents, on the other hand, determine the ability to fulfil these desires through productive activity. Where productivity is increased by individuals specialising in the production of particular commodities, that is by a division of labour, then there is an apparent separation between the individual as consumer and producer. There develops an economic interdependence between individuals necessitating exchange through markets, with relative rates of exchange or prices determined by the relative utility derived by individuals from the consumption of goods and leisure. The decisions to consume and talents to produce are coordinated using a special talent, entrepreneurship, through which productive inputs are combined in order to fulfil the demands of consumers. The owners of the inputs receive a reward determined by the utility derived by consumers from the product, and in turn productive inputs (labour services – or negative leisure – and capital services – or postponed consumption) are supplied according to the reward offered, respectively wages and interest, with enterpreneurs receiving a profit for their central role. Thus, the determinant of economic activity is the maximisation of individual utility from consumption. And, because each person has particular tastes and, therefore, preferences, this can only be achieved for society as a whole if there is free exchange with no individuals entering into a contract to buy or sell unless it is in their own interests. In such an environment, the interests of the individual (personal utility) are reconciled to the wider social interest (the utility of everyone else). There is no fundamental conflict of interest within society, with the ideal form of government being a representative assembly through which a rational consensus can be achieved. And the policy that follows from the analysis is the creation of an environment which allows maximum freedom for individual consumption decisions, with the role of the state being to remove coercion from the market place and enforce voluntary contracts between individuals.

The rejection of active government intervention in the economy is reflected in the earlier quotes from Friedman and Brittan. The values of the free market place reveal themselves as prices to which each individual is at *liberty* to respond independently of the power of the other individuals. Of course, many economists have proclaimed a fundamental confidence in the market process as the best way of ensuring the greatest happiness for all, but desired to qualify that support on some particular issues, perhaps health or education. For the purposes of this text we are primarily concerned with showing the basis of the unifying fundamental confidence. It is a rather daunting thought that, whenever an economist talks uncritically about supply and demand in a market, there is, behind those apparently uncontroversial terms, the assumption of a whole philosophy of possessive individualism and liberal politics. But why did people wait so long to discover this 'desirable' way of organising economic affairs? Human experience up to 1750 appears largely a waste of time if free markets are the key to well-being. The answer, for subjective preference theory, lies in the change of thinking, known as the Enlightenment, which occurred at about that time in Europe and North America. Intellectual energy was diverted towards understanding what we might do on earth now, rather than what we might do to regain a glorious past, or how to reach heaven in the future. By not asking 'why' for some of the time and asking 'how' instead, people have quickly made enormous changes to the physical world and discovered new possibilities in the relationship between individuals and society. The problem with asking 'how' and not 'why' is that knowledge becomes both more tentative as well as more powerful. Making statements about how a market works if left to its own devices assumes that the audience accepts that those statements are likely to apply in the future and in different places.

The point that present knowledge is always tentative is central to the philosophy of Karl Popper, who is something of a doyen among leading subjective preference theorists. His position is that, providing a theory can be exposed to a test of falsification through observation, then the theory can stand as explaining how the observation was generated. His position on the nature of 'scientific' knowledge is consistent with subjective preference theory, because it renders the untestable assumptions about individualism, on which the theory of value is based, unimportant compared with predictions about observable market behaviour. Unfortunately, there is a temptation to cross the line quickly between saying 'the world acts *as if* it were composed of independent individuals', to, 'the world is composed of independent individuals'. But the use of mathematics and its relationship to complex statistical experiments has given subjective preference theory an apparently firm methodological base, in addition to that provided by its philosophical roots. And further, the stated independence of individuals to make decisions in their own best interests means that society is seen merely as the sum of the individuals who compose it.

The problem for economic policy is, then, one of attempting to ensure that the tastes of these individuals can be expressed freely and that their talents can be exercised independently. The market must be allowed to operate unfettered by state intervention except in so far as intervention is necessary to prevent the exercise of monopoly power or to preserve an orderly monetary framework in which the delicate signals about movements in relative prices are not jammed by the background noise of price rises in general. An important part of responsible government is seen as the restricted regulation of the supply of money to prevent inflation.

Thus, society is the product of separate individuals and the government ideally the reflected representation of these individuals. The maintenance of law and order is a political precondition of economic freedom, and economic freedom is a necessary, though not sufficient, condition for political freedom. And since the components of economic freedom are timeless, the analysis of social forces or the historical experience of social development is irrelevant, and economics can be seen as a self-contained *discipline*. Thus, subjective preference theory has a durable strength which goes beyond fashion and the views of particular economists, and can claim an independent existence in its own right.

The Cost-of-production theory of value

To recognise that valuation in the market is significant does not necessarily make it desirable. The optimism over the social benefits of the market system, which developed into subjective preference theory, was countered almost immediately by a profound pessimism which was to give economics the lasting label of the 'dismal science'. This pessimism appeared in Smith's writing as a concern with the psychological impact of routine and monotonous work on the human mind. But David Ricardo, writing in the early part of the nineteenth century, had more serious cause for concern, as we shall see in Chapter 5. Returning to Smith's ambiguous formulation of the theory of value, Ricardo developed an alternative line of argument to that which became subjective preference theory. He started from the proposition that, whilst value appears in the market, it originates in and is determined by decisions to produce, rather than decisions to consume. And making two further assumptions about the nature of the physical world, namely that as the supply of subsistence goods increases, so does the size of the labouring population, and as more land is brought into cultivation, agricultural productivity declines, he reached the conclusion that the operation of free markets leads eventually to economic stagnation, with the mass of the people living at a minimum subsistence level, facing a group of landowners conspicuously consuming the economic surplus. But Ricardo, like Smith, never fully resolved the question of the determination of value, even to his own satisfaction, leading on the one hand through interpretations by Mill and Marshall to the establishment of a cost–of–production theory of value (see Chapters 6 and 7 below) and, on the other hand, to the abstract labour theory of value through Marx and Engels. The hallmarks of the cost–of–production school are:

- a central concern with the production decision;
- the subsequent distribution of output between the 'contributors';
- and the belief that market forces left to their own devices will at best lead to inefficiency and at worst to stagnation.

And it is the material environment and the state of knowledge about how to control that environment, or technology, that form their starting point rather than individual tastes and talents. The prevailing technology dictates what can be produced and how it is produced, and therefore determines the technical division of labour. The technical division of labour in turn necessitates the exchange of products, and the rates of exchange or prices will be determined by the cost of production of each good. But the cost of production of any particular good is not only determined by technical factors such as the quantity of labour time or the amount of a particular raw material required per unit of output, it is also affected by the distribution of the social product between wages and profit. And while there may be a community of interest in the sphere of production to maximise output (since everybody depends upon everyone else in a technical division of labour) the subsequent division of that output will depend upon the relative bargaining strengths of the various interest groups within society, leading possibly to social conflict. Indeed, where the livelihood of whole groups of people is threatened by technical change, there may be sectional opposition to the introduction of new techniques, thereby depriving society of the benefit of higher productivity.

For instance, 'silicon chip' technology offers new opportunities for higher output or higher unemployment, and also higher profits or higher wages. The precise outcome will depend upon the power of vested interests. If the new technology is controlled by a few industrialists or is opposed by the action of a small group of workers, then distributional gains for these people may diminish the advantages to society as a whole. Further, the reallocation of resources upon the introduction of a new technology, for instance the retraining and re-employing of labour displaced by new machines, cannot be safely left to market forces, since, cost of production theory argues, the market forces are always lagging behind the changing production conditions.

But if technical development cannot be achieved by anonymous market forces without risking high unemployment, and is also vulnerable to distortion in the interests of small groups of people, then how can society as a whole benefit from new technology? For cost-of-production theory the antidote lies in pluralist politics through which competing interests can reach compromise, and in a neutral bureaucracy seeking to remove obstacles to technical progress by establishing the appropriate institutional framework to mediate in disputes and promote new ideas and investment. Detailed state intervention in the economy is, therefore, considered as essential, and desirable, a position reflected in the writing on inflation and growth by Balogh and Kuznets, quoted earlier.

While the general principle of cost-of-production theory does show continuity, the precise detail of the theory has changed over time. With new advances in technology comes the need for new social institutions to coordinate the ever-widening division of labour and reconcile conflicting interest groups. Thus, alongside and complementing the cost-of-production theory of value are the pluralist theory of politics and the sociological theories of bureaucracy. Economics is no longer an isolated discipline, but part of a *multidisciplinary* social science. Theory then changes with society, unlike the universalist approach of subjective preference theory.

But for this school, social science itself is also a social institution with its own vested interests, especially as practised in universities, and also possesses the same conservatism that other institutions have when faced with change . This conservatism has received a formal statement in the concept of 'paradigms' put forward by Thomas Kuhn. Broadly, this concept draws attention to the tendency for groups of intellectuals to become totally absorbed in the logical puzzles of a particular theory. When outside change occurs, then the intellectuals have to be wrenched reluctantly back from metaphysical speculation to the problems of the real world and a new theoretical formulation, or paradigm, may become dominant. For instance, the intricacies of a theory suitable for an economy based on steam technology with small-scale firms run by owner-managers will not be suitable for large-scale, multinational, joint-stock corporations operating in the nuclear age. Change and adaptability are, therefore, required, and pragmatism is a virtue, in that reform may avoid confrontation and avert social collapse.

The abstract labour theory of value

Ricardo's lack of confidence in the market system co-existed historically with the development of 'socialism' as a set of ideas and political activities. Smith's positive evaluation of capitalism was being criticised on moral grounds due to the adverse effect on the lives of the mass of factory workers and on political grounds, in that increased repression seemed necessary to maintain the system. It was the work of Karl Marx which linked valuation in the market to the previously utopian socialist critique of capitalism, through what we have called the abstract labour theory of value (see Chs 8 and 9). The rigorous aspect of Marx's thought was to refuse to assume that any aspect of human activity was to be treated as given, e.g. tastes and technology, and yet still manage to say something about the nature of valuation as society changed.

Thus Marx did not start from the individual, nor from technical relations of production. Rather, his thesis was that in every society the material environment is transformed through production into things that individuals wish to use. The type of technology employed will, as in cost-of-production theory, determine the technical division of labour, but it will also coincide with and indeed be based upon a relationship of power over the use of the economic surplus, where the source of that power is the control over the means of production or economic resources of society by a particular group of people or class. The whole structure of production, distribution, exchange and consumption will reflect those *social* relations of production, and therefore economic theory has to be historically specific to these particular conditions.

There are, therefore, two interdependent relationships that have to be taken into consideration; the relation between producer and consumer that results from the *technical* division of labour, through which the material environment is transformed into products for consumption, and the *class* relation between those who control the means of production and, therefore, the use of the economic surplus and those that are dependent upon that ruling class for access to the means of subsistence. One form these relationships has assumed is commodity exchange, by which people relate to each other through markets using money. This particular form became dominant with the rise of capitalism when the majority of the people in society could no longer produce and were forced to gain subsistence through *selling* their ability to work to those who control the means of production. In such a society, both the *technical* relations of production and the *social* (or class) relations of production are expresed through market prices. The abstract labour theory of value is thus a theory of power in capitalist society.

Abstract labour theory, however, is not only historically specific, it is also dynamic. Within any society there are contradictions between the technical relations of production and the social relations of production which provide the potential for social conflict, leading to social change. Under capitalism the dynamic for social change is provided by the competition between capitalists for a share of the economic surplus in the form of profit. Either they have to innovate, or they face bankruptcy. But the drive to increase labour productivity and, therefore, improve the profitability of a particular enterprise creates a tendency for the profitability of capital as a whole and, therefore, the return to capitalists as a class, to fall. This in turn leads to increased pressure by capitalists on the labour force to increase profitability further, a move which only serves to exacerbate the situation. Thus, the apparent paradox between increased output and increasing conflict in capitalist society is resolved, a point of view that lies behind the earlier quotations from Arighi, and Bullock and Yaffe. The abstract labour theory of value, then, is not only a theory of power in capitalist society, it is also a theory of social change within and about capitalism.

Class conflict is therefore fundamental to capitalism, and this cannot be resolved by the action of the state, as in cost-of-production theory. Rather, the state reflects the imbalance of class forces and acts in favour of the interests of the dominant class. Capitalism can never rest on its achievements and is always in danger of destroying itself, but the process of destruction always lays the foundations for a new social order. Note, that central to the materialist rigour of this theory of value, is the argument that nothing comes outside social experience, whether it be God, the Seventh Cavalry or the Bolshevik Party. This raises the question of the policy prescriptions of abstract labour theory. Progress is defined in terms of ever greater control by man over the environment through the development of the technical relations of production, or what Marxists call the forces of production. But control of the environment will only come about when people can control their social relations and, therefore, eliminate conflict created by antagonistic class interests, which in turn will require a *revolutionary* change in social interests. It was Marx and Engels who derided Philosophers for only interpreting the world. The point is, they argued in *The German Ideology* (Marx and Engels 1974: 123) to change it. Certainly, self-avowed Marxists, such as Lenin and Mao Tse-Tung have attempted to do that. Indeed, the test of Marxist theory and its self-justification as scientific knowledge depends upon its effectiveness as a guide to political action. And, clearly, in this context the abstract labour theory of value is part of a more general *interdisciplinary* theory of social change. The notion of 'praxis' expresses this tension between theory and practice, and for the abstract labour theory of value, the praxis has been how to unite working class experience with working class politics. In so far as this project can be judged successful in explaining the development of capitalism through imperialist wars and economic depressions, then the abstract labour theory of value gains credibility. In so far as its adherents have failed to establish a society which transcends commodity relationships, then it still has a long way to go before it meets its own criterion of success.

1.4 To learn one theory of economics is bad enough!

The title of this section is an understandable response to this book as an introductory text. The reader might well wish that we had made up our minds as to the 'best' theory to present, and devoted our limited talents to an exposition of that theory alone. Our answer to this goes beyond the basic credibility criteria of rationalism, realism and activism, and moves towards a more comparitative framework. The ideas of the three schools have not developed in a vacuum but in relationship with each other. Economic theory is essentially a rationalisation of particular historical experiences. It is an attempt to explain and interpret observable data in terms of a causal mechanism or a theory of motivation. Economic theory, therefore, has to be understood both in terms of the historical context in which it is situated, and in terms of the theory of social relations through which this context is understood. It is no accident that economics as a distinct body of thought appeared with the rise of the market economy as the dominant expression of social relations. And it is also no accident that the appearance of the three schools of thought coincided with the rise of industrial capitalism from the mid-nineteenth century onwards. During this time, with the development of the joint-stock company, the principal social relationships within advanced economics today were established, namely between the owners of productive resources (shareholders), the organisers of production (managers, planners, etc.) and labour. And it is our thesis that each of our three theories of value reconstructs economic reality from the point of view of each of these interest groups; respectively, subjective preference theory, cost-of-production theory and abstract labour theory. Thus, each theory can be seen as having a set of core propositions to defend against criticism, barriers are created against attacks and theoretical development proceeds largely internally.

Writers have stimulated and goaded each other into strengthening and developing their theories in particular directions, and the ferocious energy which has been put into debates (which seem somewhat esoteric to the non-economist) can only be understood in this light. History, therefore, is important in this book, but it is *not* a book about the history of economic thought. Rather, history sets the context in terms of which theoretical arguments become intelligible. (For a schematic representation of the development of economic thought over time, see Fig. 1.1) The struggle to advance and prevent retreats from becoming routs *forms* the theories, and as time goes on, the core propositions of each theory are more likely to be explicitly revealed as each school attempts to assert its superiority through the statement of 'fundamental' principles. Thus the understanding of one theory is, we argue, aided by a knowledge of the others.

But even if we have to understand all of these theories, can we choose which is correct? The answer is both yes and no. No, because the core propositions are not amenable to empirical investigation, so that observation is unable to separate the theories. On the other hand, yes, because it might be argued that if the founding assumptions as to the nature of social relations cannot be proved, then at least 'facts' can be collected to determine the relative efficacy of each theory's respective policy prescriptions. However, the choice of which 'facts' to collect requires some preconceptions of where to look and what to look for. This preliminary organisation of the data is in effect a primitive theory, which in turn implies a more sophisticated theory that will resemble one of the theories already available. Observation and measurement do not offer, therefore, an obvious solution to the question of choosing between theories. And yet the theories themselves do not fail the test of logic.

At this juncture the interested reader might be tempted to consider the question of the essential nature of the propositions of each theory as foundations of scientific knowledge. Unfortunately, the term 'science' is as elusive as the term 'economics'. Amidst a philosophical jungle of epistemological bases, ontological statuses and teleological determinations, a student may feel nostalgic for the friendly forest of economics. Our investigations of the theories of knowledge as currently put forward have convinced us that they offer little help in choosing between the three theories of value. Philosophy may provide a precise language for description, but it stops short of giving clear criteria for naming a sub-set of knowledge as 'scientific' beyond the rationalism, realism and activism criteria which all three theories of value meet.

However, in terms of our thesis that each theoretical perspective implicitly serves a sectional interest, *all* theories are correct *in so far as they further such interests*. This immediately raises the question of our own claim to see the divisions within economic theory. This apparent arrogance may well owe something to the personalities of the authors, but has other explanations which situate this book in a wider context. We have already suggested above that as time passes the conflict

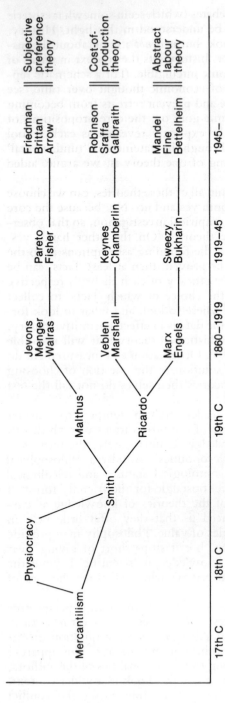

Fig. 1.1.   The historical development of economic theory

between theories becomes more acute, revealing more clearly their fundamental differences. And this is a conflict which mirrors the wider struggle between interest groups in society at large. Further, the progressive worsening of the economic situation in the world in general and in Britain in particular since the mid-1960s has thrown these differences into particularly sharp relief. Politics and their legitimation by economic theory have become noticably more ideological in content in the last few years, compared to the pragmatic reformism of the 1950s and early 1960s. Thus, in time and location, the authors stand in a particularly privileged position, and the arguments in this book are meant to be, in part, a contribution to this debate. In consequence, each theoretical case is presented in its strongest form and, fully to bring home the political significance of each perspective, the last chapter deals with a whole range of policy issues which are currently on the political agenda, but in a manner which explicitly raises the general points of principle involved.

But first, we return to the central concept of valuation, seeing how it shifted towards the market whilst retaining aspects of moral and political valuation which remain with us today.

Further reading

For a useful overview of the three schools of economics and for a good complement to this chapter, the reader is recommended to read Bob Rowthorn's excellent piece published in the 1974 *New Left Review* (see Rowthorn 1974).

Most of the texts which look at one or more of the schools of economic thought place a much greater emphasis on the history of economic thought. The reader is faced with a bewilderingly large choice. Of those written from a cost of production angle, we have found the following to be the most interesting; Barber 1967, Deane 1978 and Routh 1975. Routh is the wittiest and raciest of these, though somewhat confusing, particularly towards the end of the book. Those histories of economic thought written from a more Marxist-inclined point of view, and which the reader is likely to find stimulating are Bernal 1969 (see Ch. 12), Dobb 1973 (see especially Ch. 1), Stark 1944 (see especially pp. 1–8 and 59–76) and Therborn 1976 (Ch. 2). We found all of these, from Barber to Therborn, more useful than Roll 1973, Schumpeter 1954, Shackle 1967 and the somewhat encyclopaedic Blaug 1964.

On Popper and positivism, we recommend Popper 1969 (especially Sect. 2), Kuhn on Popper in Lakatos and Musgrave 1970 and Friedman's essay on *The Methodology of Positive Economics* (Friedman 1953). Other readings in this field which are reasonably clear are Magee 1973 and Stigler 1965 (see Chs 2 and 4). Those by Robbins 1932 and Lipsey

17

1971 are less useful. The clearest of the anti-Popper, anti-positivist views are those presented by Carr 1975, Hollis and Nell 1975 (see Introduction), reading 6 by Jones in Blackburn 1972 and Ch. 2 of Joan Robbinson's *Economic Philosophy* (Robinson 1962). We found the latter clearer than either Ch. 1 of Green and Nore 1977, or Nell's *Economics: the Revival of Political Economy*, (reading 5 in Blackburn 1972).

On Kuhn and the 'philosophy' of the cost of production school, see Chs 4, 5 and 9 of Kuhn 1962, Popper on Kuhn in Lakatos and Musgrave 1970 and Myrdal 1953. The reader may also find Blaug's 1975 article in *History of Political Economy* interesting, if a little nit-picking.

For a brief introduction to the abstract labour theory of value, it is hard to better Marx's preface to *A Contribution to the Critique of Political Economy* (see Marx 1970). But for a discussion of Marx's methodology, it is difficult to find a source which is reasonably clear and brief enough to serve as an introduction. Perhaps the first chapters in each of Fine and Harris 1979, Howard and King 1975 and Godelier 1972 are helpful for this purpose, although Godelier's first chapter is long and somewhat rambling. The reader should also be warned that the book by Howard and King deteriorates rapidly into a Ricardian interpretation of Marx after the excellent first chapter. For a broader, more wide-ranging discussion the student is tentatively recommended to look at Bhaskar's article in Mepham and Ruben 1979. The article is as broad as its title suggests; *On the Possibility of Social Scientific Knowledge and the Limits of Naturalism*, but if the student finds this too difficult, Lenin 1972 will be impossible. For articles against the methodology of Marx, look again at Popper 1969 (this time Sects 2 and 3) and at Ch. 2 of Robinson 1962. Finally, if the student can persevere with Bhaskar and finds it as stimulating as we did, then he or she might want to look at Benton 1977 (first and last chapters) or the earlier, but less satisfactory, Winch 1958.

Summary 1.1

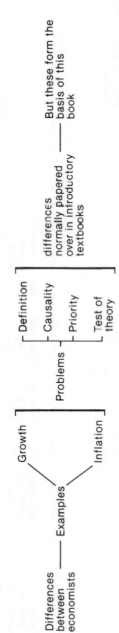

Summary 1.2

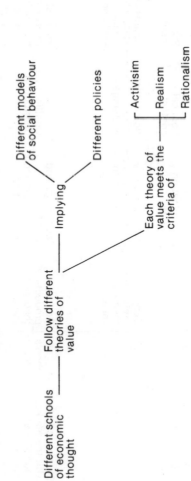

Summary 1.3

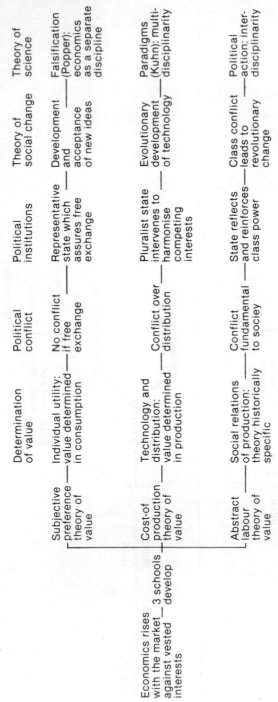

Economics rises with the market against vested interests — 3 schools develop

	Determination of value	Political conflict	Political institutions	Theory of social change	Theory of science
Subjective preference theory of value	Individual utility: value determined in consumption	No conflict if free exchange	Representative state which assures free exchange	Development and acceptance of new ideas	Falsification (Popper): economics as a separate discipline
Cost-of production theory of value	Technology and distribution: value determined in production	Conflict over distribution	Pluralist state intervenes to harmonise competing interests	Evolutionary development of technology	Paradigms (Kuhn): multi-disciplinarity
Abstract labour theory of value	Social relations of production: theory historically specific	Conflict fundamental to society	State reflects and reinforces class power	Class conflict leads to revolutionary change	Political action: inter-disciplinarity

Summary 1.4

Schools develop in relation to each other — Each represents a particular interest — Differences become apparent through political struggle — No agreement on criteria for choice

Chapter 2

Conflict and the emergence of capitalism: from mercantilism to Adam Smith

2.1 Morals, monarchs and markets

As we have said in Chapter 1, it is our intention to encourage the reader from the very beginning to see economics as a historical battle in the realm of ideas in the cause of particular economic interests. Indeed, economics as a distinctive area of knowledge itself appeared as part of such a battle. Feudal society, characterised by a hierarchical structure of control over land where lords maintained their control over the producers, the serfs, by threat of physical coercion, was primarily a system of production for use rather than for exchange. However, with the separation of towns (manufacturing) from the countryside (agriculture) and the establishment of a market economy, new interest groups emerged and economics developed as the 'science' of valuation, replacing systems of valuation founded on morality and power. The decline of feudalism and patronage, and the rise of capitalism in England, a process that took several centuries, generated new divisions in society which found their expression in contemporary writings. There is a complex interplay between morality, politics and economics in these writings, which can be broken down into a few major positions as answers to fundamental questions. Above all, two questions were of general concern. Firstly, how, with the dissolution of authority based on a hierarchical structure, was social order to be maintained; how, in other words, was individual interest to be reconciled to the wider social interest? And secondly, how was economic behaviour in an exchange economy to be judged? These questions can be simply characterised as being about efficiency and equity respectively, but the answers were not, and still are not, simple.

Around 1500, England was emerging from a series of dynastic feuds, which had decimated the aristocracy. At the same time, the fires of the Reformation, a challenge to the political and moral order in Europe, were burning in northern Europe and rapidly spreading west. A hundred and fifty years later this process had advanced significantly though unevenly. In England, a turbulent seventeenth century saw the execution of one King and the abdication of another, whilst in France the monarchy came close to absolute power in that century only to

21

collapse in the eighteenth. Thomas More was an early chronicler of this change and Thomas Hobbes observed the changes in mid-seventeenth century England. They both attempted to come to terms with dramatically changing circumstances by simplifying the complex interplay of moral, political and economic factors into 'ideal' societies.

In 1515, Thomas More published *Utopia* (More 1965) and, in 1650, Thomas Hobbes published *Leviathan* (Hobbes 1968). Neither of these writers were orthodox thinkers in their own times. Indeed, Hobbes suffered from some persecution for his views and More was regarded with much envy and suspicion. However, both reveal the main threads of the economic thought of their times. Also neither were economists, but then, their contemporaries would not have recognised that title. But both have much to say about economic activity as part of their wider perspectives on moral and political issues. It is appropriate for this book that we start with two writers who explicitly acknowledge the links between ethnics, power and valuation in the context of the early development of capitalism.

Thomas More (1478–1535) was a European in his language (he wrote in Latin) and his religion (a staunch Roman Catholic). He came from a merchant, not a noble family and advanced to a prominent position in the English State through scholarly achievement and the law. In 1515, More was sent to Flanders in an effort to remove restraints on the English wool trade and there he wrote much of his book *Utopia*. More was thus in an excellent position to experience and observe economic and social change in Europe. And not only in Europe, for Utopia was published twenty-three years after Columbus's landfall in America and at the beginning of the period which witnessed the plundering of central and south America and the subordination of the non-European empires. The politico-economic centre of Europe was moving from the Mediterranean to the Atlantic seaboard and the first centre of a unified world political economy was being created there at this time and More was a man capable of seeing the possibilities of this shift.

The central problem for More was how the government of society could be arranged to provide everyone with the physiological necessities for life. More critically examines the motivations of monarchs as the embodiment of States and thus the major effective conscious agents of change. Monarchs are assumed to calculate their own advantage in all matters (Machiavelli was virtually an exact contemporary of More's) especially in the making of war and peace. Alliances are made and unmade with the intention of extending the territory of the State to the neglect of domestic affairs. In order to raise finance for wars, kings practise deceit at home by manipulating powers, firstly over currency, secondly over the declaration and non-declaration of war and thirdly over the legal apparatus. Protests that the system can be reformed are met by More with the claim that the only cure for current evils (for More 'evils' seem to be the 'poverty, hardship and worry' of the 'vast majority of the human race') is the complete abolition of private property. The response that people will not work without the motive of personal gain and will resort to violence unless they have respect for authority is not really examined, but partially met by describing a mythical counter-example, the society of 'Utopia'.

Nobility based on landed wealth has no economic or political place in Utopia. In the list of non-productive, unnecessary roles ('necessities and comforts', not 'luxuries', are all that is consumed in Utopia) 'nobles and gentlemen' are explicitly mentioned. Thus, in a society of spartan abundance, which More wanted Utopia to be, the merchant, threatened by statute and competition in sixteenth century England, came into this own as a 'burgher', a respected citizen exercising benign authority over family and community in an atmosphere of tolerance. The standard Utopian work pattern of six hours a day at a craft and an occasional year in the countryside in agriculture would not have been threatening to many merchants whose own experience or family memory of physical labour still would be very recent. Also, confidence in becoming a member of the relatively privileged intelligentsia of Utopia would be highest among such people.

In this vision of the good society, merchants could thus unite with labourers and craftsmen against 'aristocrats' and 'goldsmiths' (who were in the process of becoming bankers). More had chosen sides in the great class struggle which was dividing the new nation-states of Europe internally, at the same moment as they were brought into existence. More chose against the nobility; the monarch could choose to join him or not. Noble patronage was not a protection for the poor and the trappings of nobility did not conceal the fundamental brutality of feudal society.

Thus, More conceived of a world using the production techniques of his own time and place which gave a 'reasonably comfortable' life to everyone, provided society was organised appropriately. But he had one outstanding problem, since 'where money is the only standard of value, there are bound to be dozens of unnecessary trades carried on which merely supply luxury goods of entertainment' (More 1965: 77) More's rejection of money as a domestic means of circulation or representation of value is total, because money has the property that it conceals human relationships and displaces the world of innocent natural behaviour which More primarily values. The pursuit of knowledge and the pursuit of money are treated as alternatives. No longer 'worried about his food supply, upset by the plaintive demands of his wife, afraid of poverty for his son, and baffled by the problem of finding a dowry for his daughter', the Utopian man shared equally in a common wealth.

More, however, saw the importance of 'money' derived from a foreign trading surplus represented by a store of precious metals, in his Utopian commonwealth. This store of specie is the guarantee of the State's integrity, even when held 'in trust' by individuals. The larger the trading surplus, the more specie would be available to the State in times of emergency. The specie is thus not used for local exchange (money is unnecessary in this society with 'wants' limited to 'needs') but accumulated to pay for mercenaries to fight wars against aggressive kings or for bribes to break up threatening alliances. There is even a place for international aid which is given as 'one seventh of total exports', and the rest of the surplus is accumulated as specie. As merchants and their supporters increasingly claimed the moral, intellectual and political leadership of English society in the seventeenth century, it was this idea of the vital importance, i.e. value of international trade which became central to the school of economic thought which has been called 'mercantilism', discussed below in section 2.2.

But if More could envisage a society whose internal harmony was fundamentally a moral order, even though international relationships had to be based on more mercenary considerations, Thomas Hobbes writing *Leviathan* in 1650 had no such consolation to offer. Starting from the assumption that hostility between individuals is inevitable as they struggle for their own ends, Hobbes deduces that there must exist an unquestionable sovereign power in order for any society to survive. So, unlike More's *Utopia*, where at least within a national society there is the possibility of a common interest giving rise to common wealth, Hobbes' *Leviathan* describes a society where relative scarcity forces all to compete for wealth and thus requires a strong authority for any internal civil order to prevail.

In the second part of his book, Hobbes examines how this civil order may be preserved. In Chapter XXIV, Hobbes talks directly about the sphere of economics. His discussion emphasises the absolute right of the sovereign to distribute and redistribute means of production (especially land and international trading opportunities) among subjects, the right to property is thus not absolute, at the discretion of the sovereign. However, the production of commodities and their exchange between subjects beyond this initial distribution is to be based on mutually agreed contract, albeit within a framework provided by the sovereign. Contract is the practical expression of Hobbes' second Law of Nature in which 'men are commanded to endeavour Peace' despite their natural right to seek private ends through war, which is the basis of the first Law of Nature (Ch. XIV). But the preservation of peace is in the hands of the sovereign and cannot simply be left to contractual exchange, there can be no binding social contract between sovereign and subjects, since the existence of such a contract itself denies sovereignty. Also the right of the sovereign to raise taxes is not open to question by the subjects, as it is part of the absolute right of the sovereign over distribution. The coining of nationally circulated money (as distinct from the gold and silver used in international transactions) is itself under the control of the sovereign, but once in circulation, then the sovereign may use force to raise taxes in the public interest from reluctant subjects, especially where concentration of wealth gives some subjects a potential power to challenge the sovereign. Thus, for Hobbes, the organisation of the economy was dominated by the absolute power of the sovereign over the original distribution of wealth, with subjects being free to exchange through mutually agreed contracts. As mercantilism is in some ways the economics of More's *Utopia*, so the school of economic thought called physiocracy has strong connections with the implicit economics of Hobbes' *Leviathan*. Physiocracy is discussed explicitly in section 2.3 below.

Thus, from the very start of the capitalist epoch, the divisions in society found expression in contemporary writings. A complex interplay between morality, politics and economics in the realm of ideas and the connections between ideas, policies and events can be seen. More and Hobbes both saw limitations in private property and mutual contract as the basis of harmonious economic relationships, but their visions of how to overcome those limitations were very different and the actual course of events was different again as capitalism developed. But this does not make either or both wrong in any simple sense, since the thought of such people itself contributed to the events which did take place. A more *objective*, less confused set of ideas was not possible at that time, not because the thinkers were inadequate, but because the material conditions in which they framed their ideas were specific to a particular time and place. It seems bold to suggest that in our own time we have transcended such socio-historical limitations. Indeed, the conflicts, between liberty and authority, private property and common wealth, competition and cooperation, still exist today and are still no further towards resolution.

2.2 Mercantilism and the rise of an English trading interest

We can understand *mercantilism*, like all sets of ideas making prescriptions for the whole of society, as an attempt to present the interests of a particular group, in this case merchants, as the interests of a whole society. But mercantilism is especially significant in that it is the first attempt to formulate a specifically *economic* theory. That is, it is based on a theory of value closely bound up with market price. Hitherto (before the sixteenth century) economics or *oikonomia*, in accordance with its Greek origins, only referred to household management, but now it was applied to society as a whole. Now that social relationships increasingly involved exchange of goods reaching not only beyond the household but over the whole world, then the rationalisations and justifications of particular forms of these relationships had to address themselves to the determinants of the *value* of such exchanges and, therefore, the *rate* of exchange, which in turn would explain the size and distribution of the social product.

Merchants can be defined as the economic agents, who gain a share of the social product by buying goods cheap and selling them dear. There thus has to be some barrier between the direct producer and the final consumer to allow for this margin. Initially, this barrier may be natural, for instance geographical distance, but sooner or later it has to be political. For, as more and more merchants enter into a *particular* trade, each merchant will try to capture a greater share of the market by undercutting competitors. Thus, in trying to protect individual interests, each merchant, by reducing the profit margin, undermines the interests of merchants as a whole. One resolution of this contradiction lies in State-guaranteed exclusive rights of trade.

Thus, on the one hand, merchants *in general* demanded a State strong enough to break down feudal barriers to the expansion of trade, but, on the other, individual merchants sought monopoly privileges over particular trade routes and particular commodities to protect their own profit margins. For all merchants there is a common interest in the expansion of trade in general alongside individual interests in protection. There is the possibility of a theory of value common to all writers supporting merchant interests, namely that value is identified with the ability to exchange flexibility, i.e. control over specie. The mercantilist theory of value, in line with the activities of merchants, identified wealth with power to exchange, particularly control over precious metals. From this it followed that trade for any individual or nation should be regulated to maximise the trading surplus in the form of weights of such metals.

Increasingly in the sixteenth, seventeenth and first half of the eighteenth centuries, the State in west European countries took an active role in promoting trade and, in general, merchants' interests, although this development was perhaps most marked in Britain. This intervention on the one hand took the form of integration of the national economy but, as importantly, the establishment and protection of particular national monopolies in international trade, wherever it was possible to exclude competition, perhaps the most well-known example being the East India Company's trading activities in India. So, with regard to domestic policy, there was continuous pressure throughout the sixteenth century to reduce the power of guilds (largely self-regulating organisations of craftsmen in particular trades) to limit the manufacture of certain commodities through rules relating to apprenticeship and local rights of taxation of commodity movements. But at the international level, the history of Europe between the sixteenth and eighteenth centuries is a succession of wars between nation-states attempting to gain control of trade routes for their merchants: Anglo-Spanish wars over trade routes to the West Indies, Anglo-French wars over the trade routes to India and North America, and the Anglo-Dutch wars focusing on the trade routes to the East Indies.

Thus, Thomas More's comfortable burghers found wealth in a changing society but without the accolade of moral superiority he had predicted. Internationally, merchants actively used the sword and lash to persuade those reluctant to accept the virtue of trade. If the quiet, domestic, ordered life of Utopia was seen in the Bristol merchant's mansion then it was intimately related to the horrors of the slave trade and mutilated bodies on battlefields in four continents. Mercantilism helped push the world towards a bloody unity. Many today would say this was progressive. The eclipse of mercantilism was due as much to the loss of its power to mobilise political support, as its moral hypocrisy or logical flaws.

2.3 Physiocracy and the collapse of French aristocratic interests

In the eighteenth century, the French monarchy had effectively reduced the nobility to courtiers and ruled in absolutist manner through a bureaucracy which constricted the rise of merchant interests. But the opulence of court life and the crippling cost of major land wars left the state constantly short of money. Finance was raised by the selling of posts in the bureaucracy to people from outside the aristocracy and through loans from financiers with large incomes from trade who themselves held office in the Treasury. The other source of revenue was the taxation of the peasantry. But the peasantry were also subject to share-cropping type arrangements by which the feudal nobility appropriated a proportion of the agricultural product, plus numerous local dues, tithes to the clergy, 'corvée' or obligatory labour services supplied to the state for such purposes as road building and, in addition, each area had to supply a quota of men for the army. Thus, on the one hand the monarchy was increasingly losing control of the State to a rising bourgeoisie and, on the other, there was a constant threat of peasant revolt and a decline in agricultural production. The latter tendency was, if anything, accentuated by the experiment with mercantilist policies towards the end of the seventeenth century, notably under a chief minister named Colbert. This experiment discriminated against agricultural producers in favour of manufacturers and traders.

   The real possibility of political revolution which could not be overcome and the existence of continuing economic crisis encouraged the court interest around the monarch to accept ideas which, in an opportunist form, resemble those advocated by Hobbes for the absolute sovereign over the social Leviathan. In these circumstances, Francois Quesnay (1694–1774), a physician to the court of Louis XV who wrote extensively in the field of medicine, at the age of 62 turned his attention to political economy, and in so doing became the leading light in what has come to be known as the physiocratic school of thought. The rationale for a new policy came from a model of the economy he constructed, called the *Tableau Economique*, first published in 1758. The basic assumption behind the model was that there exists a 'natural' social order, analogous to the concept of the natural order that gives regularity and harmony to the physcial world. Except that whereas the latter operated independently of man's will, the former must be based on a conscious desire to let the 'natural' order prevail, in which man would choose to live in the best of all possible worlds. It was Quesnay's intention, through the 'Tableau' to make this natural law explicit, thereby providing a rational basis for an economic policy which seemed conducive to the maximisation of the potential for general economic plenty if individual choice was exercised under the firm guidance of the monarch.

The physiocrats did not subscribe to the mercantilist view that value was synonymous with money and that trading was productive because it yielded surplus specie over what had been expended. Rather, value was defined in terms of the production of *physical* goods and productivity in terms of the production of a physical surplus, that is, the gift from a bountiful physical environment. It was a view that accorded well with the interests of the nobility, whose income comprised a share of the agricultural surplus, and who thus could say their wealth came from God, not from the toiling peasantry.

Essentially, the argument went as follows (see Fig. 2.1); the agricultural product, as the source of all wealth, was initially distributed as inputs back into the agricultural sector (seed, peasants' subsistence, etc.) and then as income to the proprietary class, which included landowners, state officials and the clergy as trustees of the monarch and hence of society. In turn, part of the inputs into agriculture was passed onto the manufacturing sector to be transformed into products to be returned to agriculture (e.g. plough shares) and part of the income of the proprietary class was transformed by the manufacturing sector into goods for consumption.

The policy prescriptions were clear. Economic prosperity depended upon a successful agricultural sector. Consequently, there should be no economic discrimination against agricultural products. Thus, Ques-

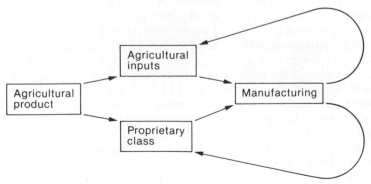

Fig. 2.1   Outline of *Tableau Economique*

nay's policy was specifically directed against the very monopoly privileges that mercantilism supported. Quesnay argued that all trading should be carried out at 'just' prices which would be determined by the free operation of the forces of supply and demand. Further, there should be no hoarding of wealth, since this reduced the flow of resources and, therefore, the size of the economy, a conclusion directed against financiers and merchants who held money in order to make more money. And finally, all taxation should be levied on the nobility who received the economic surplus in rent, and not on the tiller, who should be encouraged to invest as much as possible to increase the size of the agricultural product. This measure, if adopted, would have taken the pressure off the peasantry and reduced social tension, although it is clear from their writings that the physiocrats also had in mind the reorganisation of agriculture along capitalist lines. The monarch, as the only person or institution free from sectional self-interest and who could, therefore, rule according to these precepts, was the linchpin of the whole system.

In terms of economic theory, there were a number of original contributions. Firstly, wealth and, therefore, value could only be increased through investment in production and not in trade or finance. Secondly, they saw the exchange process as subject to laws, which implies on the one hand that the economic system is integrated, recognising the interdependence of individuals within society and, on the other hand, that the operation of the economic system is independent of any one individual save the sovereign, recognising the fact that the social relations of interdependence have taken the form of exchange relations.

At the political level, however, they were less successful than the mercantilists. Their influence reached its peak in the 1770s when Turgot, a physiocrat, was appointed Chancellor to Louis XIV in 1774. But he only remained in office for two years, after which time physiocratic influence declined rapidly, not least because their policy prescriptions adversely affected in one way or another just about everyone; financiers, manufacturers, merchants, landowners and even common people, since free trade in corn led at this time to an increase in the price of bread. By trying to support the *monarchy*, whose position depended upon no particular class being in a dominant-position, they were unable to win the full approbation of any interest group and, therefore, necessarily had little lasting support. More publicised than practised, physiocracy exerted influence on subsequent thinkers, not the social order it attempted to preserve.

2.4 Power to the market?

In Britain, the commercialisation of agriculture was far more advanced by the mid-eighteenth century, as were rural property relations, with land enclosed into large landholdings, often worked by tenant farmers employing wage labourers. The feudal lord-peasant relationship characteristic of France had already ceased to be the dominant relationship in English agriculture by the end of the sixteenth century, and the agrarian situation as such raised neither the same physical nor political questions after that time. The economic organisation of manufacturing in sixteenth and seventeenth century England was, however, characterised by a complex web of restrictive practices. In medieval times, the right to engage in manufacture was commonly purchased individually or collectively from a lord or the crown, and this right was protected from interlopers by strict regulations on apprenticeship and the coercive power of the State. As we have seen, merchants, while seeking the protection of the State against international competition, also sought the removal of obstacles to the easy local movement of goods and thus the creation of a national market, a common legal system and standardised weights and measures. But while the State was relatively sympathetic to mercantile interests with regard to foreign trade, especially as many of the richest merchants acted as financiers to the government, in the British economy successive monarchs still tended to obstruct movement of goods and people in their pursuit of tax revenues and political stability.

To avoid these restrictions, a 'putting-out' system of manufacturing developed, mainly in rural areas to avoid the guild statutes of the towns. Merchants would supply raw materials to craftsmen who worked in their own homes, returning later to collect finished goods and supply more raw materials. Often this relationship was maintained by the indebtedness of the artisan to the merchant. But these changes were not smooth; putting-out was attacked with varying degrees of success, with only in some areas urban guilds being subordinated to trading companies leading to a relaxation of trade restrictions. Merchants were joined by relatively prosperous craftsmen attempting to expand their activities by employing poorer craftsmen and moving into trade, who therefore also wished to sidestep the guild regulations on restricted entry, which operated to the advantage of the independent artisan. Further, an increasing number of new technologies developed which required relatively large investment and could avoid the restrictions of conventional guilds; for instance, iron smelters and the newer, deeper coal mines. The circle of interests which were thus obstructed by existing individual and collective privileges was widening and the antipathy of these growing sectional interests to particular restriction found a common front in a general movement against monopoly.

At the centre of these developments lay the emergence of a new economic relationship; that of wage-earner to employer. The nature of the technology in manufacturing industry still on the whole closely resembled methods developed within the guild system, and the industrial revolution was yet to leave its mark, but the *control* of technological change had shifted. The means of production (raw materials, tools) were *owned* by a new class of capitalists, who *employed* labour, and not by the craftsmen themselves. The economic surplus, which might have been used by the independent producers for their own consumption, was appropriated by the capitalists through contract in the form of profit and used to put other labourers to work, yielding greatly increased output which often necessitated the active search for markets. The rallying-cry of the rising manufacturing capitalist class as a whole was that of free trade, although, of course, this demand was suitably modified by particular capitalists in furtherance of specific sectional interest. Thus, the political motivation for such a movement came from the emergence of a distinctive class of manufacturers, and its theoretical rationale came from Adam Smith (1723–1790).

The question of free trade again brought to the fore the relationship between the individual and society, between self-seeking and altruism, between conflict and cooperation. In this *Theory of Moral Sentiments* published in 1759, Smith argued that for people to live in society as free individuals, there must be an element of perceived common interest in order to make social life tolerable and possible. But this common interest was not to be found in More's universal altruism or Hobbes' unbridled self-interest mitigated by fear of a sovereign power. In common with the physiocrats, some of whom he knew personally, Smith believed in a system of natural law through which the individual was reconciled to society. The hand of God was present in the world and could be discovered through empirical regularities which were the expression of these natural laws. And these laws acted as a ladder between the reflecting individual (cf. More) and the punishing society (cf. Hobbes). The first step on the ladder is self-judgement. We have a capacity for internal reflection which informs us when an act done to another would be unpleasant if the roles were reversed. A second step is when the judgement of other people is brought to bear on us, confounding any capacity for self-deceit. In society such judgements become a code of behaviour, so that social morality, the perception by all individuals that it is in their own interests to conform, becomes the third step. The fourth step is the power to punish those who do not conform to the generally accepted norms, although individuals still possess the right not to conform depending upon their estimation of the benefits of an action and the cost of punishment. The argument runs from the individual to society and ideas of morality and power are no longer separated, but are the products of the experience of active people pursuing their own ends.

But with regard to the operation of the economy, what is this social morality or natural law, the observance of which ensures that private gain is not at the expense of social advancement? Or perhaps the first question should be, how is the economic development of *society* dependent upon *individual* economic behaviour? For Smith, wealth was not synonymous with the accumulation of money, as in mercantilist theory, but was dependent upon the ability of labour to transform the natural environment into products for use. In *Wealth of Nations*, which was published in 1776 after some ten years of preparation, Smith argued that an increase in wealth depended upon an increase in the physical productivity of labour, which in turn depended upon an extension of the *division of labour*, most simply seen as craftsmen becoming more and more specialised in the production of particular goods, but more significant when labourers are required to only repeat very specific tasks. Undoubtedly, this thesis was based upon the experience of the emerging manufacturing industry where the work was still being organised into a number of separate processes (see Smith 1974: Bk 1, Ch. 1). The problem is then clearly that as labourers become more and more specialised, they also become more and more dependent upon each other for the products they consume. A carpenter depends upon, not a cobbler, but several specialised labourers for shoes, who depends upon, not the baker but other specialised labourers for bread, and so on. Individual gain cannot be simply associated with social position or individual effort and cannot be separated from social prosperity. Smith asked the socially obvious question, how can a large number of interdependent individual economic decisions be coordinated in order to achieve the maximum benefit for society as a whole?

The extension of the division of labour requires that individuals enter into exchanges to obtain the other commodities they desire to use. And the more people who can engage in exchange, the more can each specialise and thus the more products will be available for the group to divide out in total. Therefore, the division of labour is related to the extent of the market and the size of the market is related to the amount of commodities and number of people coming together to exchange. But to ensure the maximum extension of market relationships and, therefore, of the division of labour, what should be the basis of such exchange – might there be a natural law by means of which social production can be reconciled to private consumption?

To answer this question, Smith had to consider the factors which determine the rate of exchange or price relationships of products. To understand Smith's theory of value one point must be made clear. In discussing the increase in the wealth of a nation, he was concerned with the physical *productivity* of labour, the amount of any product produced within a particular time period by a labourer. This goes beyond the physiocrats who only considered the physical *product* and, identified agricultural production as the primary source of all goods and, therefore, as the only productive activity. Thus, for Smith, labour is the most important natural resource and, agriculture and manufacturing are productive activities in that they involve physical goods being produced by labour. Service industries, on the other hand, are non-productive, since there is no physical product (see Smith 1974: 430).

Smith's position on the determination of value, however, was ambiguous. He never fully resolved whether the value of the goods produced was determined by the labour time taken to produce them, or the value of the labour time given by the number of goods produced.

If value is determined by the labour time required for production or labour *input*, then profit, the return to the capitalist or, in Smith's terminology, the owner of stock who supplied the raw materials and subsistence of the labourers (wages), is a *deduction* from the product of the labourer. 'The value which the workmen add to the materials, therefore, resolves itself in this case into two parts...wages...profits' (Smith 1974: 151). And in agriculture, where there is also an additional gift from nature, '... rent makes the first deduction from the produce of the labour which is employed on the land...profit makes a second deduction' (Smith 1974: 168). This, in turn, is consistent with the statement 'In every society the price of every commodity finally *resolves itself into* some one or other, or all of those three parts, [wages, profit and rent]' (Smith 1974. 153, emphasis added) (see Fig. 2.2).

Alternatively, if the value of labour is equivalent to the physical products produced by that labour, then the way is open for stock to be productive in its own right, thereby avoiding the awkward (for Smith) political conclusions that follow from the first argument. That is exploitation of labour by the capitalist, who only receives profits due to an unjustifiable deduction from the product of labour. The more comfortable alternative analysis is that stock, land and labour are independent sources of value combined together in the production process to produce goods. Thus, in so far as the input of labour is responsible for the final product, wages are paid, and in so far as stock is responsible, profit must be paid to bring stock into that employment. The value of the good is then greater than the labour input and, therefore, the total cash realised from the sale of the product would be naturally greater than the wages component, so that, if all that cash were used to employ more labour, the amount of labour thus *commanded* or bought, would be greater than the original labour input into the commodity. 'The real value of all the different component parts of price...is measured by the quantity of labour which they can, each of them, purchase or command' (Smith 1974: 153). This is the labour *commanded* theory of value, as opposed to the earlier labour *input* theory of value. Although the two theories of value appear side by side, it is the labour commanded theory with its implied rejection of exploitation of labour which forms the basis of his analysis of the determinants of the wealth of nations and, thus, is more important for Smith. To consider this analysis, Smith looked at how the price mechanism guides individuals

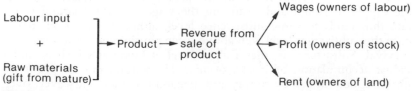

Fig. 2.2   Smith's labour input theory of value

to allocate resources to the greatest social advantage. Smith distinguished two types of price: natural price and market price. The former was never satisfactorily analytically defined, but corresponds statistically to an average price for the product. 'The natural price...is...the central price, to which the prices of all commodities are continually gravitating' (Smith 1974: 160). Market price differs from natural price according to the dynamic forces of imbalanced supply and demand. Where demand is temporarily greater than supply for a commodity, consumers will bid that price up so that market price (Pm) is greater than natural price (Pn). This in turn implies that one or more of the inputs into production (labour, stock, land) are receiving more than their average (wages, profit, rent). If, for instance, it is rent that is relatively high because land in that use is in short supply, then more land will be allocated to producing that commodity by landowners in the belief of a higher individual income, production will increase and the Pm of the product will fall towards Pn. On the other hand, if the commodity is in temporary excess supply, capitalists, to dispose of their extra stocks, will have to lower the price and at least one of the inputs will, therefore, receive less than its average return. That input, say stocks of raw materials, will, therefore, look for employment elsewhere at the higher average profit rate, and consequently output of the commodity will fall and the Pm rise towards Pn.

Notice that the adjustment of Pm towards Pn depends upon the re-allocation of productive inputs motivated by the self-interest of the owners of those inputs. The natural price of a commodity, therefore, 'is neither more nor less than what is sufficient to pay the rent of the of the land, the wages of the labour and the profits of the stock employed in raising, preparing and bringing to the market [the commodity] according to their natural rates...The commodity is then sold precisely for what it is worth' (Smith 1974: 158). The reallocation of resources achieves the lowest price for the product, whilst each input receives as high a reward as it could in any occupation.

To solve the riddle of the natural market price, Smith tried to fix the natural rewards to each input which, when multiplied by the quantity of input used, would give in total a natural price for all commodities. In the labour market, the supply of labour depends upon the size of the population, and Smith assumed that men, like all other animals, reproduce in proportion to the means of their subsistence. Thus, when there is excess supply of labour and the wage rate is bid down, the resulting poverty will discourage marriage and procreation, eventually reducing the supply of labour and steadying the wage rate. The natural wage rate thus tends to some subsistence level, although education might raise this subsistence level well above some physiological minimum for survival. Subsistence is, therefore, a level of living at which no individual accumulation of stocks occurs. The natural rate of profit is, likewise, determined by supply and demand for stock. However, over time, if the total stocks of a particular society increase with continuous investment in production, for instance advancing subsistence to many labourers employed in a complex division of labour, the natural rate of return on stock, or profit, will exhibit a long run tendency to fall. But his theory of profit seems somewhat lacking in rigour, and he had even greater problems with the theory of rent. 'Rent...enters into the composition of...price...in a different way from wages and profit. High or low wages and profit are the causes of high or low price; high or low rent is the effect of it' (Smith 1974: 249). There seems, for Smith, to be no element of *extra* cost involved in the payment of rent, which makes it unable, within the labour commanded theory of value, to be a part *cause* of price. The explanation of profit and rent within a *labour commanded* framework had to wait another 100 years or so for the development of subjective preference theory (see Ch. 3) but Ricardo was to attempt the reconciliation within a *labour input* framework early in the nineteenth century (Ch. 5).

We are left, then, with natural price being some sort of average price resulting from the operation of the forces of supply and demand, from the competition of individuals trying to maximise personal income. This lack of analytical precision would certainly not satisfy an economist today, but Smith's concern was less to show how prices were fixed, but more to answer critics who claimed that markets left to their own devices produced prices that were unstable and erratic and, therefore, allocated productive resources in an arbitrary manner. Smith set out to demonstrate that although market prices did move, these moves were due to changing economic circumstances and the outcomes were to the benefit of society, and required no direct government controls.

But Smith had no wish to abolish government altogether. Rather he was a sympathetic and complacent observer of the British political status quo, suggesting reforms which were attractive to many contemporary politicians. For instance William Pitt, the British Prime Minister in the revolutionary years at the end of the eighteenth century, praised Smith as an advocate of good management rather than condemning him as a revolutionary. Certainly Smith was in favour of a reduction in State expenditure in those areas which he considered counter-productive to the process of accumulating stocks, but law and order, transport projects and even elementary education were legitimate areas for government intervention. His definition of productive labour (the production of a physical good) logically seemed to condemn the sinecures and privileges of large numbers of people receiving incomes on the fringes of government, although he accepted such income in later life. The conspiracies which traders and manufacturers entered into to keep prices high were only effective when backed by the State and enforceable through law and the suggestion that the State should abolish rather than create such monopolies, did have a radical sound in its attack upon the vested interests of established merchants. However, events at Smith's time, such as the loss of the American colonies and the scandals surrounding the East India Company, were demonstrating very clearly and much more practically the limitations of the mercantilist position to contemporary politicians.

But even in this field of international economic relations where Smith was scathing in his attack on mercantilist ideas, he still recognised the need for government activity. The Navigation Acts of the seventeenth century restricted colonial trade with Britain to British ships, but Smith in his attack upon the cruder bullionist theories of mercantilism, which virtually raised the hoarding of gold and silver to a desirable end in itself, still did not oppose the Navigation Acts, seeing them as a necessary piece of legislation to increase the wealth of the British Isles. In the debates of his time Smith may have favoured freer international trade but tempered by the recognition that political economy was centrally concerned with increasing the wealth of one's own nation, not all nations, and Smith accepted this increase in wealth required considerable national 'defence' forces.

So, Smith's idea of laissez-faire government, rather like it had been for the physiocrats, gave plenty of room for a sovereign to undertake the defence of personal and national liberty. Therefore, the question remains; in whose hands should such power be vested? Smith then took his economic categories into the realm of politics to evaluate their suitability. Firstly, labourers in general had an interest in social progress. They had nothing to lose, and indeed might have something to gain if they could obtain some of their productivity increases through higher wages by improving their weak bargaining position with employers, certainly over the short term before the population, and hence the labour supply, expanded in response to higher standards of living. But Smith considered them to be insufficiently educated or articulate to express their own interest non-violently and, therefore, responsibly wield power.

In contrast, profit-receiving capitalists, whether they were traders or manufacturers, were considered by Smith as much more dubious as a progressive force in the political arena. In so far as they acted wisely and ventured their property in productive enterprises, they were worthy of economic reward. But when they applied their joint energies to manipulating market prices as they were always tempted to do in small groups, then their reward was at the expense of society's well-being. And even more damning was the general association of economic development with the accumulation of stocks and the resultant decline in the rate of profit which gave capitalists a material interest as a whole class in arresting the associated fall in natural prices. Thus, somewhat paradoxically Smith appeared to come to the conclusion that we should be in favour of capitalism but against capitalists.

Finally, landlords, Smith concluded, had a collective material interest in the increase of the wealth of the nation. For, as population grows, the demand for agricultural products will increase, leading to an upward pressure on agricultural prices and thus increases in land rents. In addition, because landlords were an educated section of society, they

would be enlightened and able to rule responsibly. Progressive government could be left in the hands of the landowning aristocracy. Such
a conclusion would not have worried the British Parliament of Smith's
time and the French revolutionary slogan of 'liberté, egalité, fraternité'
found only a very muted and politically acceptable echo in Smith's conclusion as 'freedom of contract, equality before the law, wide division
of labour'.

What, then, has been Smith's legacy to economic theory and policy?
Both his lack of rigour as to the determination of relative prices and
the historical specificity and convenience of his political conclusions
have already been noted. Firstly, by formulating the labour commanded theory of value, he raised the idea that value was not *determined*
by the amount of labour that went into producing the commodity,
which implied a primary role to labour, but relegated labour to a *measure* of the value produced by the combination of three independent
inputs: labour, stock and land. Thus, the value of a good was measured
by the amount of labour that could be bought by *selling* the commodity
– that is, by what people were willing to pay for the product and for
what wage rate people were willing to work. But he still focused his
attention on production, not consumption, that is, on the natural prices
of the independent productive inputs and found difficulties, especially
over the determination of natural rates of profit and rent. But as we
shall see in Ch. 3, a theoretical perspective which starts from what people are prepared to pay or to accept for a commodity (be that commodity a finished good or a productive input) has to develop a theory
of the valuation of commodities in *use* or in *consumption*. The logical
outcome of this trend is to stress individual choice within a framework
of markets regulated by competition, with the valuation of commodities determined by the particular subjective tastes of the individuals
concerned.

David Ricardo developed his fundamental economic principles from
Smith. But as we shall see in Chapter 5 Ricardo rejected the labour
commanded approach and instead pursued Smith's question about rent
and profits by stressing the labour input theory of value which Smith
had never quite rejected. He also, however, failed to resolve the problems but in doing so, provided the formal foundations for two rival
theories of value; cost-of-production theory (see Ch. 6) and abstract
labour theory (see Ch. 8).

Cost-of-production theory, like abstract labour theory, keeps from
Smith an emphasis upon the division of labour as the centre of economics. But for cost-of-production theory, production is seen as a *technically ordained* set of relationships in the workplace, so that market
relationships are temporarily suspended or superceded. The value of
the product when produced is determined by the inputs required in
production and the prices of inputs. These input prices are not simply
the outcome of market relationships, but include considerations of relative power between owners of inputs. A successful society is not

found in the mind of individuals enjoying freedom, but instead is seen (as Smith might have also seen) as a large population employed in ever more complex production units achieving ever greater levels of output under the guidance of an educated elite who moderate struggles over distribution.

In contrast, abstract labour theory focuses on the *social* relationships inherent within a division of labour, identifying the sectional interests which motivate economic behaviour and the social conflict which results from their incompatibility. Thus, a state of society which is favourable to capitalists may be judged undesirable by labourers whose wages are low, their future insecure and their minds depressed by routine, as Smith himself pointed out. Valuation is, then, largely the result of political struggle in which opposing classes find expression, a struggle in which nobody can be a referee or a mediator.

Thus, in a theoretical sense, all modern schools of thought can, and do, trace themselves back to Adam Smith, the 'father' of economics, although each stresses aspects of Smith's writings in a particular way. Perhaps if the 'real' Adam Smith were to stand up, then nobody would recognise him, although all would still claim to be his offspring. It is perhaps this confusion which makes Smith the first 'real' economist, not the certainties. But he must be given credit not only for his breadth of investigation, embracing explicitly the moral and political implications of his work on price formation, but also his methodological breadth attempting to combine analytical rigour with careful attention to historical detail. In these areas certainly we can all learn from Smith.

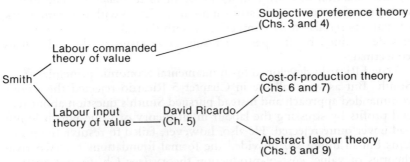

Fig. 2.3   Smith's theoretical legacy

Further reading

There is no substitute for reading the works of great social thinkers as close to the original as possible. Firstly, they are often an antidote to the arrogance that serious thinking only began in the twentieth century, but also they are wiser, more complex and more human than modern attempts at summary (including our own). We recommend the relatively easily available (in the United Kingdom anyway) editions of More's *Utopia* (More 1965), Hobbes' *Leviathan* (Hobbes 1968) and Smith's *Wealth of Nations* (Smith 1974). More's book is very readable in this edition and, whilst the image of the world tends to the ideal, it is very much the mercantilist ideal. Hobbes' book is a massive cathedral compared with More's simple chapel, and only parts of Part II are immediately relevant here, but the ambition of his project may attract some readers to other parts of his book. The edition of Smith recommended leaves out his policy recommendations, but the major analytical points are contained in Chs. V to XI of Bk 1, and the introduction by Andrew Skinner does put the book into its wider intellectual context, including Smith's own writing in *The Theory of Moral Sentiments*.

Having looked at these originals, the reader can go in three directions. The first is towards modern attempts carefully to synthesise the essentials of mercantilism and physiocracy. On mercantilism we recommend Ch. 1 of Buck 1964 and the introduction to Coleman 1969. Physiocratic thought is explicitly dealt with in Deer 1939 and Meek 1962 and Meek 1968. The second is towards attempts to summarise the enormous changes which were occurring in the United Kingdom and France. The parts of books we would recommend are, Part 1, Ch. 4 of Anderson 1974, Chs 1–3 of Dobb 1963, the pieces by Dobb and Hobsbawm in Hilton 1976 and Hill 1969. These are all written from a Marxist perspective, which broadly sees the period as one of a transition from feudalism to capitalism with the formation of new economic classes producing fundamental repercussions in the realms of politics and ideas.

The third direction is one which tends to reduce mercantilism, physiocracy and Smith to steps in the development of economic thought This applies least to Stark 1944: 1–35, which explicitly links the concept of a transition to capitalism to the development of economic thought. Other texts on economic thought, such as Barber 1967, Dobb 1973, Roll 1973, Routh 1975 and Therborn 1976, all contain sections on at least Smith, but we really urge the reader to spend some time reading Smith, preferably in a lowland Scots accent.

Summary 2.1

```
                    Rise of the market        Resolution of
                    economy and new ——— individual and ———
                    vested interests          social interests
```

Summary 2.2

```
Mercantilism ——— Expression of      ——— Merchants' surplus from ———
                 merchants' interests      buying cheap/selling dear
```

Summary 2.3

```
                                  By selling posts        Increases
                                ┌ in the bureaucracy ——— power of ┐
                                │ + loans                 bourgeoisie │
Physiocracy ——— French monarchy ┤                                    │
                raise money     │                                    │
                                └ By taxation    ——— Increases threat ┘
                                                     from peasantry
```

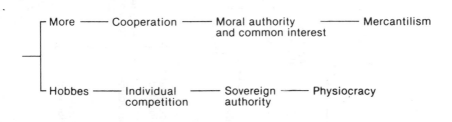

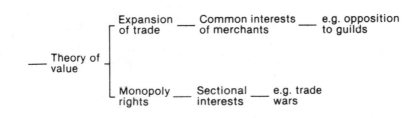

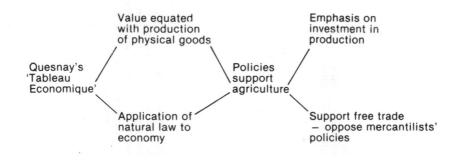

Summary 2.4

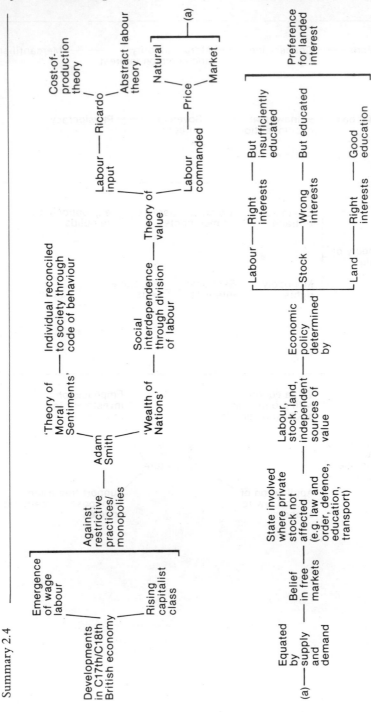

Chapter 3

Freedom is the market:
the subjective preference theory of value

3.1 From labour commanded to subjective preference theory

When Adam Smith's book *Wealth of Nations* was published in 1776, production was characteristically carried out in small workshops where the skill of the individual labourer was important. The widespread systematic application of inanimate power and machinery to production, so that the activity of the labourer was governed by the work rate of the machine, was yet to occur. It was rather against the background of the European Enlightenment's nationalist humanism that Smith attempted to reconcile the principles of individual conscience and right to personal liberty, placed on the agenda by the English revolution of the seventeenth century, with the achievement of social harmony and justice. For those economists who see the essence of our present society, not in an Enlightenment, but in an 'industrial revolution', this is a crucial limitation on Smith's insights.

In the nineteenth century, there certainly were dramatic events associated with the growth of the manufacturing industry, which put Smith's ideas into abeyance. These included the increased use of machinery and the concentration of labour in large factories, and the associated creation of a national trades union movement as one of the expressions of a politically organised working class in Britain. Economic demands for shorter hours, higher wages, better working conditions and the restriction of child labour, were closely linked to political demands for the extension of the Parliamentary franchise and the development of various theories of socialism. The intellectual support for this movement in economics derived from radical versions of the labour input theory of value with its tendency to attribute the worth of a product solely to the labour which had been employed in manufacture. David Ricardo (see Ch. 5) analytically honed this approach to valuation into a double-edged sword in the early years of the nineteenth century, capable of being used later by reformist socialists and liberal manufacturers, not only against the last remnants of the aristocracy and absolutist monarchies, but also against each other. As the combat between the bourgeoisie and the working class moved to the centre of the formal political stage in the latter part of the nineteenth century with identifiably working class struggles throughout the industrialising world, economics broke apart into the three distinct theories we see today, and Smith's labour commanded theory re-emerged as the basis for the defence of conservative interests.

Thus, between 1776 and 1870, Smith's labour commanded theory was largely eclipsed by the dominance of Ricardian economics and underwent little active development. However, the changes it did undergo were significant in reversing Smith's conclusion about the progressive role of the labourer as opposed to that of capitalists and to strengthening the emphasis on consumption as the determinant economic activity. In Britain writers like Bentham (1748–1832) and Malthus (1776–1834), virtually contemporaries of Smith, helped give some credibility to the idea that value arose at the point of consumption, not at the point of production. However, the confusions they caused were as great as their contributions, Bentham because he insisted on the measurability of consumer satisfaction as an assumption of his theory; Malthus because he used this idea to justify the existence of landowners because they consumed without producing themselves, i.e. they commanded others' labour to be put to work which would otherwise have been left unemployed. Both these writers also left an inheritance which is now something of an embarrassment to subjective preference theory. Bentham concluded that as all human beings have a roughly equal capacity for pleasure and pain, therefore equality in consumption was desirable for the greatest happiness of the greatest number. Malthus concluded that since the mass of human beings are irresponsible begetters of children, that massive inequality in consumption is both inevitable and desirable. In our time it is interesting to note that Bentham's conclusion is apparently the greater embarrassment to economists of the subjective preference school.

Less ambiguous contributions were forthcoming though. In France, Jean-Baptiste Say (1767–1832) gave Smith's ideas to a post-Revolutionary France cleansed of their pre-Revolutionary Physiocratic origins. Say argued more explicitly and forthrightly than Smith that the worth of a good depended upon the value of the good in use. This value was indicated by the amount of alternative commodities that would be voluntarily exchanged for a single unit by its individual owners. He also concluded that since every transaction involves a buyer and a seller, then if all transactions are voluntary, the desired supply and desired demand must be equal. He used this argument to place values on productive 'agents', or inputs, which he categorised into industry (or labour) which received a wage, capital which received interest and land which received a rent. In the act of production these three 'agents' would be combined by an entrepreneur who would receive 'profit' as a combination of rewards for the use of own raw materials (a share of interest), own land (a share of rents) and own organisational skill (a wage for a particular type of industry or labour). Thus, according to

Say, value is not intrinsic to a commodity, and all productive inputs are placed on an equal footing, each being paid what they are worth in terms of demand for them derived from usefulness in final consumption. This conclusion removed the conflict of interest between the various classes of income receivers which had concerned Smith.

In Britain, Nassau Senior (1790–1864), a lawyer who became a professor of Political Economy at Oxford in 1852, went one stage further in the theoretical justification of interest as a form of economic reward, by arguing that the supply of capital was the result of abstinence from consumption, or saving. A process every bit as painful as labouring and, therefore, deserving of a reward, not only because it gave pleasure through helping produce goods demanded for consumption, but also because it cost pain in being supplied. Whilst Senior's economic theory gave the appearance of even-handedness, his political activities were much more partisan. On the Poor Laws (legislation on unemployment), the Factory Acts (basically legislation on hours of work) and on trade unions' rights, Senior came down solidly against working class interests.

This combination of classless theoretical economics and divisive practical politics is perhaps the inevitable conservative response to a challenge. For instance, both mercantilists and physiocrats could argue, when attacked, that legislation enacted in the interest of one group was in the interest of all. In 1871, bourgeois Europe had been shaken by the first explicitly working class revolutionary challenge to the legitimacy of its rule, in the form of the Paris Commune. It is perhaps not surprising, therefore, that the 1870s also produced the rebirth of Smith's once revolutionary labour commanded theory of value in a form suitable to defend the bourgeois order against the socialist offensive by claiming that this order was essentially classless and, further, that this claim could be scientifically substantiated. Smith's project to reconcile the pursuit of individual self-interest with social harmony was now revived to demonstrate that 'class' need not be a central analytical category of economics. But now this project was to be expressed in mathematical terms and thus gain both the credibility and mystique of a science.

The widespread socialist challenge, rather than the international exchange of knowledge, helps explain why William Stanley Jevons (1835–82), a British economist, Carl Menger (1840–1921), a professor of economics in Austria-Hungary and Leon Walras (1834–1910), professor of economics in Lausanne, Switzerland, all published books in the early 1870s, expositing ideas which were apparently worked out independently, and yet which bear a striking similarity. For all three writers, as for Smith, Say and Senior, commodities have value because they are wanted, and wanted because they have usefulness (technically named 'utility') for individuals. For any individual the intensity of the want for an *additional* unit of a good declines as more of that good is consumed relative to others, since each additional unit is assumed to be less useful to the consumer than the unit before. The intensity of want for that additional unit is the measure of value and can be given the technical name, marginal utility, amenable to analysis in mathematical terms. Indeed Jevons, like Bentham, believed that it would eventually be possible directly to measure these changes in utility, so that economics would have the precision and observability of a physical science. Menger and Walras, on the other hand, saw utility as only relative, something preferred to something else, with relative utility indicated by relative prices. This idea of relative utility was taken up by the Italian, Vilfredo Pareto (1848–1923), who demonstrated that all the major conclusions of utility theory did not require measurability.

Walras made an early attempt to demonstrate Smith's conclusion of social harmony through an algebraic model of an economy. Every market was represented by a single hypothetical equation which, when simultaneously solved, indicated the equilibrium prices and quantities for all goods. This still left the problem for Walras, that if every individual's decision to buy or sell depends upon everybody else's decisions, how does the individual find out what everybody else is doing? He abstracted away from this problem by conjuring up an all-seeing, all-hearing 'auctioneer' who would adjust prices for all commodities until desired supply was equal to desired demand in all markets, a condition known as 'general equilibrium' (we shall return to this concept in Ch. 4). Menger, on the other hand, accepted that perfect information would not be available, and consequently did not construct a general equilibrium model of the economy, although he did hypothesise that autonomous price movements would be such as to move towards equating desired levels of supply and demand. Thus, while for Walras economics was a sub-set of mathematics with the potential for being as precise, Menger compared economics to astronomy, suggesting that by study of the visible movements of prices (planets), we could deduce something about the nature of the invisible force of utility maximisation (energy). Jevons, a phlegmatic Englishman, would only stake his claim for scientific respectability at the level of weather-forecasting.

Thus, in the 1870s, historical necessity (the requirements for a defence of vested interests against fundamental criticism) and methodological legitimacy (the mantle of science associated with mathematical formulation) combined to give strength to a school of economic thought which has remained powerful for a century and dominated policy making in many countries for much of that time: the subjective preference theory of value. The discussion of this theory which follows incorporates the major developments since 1870, including the contributions of four eminent American economists, J. B. Clark, Irving Fisher, Milton Friedman and George Stigler. We feel our ahistorical, analytical approach to be justified because it produces a unified exposition of the basic theory, which is in the spirit of the subjective preference theory scientific method. This method asserts that the great breakthrough of the European Enlightenment found an expression in economics most closely associated with Adam Smith's writings. Since then knowledge of economics has advanced incrementally as a shared research programme, albeit with some mistakes by Marx and his followers, illuminating the eternal verities of human activity in this world which were discovered in principle two hundred years ago. From the point of view of subjective preference theory, this chapter so far has been irrelevant, from now on for the rest of this chapter we ask the reader to become a subjective preference economist and see the world from that perspective. If you feel that this stretches your credibility, go to any newspaper stand, pick up a 'conservative' newspaper and read it. What follows is the basic economics of that newspaper.

3.2 The nature of subjective preference theory

Subjective preference theory rests on the assumption of rational indi viduals as the basic atoms of economic knowledge. The term individual is conceived to be a decision-making unit, which may be a single human being or a group of human beings, such as a household. In the latter case questions about equality and liberty are suspended within the group, often leading to an impression that there is a head of household (feminists and sympathisers may note the frequent use of the masculine gender in subjective preference writing) who makes decisions for the whole group. The sensations that express usefulness, i.e. the property of utility, for any individual, will depend upon the particular, unique tastes of that individual. Utility is not directly observable, but is revealed in behaviour by choice between alternatives. It is, therefore, an *ordinal* concept, in that we are able to say that a specific combination of goods and services provides more, or less utility for a particular individual than an alternative combination; it is not a cardinal concept so that a numerical value cannot be placed on the amount of utility derived by that individual from the consumption of a given combination of goods and services. Since the specification of utility is subjective for each individual, and cannot be valued independently of preferences revealed in active choice, we use the term 'subjective preference' to describe this theory of value.

Any item of consumption that provides utility for an individual will be compared by the individual with the loss that individual as a consumer is making in terms of missing or sacrificing alternative sources of utility (i.e. an opportunity cost). Thus, for an extra hour of leisure time, the opportunity cost is the *utility* of goods and services for consumption, which are given up by not labouring for another hour. The rate of trade-off between two commodities as sources of utility is the amount of one commodity that an individual is willing to forgo in order to obtain an extra unit of the other commodity without the individual feeling a loss of satisfaction. This provides a valuation of the second commodity in terms of the first, which indicates the strength of preference and, thus, the tastes of that particular individual.

But individuals are not only endowed with tastes and, therefore, desires, they also possess talents by which, through engaging in production, they might better fulfill these desires. The sphere of production is analysed as the application of talents as a worker (various types of skill *and* desire to work) to the material environment (non-reproducible resources) over time (seen as services derived from savings, another type of talent) in order to satisfy tastes (patterns of consumption). Each of the productive inputs, labour services, non-reproducible resources and services of savings, will be valued by the individual owner according to the opportunity cost (i.e. the utility) forgone in the act of supplying another unit. It is this opportunity cost that determines the value of the input for the individual supplier in utility terms. Thus, the individual as consumer is not only making a judgement of the benefit received from the consumption of alternative sources of utility, but also judging the cost in utility forgone of supplying inputs to production. And it is the talents of an individual, i.e. the ability to transform productive activity (experienced as utility costs) into desirable products for other individuals (experienced as utility benefits) that give the individual command over the products of other individuals' labour.

Thus, even with economic rationality being essentially individual and presocial, there is the possibility of economic systems in which there are complex interrelationships between many individuals. One explanation consistent with the assumptions of subjective preference theory is that there are differential tastes between individuals for items of consumption (including the opportunity cost attached to supply of productive inputs), and that each individual has specific talents. Thus, particular individuals may not be able to satisfy greatly their own tastes by applying their specific talents. There is, therefore, a possible advantage from specialisation in the sphere of production, with the total supply of inputs by individuals with appropriate talents to particular lines of production being regulated by the total demand for those goods by individuals unable to produce those goods but able to produce others. Consequently, individuals, in order to maximise utility, are willing to supply particular inputs towards the production of a variety of goods and services for the satisfaction of other people's tastes, in the expectation of being able to exchange for goods and services they desire. Social relations can then be caricatured as relations of exchange between individuals as eccentric consumers and individuals as peculiarly talented producers, where everyone feels there is a personal benefit from their particular role in transaction.

This model of specialisation in production according to specific talents gives rise to the type of *division of labour* most obviously resembling a community of small farmers and artisans. In such an economy, producers using their own inputs specialise in the production of particular goods, so that there is a division of labour in the production of different consumer goods, leading to the exchange of final goods between producers and interdependence in consumption. Beyond this simple society comes the more complex case of interdependence in both consumption and production that is found in contemporary societies. Thus, the production of any particular consumption good which is a source of direct utility, is broken down into a number of processes carried out by different producers, so that there is a division of labour *within* the production of a consumption good and exchange of both productive inputs and final consumption goods. It is a model of this type of society which we will attempt to construct in this chapter and the next.

Before proceeding with more detailed analysis, it is worth emphasising three points. Firstly, the fundamental assumption of subjective preference theory, the existence of utility maximising individuals endowed with tastes and talents, *is* an assumption and *not* a hypothesis. It is not open to question or refutation, but forms the starting point from which it follows by logical deduction that, firstly, such individuals acting in their own private interests also serve the wider social interest as long as there is free exchange and, secondly, some statements amenable to observation and falsification are generated. It is accepted that individual economic behaviour is often constrained by social institutions which limit free exchange; for instance the monopoly privileges extended to merchants in the sixteenth century, or the activities of large corporations or trade unions in our own time. But the aim of the theory is not to *describe* economic behaviour except in terms of the broadest falsification criteria, but to explain it, and thereby show that only economic institutions which give a framework for the operation of 'free markets' are desirable. Only then can all individuals maximise utility simultaneously, subject only to the constraints given by their innate individual talents.

Secondly, in principle, the analysis can be applied to any economy. The starting point of subjective preference theory is the individual innately endowed with tastes, talents and a propensity to maximise utility, which provides a conception of rational economic behaviour that is independent of any social, political or historical situation. The analysis of this essential *presocial* rationality can, therefore, legitimately ignore social, political and historical factors, with the motivation for economic behaviour, i.e. utility maximisation being seen as universal. Where general patterns of tastes and talents differ fundamentally from one place and time to another, there lies a possible subjective preference explanation of 'underdevelopment' as an expression of a pattern of tastes and talents neither highly valuing nor conducive to material affluence.

Lastly, it is important that both characteristics of the individual, the endowment of tastes and talents, *and* the motivation to maximise utility are recognised as the basis of subjective preference theory. In much writing on economic theory, it is only the latter characteristic which is emphasised in the identification of a school of thought called neo-classical economics, where maximisation, emphasising the use of differential calculus, is taken as the hallmark of a unified school of thought. While neo-classicism by this definition certainly includes subjective preference theorists, it also includes a number of other writers such as Alfred Marshall (see Ch. 6), who, while accepting maximisation as the motivation of economic actors, did not see the basis of social relations as independent individuals with given tastes and talents and, therefore, did not see social relations as simply exchange relations, either in practice or as an ideal. We will return to Marshall's work in Chapters 6 and 7.

With this overview and these qualifications in mind, we can construct the general analytical framework of subjective preference theory in more detail. In sections 3.3., 3.4 and 3.5, analyses of consumption and production are undertaken in terms of utility accounting. In section 3.6, social implications of maximisation of utility by an individual within the system as a whole are examined. As these sections are expressed in terms of utility, they could be said to deal with the invisible motivational forces underlying visible behaviour. In sections 3.7 and 3.8, the way in which this invisible motivation becomes visible phenomena in the form of firms, markets and prices is described, and in 3.9 some of the problems of varying the assumptions involved are examined. Obviously in a book of this length our presentation is bound to be rather schematic. We would recommend Chapters 1 to 8 of Kelvin Lancaster's introductory textbook (Lancaster 1969) as an excellent accompanying text. The reader may be a little confused, however, by the fact that Lancaster starts with the market for water melons and ends with the concept of utility. We feel happy to leave it to the reader to judge where the water melons should come in subjective preference theory.

3.3 From unobservable utility to possibly observable demand relationships

For subjective preference theory, Smith's idea of use value becomes the concept of utility. Utility is the accounting unit by means of which different combinations of goods and services can be made commensurable and evaluated by an individual. Utility, thus, summarises the structure of preferences of each individual and is specific to the unique tastes of that individual. The major theorems of subjective preference theory only require utility to be ordinal and do not need to allow comparison between individuals. All that is required is that individual choices be rational in the sense that the broad structure of preferences obey certain general rules.

Firstly, the individual as consumer is assumed to be insatiable and, therefore, because of the resulting scarcity is forced to consciously choose between many combinations of goods and services (hereafter called 'goods') representing different levels of utility. This does not necessarily mean (although it often seems to in subjective preference theory) individuals are gluttons for material goods; leisure and pleasure in altruism may both be sources of positive utility. However, the second assumption tends to rule out an excessive indulgence in either of these activities and, thus, maintains the tension of scarcity and hence competition in the economy. This second assumption is technically called the assumption of diminishing marginal rates of substitution between all goods. This states that as the consumption of one good rises relative to others, then the consumer will be willing to give up less of the others in order to obtain another unit of that good. This formulation in terms of 'one unit more' is close to the mathematical concept of a *marginal increase*. A marginal change is a very small change in the total quantity of a variable, and marginal analysis, which lies at the heart of subjective preference theory, is the analysis of the relations between marginal changes in variables. Marginal analysis is important, not because it reveals the way in which individuals make decisions, but because it is amenable to mathematical handling to reveal the properties of a maximised situation. In other words, if an individual is assumed to maximise utility, then marginal analysis can say something about the general properties of the resulting situation, even if the individual was not using marginal analysis consciously to make the decision. The assumption of a diminishing marginal rate of substitution can be roughly considered to be an assumption of moderation in consuming any particular good. That is, summarising the first two assumptions, whilst we are rather greedy, we are not totally obsessed with consuming any particular good.

Now, these assumptions can be represented graphically if we assume only two goods. The reason for this change in mode of presentation is that it permits both the precision of mathematical logic and the simplicity of hieroglyphics. The argument could be carried on more generally in either verbal or algebraic terms, but we subjectively prefer the pedagogic force of geometry. For those many readers who find difficulty in seeing three lines on a piece of paper as summarising the human condition, we have much sympathy. For those who wish for the elegance of algebra and the differential calculus, we refer them to the annotated bibliography at the end of the chapter. For all readers, we emphasise that the conclusions drawn from the analysis of two goods are generalisable to many goods.

If both goods are sources of utility for an individual, the utility provides a common accounting unit, and the satisfaction from consumption of different combinations of the two goods can be compared. Because of the assumption that utility is only ordinal in its nature, the individual can only say whether one combination is similar in utility terms to another or better or worse. For the case of similarity, then the individual can be said to be indifferent *between* these alternatives (NB: not 'indifferent *to*'). If assumptions of continuity (i.e. easy divisibility so that small amounts of goods can be exchanged) and diminishing marginal rate of substitution are built in, then this relationship takes on a particular regular shape when drawn on a graph with quantities of the two goods on the axes, see Fig. 3.1.

This relationship, or iso-utility curve, is equivalent to a contour on an ordinary map, except that it joins points of equal utility not equal height. Such a situation is shown in Fig. 3.1, note the curve is smooth (represents ease of division), downward sloping (represents insatiability) and curves inward towards the origin of the graph (represent diminishing marginal rate of substitution). To check that the shape on the graph corresponds to the assumptions, we ask the reader to consider four combinations of different amounts of goods A and B. Combination 1 involves less of good A *and* good B than point 4 and thus must have given a lower level of utility if the individual is insatiable, i.e. always prefers more to less. Conversely, combination 1 involves more of good A *and* good B than combination 3 and thus must give more utility, although we cannot say how much more. Combination 2 has more of good A than combination 1 but less of good B and thus is a candidate for indifference as indifference is not immediately ruled out by the insatiability assumption. The case for indifference is strengthened because combination 2 involves a relatively large total amount of good A to good B compared with combination 1, and the minimum amount of B required to get the individual to voluntarily accept one more unit of good A is much smaller for combination 2 than combi-

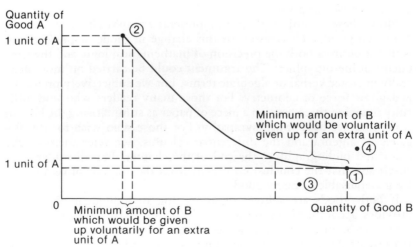

Fig. 3.1   Iso-utility curve for one individual choosing between two goods

nation 1, and thus meets the assumption of a diminishing marginal rate of substitution.

Using this framework alone, it is possible to derive the first falsifiable prediction of subjective preference theory. Let the individual be given as a social fact a barter exchange rate between the goods. In Walras' simple model of an exchange institution, this fact would be the auctioneer shouting out how many units of B will exchange for one unit of A. Now constrain the individual by stipulating a maximum level of satisfaction, but let the individual be free to choose any combination of amounts of goods A and B which satisfy this constraint. Thus, the problem is to describe the combination which will give the individual the maximum personal benefit possible given the individual's own tastes, but subject to the outside constraints of a given rate of exchange and a given maximum level of individual satisfaction. On the graph in Fig. 3.2, the given barter rate of exchange appears as any straight line of a given slope.

Figure 3.2 shows four examples of relationships (lines 1, 2, 3 and 4) which correspond to a fixed exchange rate between two goods. In all four cases giving up one unit of A always involves getting the same extra amount of B if we are to stay on that particular line.

In Fig. 3.3 the information on Fig. 3.1 and 3.2 is combined to produce the choice situation for the individual. The individual would be equally satisfied at points a and b because they both lie on the same iso-utility curve. But in a situation of general scarcity and competition, there are pressures on the individual to change the combinations these points represent. At point a the individual will give up relatively large

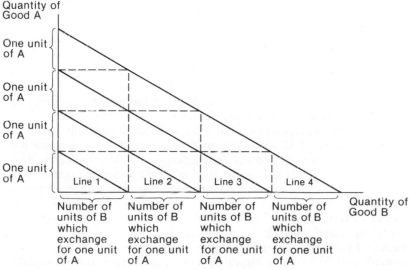

Fig. 3.2   Representing a constant rate of exchange

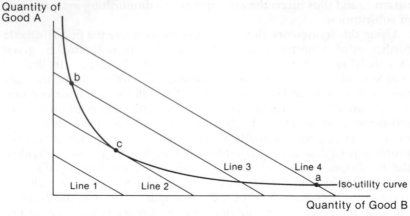

Fig. 3.3   A constrained choice for an individual

amounts of good B for a unit of good A and not feel any loss of satisfaction, thus more good B will become available to others than it costs them in good A at the going exchange rate. At point b the individual is willing to sacrifice a large amount of good A for a unit of good B and thus more good A could become available to others without much sacrifice of B. Only at point c, where the slope of the iso-utility curve equals the slope of the exchange rate line, will the individual be unwilling to change from the combination of goods at the going exchange rate. At that point only can consumption be considered 'efficient' with nobody else able to become better off without this individual becoming worse off. In a competitive society there will be pressures for all individuals to move towards combinations of goods like c.

But suppose the given exchange rate changed, then all the exchange rate lines would have a different slope. For instance, if a unit of A could only be exchanged for fewer units of B, then all the exchange rate lines would become steeper in our example. A new 'efficient' combination will now be found and, given the shape of the iso-utility curve, this combination must involve more A and less B (see Fig. 3.4).

We can logically conclude that if an individual (and this individual is representative of all subjective preference individuals) is faced with a choice in which one good has become relatively more expensive compared to other goods (i.e. good B in our case as fewer units of good B can be obtained for the sacrifice of a unit of good A), then we predict that the amount consumed of the relatively more expensive good should certainly not rise! Although this may not seem the most earth-shattering conclusion, it is important for the subjective preference theory of value. Firstly, methodologically, we have moved from unobservable utility through a logical process of deduction to an observable, falsifiable statement or hypothesis. This meets the Popperian criterion

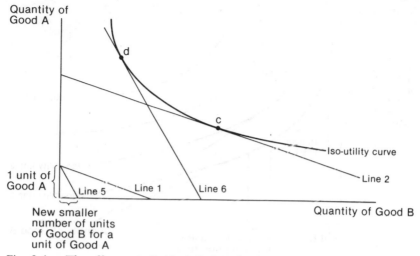

Fig. 3.4   The effect on individual choice of a change in exchange rate

of scientific method. Secondly, it is the only falsifiable statement obtainable from utility theory. Thus, if this statement is falsified, then utility theory, with all its implied attributes of competitive individualism, would have to be discarded. Up to this time, as far as the authors know, nobody has succeeded in falsifying this hypothesis and, thus, subjective preference utility theory survives its own test as scientific knowledge. The fact that other theories may predict the same observation does not detract from the statement that 'the world behaves *as if* it consisted of individuals rationally maximising utility in a framework of well-ordered preferences'.

So what is to prevent critics of subjective preference theory from a concerted empirical attack which would destroy it by its own definition of scientific knowledge? The answer lies in the experimental conditions that would be necessary, most crucially the assumption that the individual remains on the same iso-utility curve. For every level of utility there is an iso-utility curve which joins all combinations of goods giving equal satisfaction according to the assumptions of rational preferences. Earlier an iso-utility curve was compared to a contour line on a map, and as every height can have its own contour, so every utility level can have its own iso-utility curve. If it is assumed that iso-utility lines, like contours, cannot cross, an assumption called transitivity which assures that rational choice cannot involve one combination being simultaneously preferred to *and* considered indifferent from another combination at the same time, then a whole preference 'map' can be constructed as in Fig. 3.5.

This figure shows that even with all these assumptions, there is still no necessary reason why the individual should reduce the consumption of good B, if the 'price' of good B rises in terms of A (that is, fewer

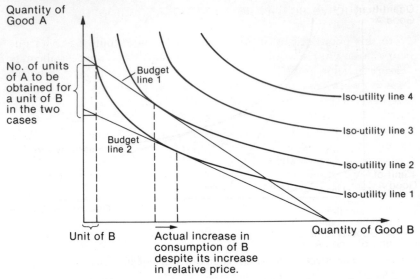

Fig. 3.5   An individual's indifference map: showing an increase in the price and quantity consumed of good B

units of A have to be given up to get a unit of B). The individual can choose to consume more B at a new equilibrium point on an iso–utility curve closer to the origin of the graph. This situation is logically accept-able for subjective preference theory and faces the critical experimenter with the task of controlling the level of individual satisfaction, such that the choices compared are constrained along a single iso–utility curve in order to test the theory. The amenability to rigorous testing of subjective preference consumer theory is thus much more limited than at first appears. And if this difficulty is true at the level of the individual, then it becomes an impossibility at the level of all individ-uals interested in a particular good. Then falsification of the hypothesis requires all consumers to have remained on their individual unobserv-able iso–utility curves, which is an experimental condition impossible to fulfill. Thus, the vital proposition for subjective preference theory that lowering the price of a good will increase the amount of that good consumed (i.e. the demand relationship) remains cloudy in rigorous analysis, except that it can be deduced there is one force certainly push-ing in that direction. But then the major purpose of this analysis is not to derive powerful predictions useful for policy-makers, but to exposit a plausible model of human behaviour in which price changes produce orderly, systematic, voluntary responses, and thus make policy-making unnecessary.

3.4 Productive activity as a form of consumption

Up to this point, Adam Smith might well have recognised the argument as his own. He would have gone on to argue that the best ultimate measure of value, noting that so far our analysis has only been in barter terms between two goods, is how much of the good is socially, i.e. generally, necessary to command a day of unskilled labour. Thus, Smith's confidence in the 'invisible hand' of the market, allocating resources smoothly, is totally consistent with the responses of utility maximising individuals to price changes. The step beyond Smith for subjective preference theory was to unify the final consumption choice with the productive activity choice in a single decision for each individual, and thus finally dispose of the labour input theory of value. Every activity an individual undertakes can then be seen as an act of consumption, giving utility. Consumption, not labour, is in command; people do not work, they forego the consumption of leisure; people are not savers, they are abstainers from immediate consumption. Production occurs because individuals are persuaded by material rewards to overcome their love of leisure and impatience for consumption. With this formulation, it is possible to use precisely the same analytical framework for choices of productive activity as was used in the previous section to examine straightforward final consumer choice.

Firstly, the opportunity cost incurred in the supply of any averagely unpleasant labour service for a given time for an individual is determined by the utility of the equivalent amount of leisure time that is sacrificed. Given the desire to maximise utility, the individual has to receive a source of positive utility in the form of a wage if work is to be undertaken. The individual, therefore, can be looked on as choosing between the utility associated with a lost hour of leisure time (assuming all work is equally unpleasant), and the utility derived from using the extra purchasing power from the wage to obtain goods and services for consumption. The iso–utility curves in Fig. 3.6 show the individual's structure of preference between these two sources of utility as a typically shaped iso–utility curve. The corresponding utility maximisation position is shown as point a for wage rate 1.

The marginal rate of substitution in this case places a value on leisure time in terms of lost purchasing power and, therefore, indicates that an increase in purchasing power per hour of leisure given up (i.e. a rise in the wage) would be predicted to decrease the consumption of leisure if the individual remains on the iso–utility curve. But the diagram also shows that an increase in leisure time (i.e. a reduction in work time) is quite compatible with an increase in wage rate without breaking any of the assumptions about rational consumer preferences providing the individual can move between iso–utility curves to point b from point a.

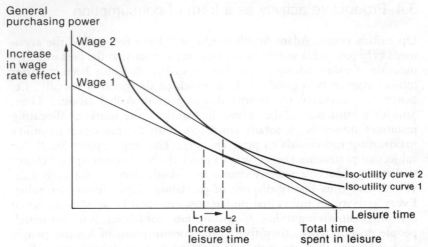

Fig. 3.6   Iso-utility curve and the supply of labour showing an increase in
leisure time with a rise in the wage rate

Similarly, when considering the framework for explaining saving, subjective preference theory sees the decision as one of abstaining from immediate consumption. Thus, in receiving an income the consumer has two possible courses of action, either to consume immediately, or to postpone consumption, i.e. save. It is assumed that the waiting associated with saving involves an opportunity cost in utility terms, individuals being generally impatient, which requires a reward if it is to be undertaken. In this case the extra purchasing power gained is called interest, conventionally proportioned to the volume of saving as a rate of interest. The relationship between the consumer's prefer-ence, for consuming something in the present and consuming more in the future, is represented by the iso-utility curves in Fig. 3.7. The budget lines in this case show the trade-offs between present con-sumption and future consumption for two interest rates when all income is earned in the present and then allocated between present and future consumption.

The marginal rate of substitution measures the value of future pur-chasing power (saving + interest) in terms of a unit of present con-sumption. Moving along any one iso-utility curve shows an increasing rate of interest which makes the line more shallow, and will produce decreased present consumption, i.e. increased saving. The full shift between the curves due to a rise in interest rate to r_2 shows the effect in this case operating in the opposite direction compared with move-ment along the single curve. Again such a result does not falsify sub-jective preference theory prediction as the assumptions of subjective preference consumer can be seen to hold.

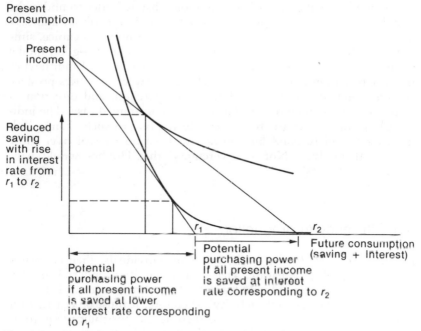

Fig. 3.7   Iso-utility curves relating the supply of saving and the rate of interest

Only when the productive activity is incapable of being increased in response to an increase in reward can this model of quantitative responsiveness to price change break down. Then, the increased reward for the individual owner of the input, once it is being used to capacity in the production of a consumption good, is determined *solely* by the utility derived in the consumption of the final product and, therefore, limited only by what consumers are willing to sacrifice. Such a return above that which compensates the supplier for any loss in utility incurred (i.e. the opportunity cost) is termed an *economic rent*. The concept of economic rent can be used to explain the return to a particular, apparently non-reproducible skill, such as an exceptional ability to sing or paint, and thus the fee paid to top singers, artists, etc. can be considered analytically in part an economic rent, a payment in excess of the wage rate sufficient to induce the individual to work, which alone would be the opportunity cost for the loss of utility in leisure foregone. Only in these limited cases can rewards be criticised as unjustified; no degree of inequality in rewards in other cases is acceptable, providing that the individuals entered into the contract to supply productive inputs voluntarily.

The meaning, and limitation, of the concept of consumer sovereignty in subjective preference theory should now be becoming clear.

The individual makes a single decision on what activities to undertake as a demander of goods and services *and* a supplier of labour and savings. This decision can be seen as a complex consumption choice, simplified in this chapter for expositional purposes to a two-good model of individual utility maximisation, iso-utility curves and indifference maps. Changes in barter rates of exchange between activities produce smooth voluntary responses, although the strength and direction of response is not certain in any but the most constrained case. The individual has the liberty to choose how to respond to such change and, in general, will respond but appears to have no control over those changes themselves. Not a 'sovereignty' that Hobbes would have recognised perhaps!

3.5 Efficiency in production

If valuation is left totally in the heads of individuals, then efficiency takes on a tautological nature. That is, if an activity is undertaken, then it must be because an individual gets more satisfaction from that activity than any other possible activity. Therefore, it must be efficient for at least that individual. Of course, there is the possibility that some other individuals may be inadvertently affected by the activity, i.e. an action may have implications 'external' to the immediate participants. However, subjective preference theory assumes that these implications are likely to be rare or easily observable , and often remediable through individual negotiation. If this is the case, then the basic condition for efficiency is precisely the same as that for social equity, that is, the maximum amount of liberty for individual action subject to the constraints of voluntary contract. To go beyond this statement in rigorous subjective preference terms requires caution if the primary concern with individual liberty is to be kept firmly in view, and deviations towards some form of 'technological' necessity or determinism avoided. In a subjective preference world we can all be poets and philosophers for the short period before we starve to death if that is what the individuals involved want. There are no such things as necessities or luxuries outside the desires of individuals; therefore, no economist or engineer can specify that any good is essential or basic, and thus analyse 'efficiency' in production as a technical exercise independent of consumer preference.

But, keeping this vital qualification in mind, it is possible to describe a production system in broad terms starting from an assumption that there are physical limitations imposed by the natural world and the general state of knowledge on individuals at any point in time. Starting from this assumption, it follows that using any given combination of inputs either involving one individual or, more realistically, many individuals, in a particular production process will have a maximum physical output. This provides the starting point for describing the structure of production from the subjective preference standpoint.

To analyse this structure, a similar form of presentation is used as that developed for the consumer in the previous section. The diminishing marginal rate of substitution in consumption has a parallel in a 'law' of variable proportions in production. This assumption implies that, if the total amount of one input utilised in production is increased relative to another, then the amount of the first input required to maintain physical output for a unit reduction in the second also increases. Also parallel to consumer theory is the assumption that inputs are highly divisible (by perhaps assuming that inputs are measured in terms of time, e.g. an extra hour of a lathe's service, not an extra lathe), which allows gradual adjustment to changing external circumstances. The assumption that any additional input always increases output ensures that production, parallel to consumption, never being 'satiated' in outputs, can never lose the tension of overall relative scarcity of all inputs.

In the analysis of consumption we developed a framework to structure the alternative combinations of any two sources of utility that would provide the same level of utility, as represented by the iso-utility curve analysis. In parallel the analysis of production starts from a structure showing the alternative combinations of any two inputs that will provide the same level of total output. This relationship is represented by an isoquant curve (see Fig. 3.8).

This shows alternative combinations of hours of two types of labour input L' and L'' to provide a level of output A. The isoquant shows all combinations of inputs which are *technically* efficient for pro-

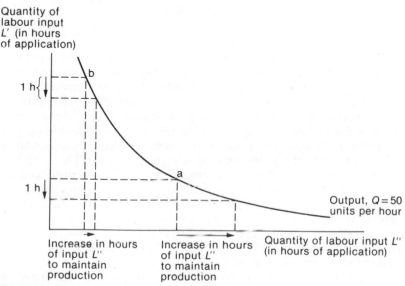

Fig. 3.8   Isoquant joining points of equal production

ducing Q, i.e. reducing either or both the inputs will reduce output. Note that in the analysis of production it is possible to make the new assumption that for most goods and services some measure of output can be attached to each isoquant, that is physical production can be assumed to be cardinal, whilst utility was assumed to be only ordinal.

As the iso-utility curve was able to tell us something about relative valuation of outputs, so the isoquant can say something about the relative value of inputs. In Fig. 3.8, at point a, giving up an hour of labour input type L' requires a relatively large addition of time from labour input type L'' compared to the combination represented by point b. Thus, in a situation where labour type L' was easy to obtain and L'' difficult, it would be expected that production would take place using the combination represented by point b rather than point a. If L'' then became more accessible compared to L', pressures would exist for a change in production technique involving the use of more L'' and less L', i.e. a move towards the combination represented by point a. In a market system, relative abundance and scarcity are experienced as relative prices and the argument would involve changes in the relative cost of an hour of input L' against an hour of input L''. For instance, if fewer individuals with the talent for L' are born and/or such individuals develop a greater liking for leisure, then labour time of type L' would only be provided for a higher reward. In such a situation, this analysis suggests that output can be maintained at the previous level, even though the particular process used may change as a result of adjustment to the change in relative input prices, i.e. the market mechanism will operate to encourage the substitution of L'' labour time for L'.

Just as in the analysis of consumer choice an iso-utility curve is part of a wider indifference map, so for the analysis of entrepreneurial choice any single isoquant is one of an infinite number of possible isoquants, one for every possible level of output. The assumption of measurability allows the concept of *returns to scale* to be discussed as a description of relationships between isoquants. Subjective preference theory is best served when constant returns to scale are assumed, that is changing the quantities of *all* inputs by a uniform proportion will change the output by the same proportion, e.g. doubling all inputs will double output. The major reason for this preferred assumption is that it ensures relative ease of entry into the production of any good on a small scale of new enterprises and, thus, allows both the existence of competition and the sensitive, gradual responses in production to price changes which are so important to subjective preference theory. It is also theoretically possible to have *non-constant* returns to scale. The implications of non-constant returns to scale are uncomfortable for subjective preference theory and have formed the basis for one important strand of cost-of-production theory (see Ch. 6).

A constant returns to scale production function is illustrated in Fig. 3.9 for the two input/one output case.

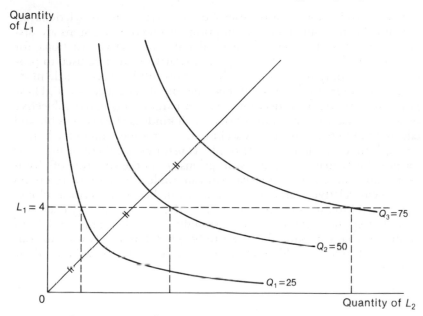

Fig.3.9   Three isoquants showing constant returns to scale

Graphically, the property of constant returns to scale throughout all production possibilities means that going out along *any* straight line from the origin of the graph will cross isoquants representing equally spaced levels of output (25 units in Fig. 3.9) at equal distances from each other. If, however, instead of moving along a ray, a horizontal or vertical line is followed, then this equal spacing of iso-quants representing equal changes in output cannot occur for the constant returns to scale example. For instance, Fig. 3.9 uses a horizontal line from the point on the L_1 axis, $L_1 = 4$, and shows that the amounts of L_2 needed to obtain equal increases in Q change. In words, this means that the relationship between the level of output and the amount of one input, given other inputs fixed at certain levels, is one which varies even if there are in general constant returns to scale. More specifically, no matter what the initial conditions, if one input only is increased then at some stage the amount of extra output per additional unit of input will *fall*. This property is called diminishing marginal physical productivity. Thus, although 'untalented' labour can always be substituted for 'talented' labour to maintain output, the substitution is not perfect and becomes increasingly difficult if total output expands on a restricted base of talented individuals justifying a relatively high reward to attract more labour time from those individuals with rare talents. The smooth operation of the price system even in a growing economy may thus produce increased inequalities in reward, which can be justified in subjective preference theory on the basis of relative scarcity of talents.

Thus, production considerations do involve some restrictions on individual behaviour. Like consumption, production decisions are discussed in terms of marginal, restricted and comparative situations; for instance, shall a little more of this input relative to that be used to produce a given output, or, what is the relationship between a little more output and more of this input if this other input is held constant? These physical restrictions on decisions are not paramount, given subjective preference assumptions. Substitution of all kinds is always possible and talented individuals are always seeking to overcome temporary bottlenecks, if they should occur. Also, like consumption, there seems to be the possibility that, given the assumptions about the structure of physical production, the price mechanism can guide allocation of resources to prevent relative scarcities of inputs from becoming critical blockages. Therefore, for subjective preference theory, technology is at most a limitation and certainly never a straightjacket. The only final limitation on what is produced appears to be what individuals want to consume. But why should individuals form societies to achieve these wants?

3.6 The basis of social organisation: what's in society for me?

Subjective preference theory sees no imperative for individuals to live in society. Robinson Crusoe's situation is not only a convenient pedagogical device for teaching students the principles of economics, but also a real potential for us all. Individuals are equipped with innate talents which can be used independently of society to meet their tastes to some degree. In choosing to participate in society the individual must see some personal advantage. Individuals voluntarily enter society only because of the net benefits in terms of extra utility they can achieve. Nobody is forced to join; therefore nobody has legitimate cause to object to her or his own position in society as everyone is free to leave once existing obligations have been fulfilled. There is a slight complication in that by leaving society the individual actually alters the nature of society marginally, for instance by reducing competition for wage work with others possessing a similar talent, but for the purposes of this chapter it is assumed the impact is not significant.

The subjective preference individual meets the ideal society at two levels. The first level is the framework of voluntary contract enforced by law as a fundamental condition for social existence. The second level is the mass of social facts called prices (which include wage rates, interest rate and economic rents). The individual can then calculate the meaning of these prices in terms of utility by bringing in consumption possibilities, given the specific tastes and talents of that individual. This calculation will indicate whether it is worth that individual participating less or more in society. In the extreme case, where an individual talent is by some divine miscalculation utterly incapable of satisfying that individual's tastes, then the question becomes academic. But for most people, the decision will not be of a qualitative, but a quantitative nature; a little more wage work or a little less, a little more saving in the bank, or a little less.

This decision can be pictured as a set of formal general propositions that link the analysis of individual preference with the social facts of prices. In section 3.3 we introduced the concept of marginal rate of substitution to indicate the relative strength of preference in utility terms between consuming combinations of two goods when moving round an iso–utility curve and in section 3.4 showed how this also applied to supplies of inputs. It was also suggested there that the individual experiences 'prices' as external trade-offs when deciding what combination of goods to consume. The relationship between the subjective trade-off between two goods as sources of utility and the objective experience of prices as social trade-offs must be one of equality if the individual is to cease seeking further trading opportunities. Similarly, in using amounts of individual talents, including the talent of saving (as sources of disutility), to produce goods (as sources of utility), the individual will equate the subjective evaluation of turning extra pain into extra pleasure in every activity in net utility terms with the objective, socially given, relative rewards in wage/price and interest/price terms.

If these equations do not hold, then it is in the interests of the individual to adjust behaviour. This could involve consuming more of a relatively highly valued good in marginal utility terms and giving up some of a relatively lowly valued good, or by increasing activity in social production if prices of consumption goods are relatively low compared to wage and interest rates in terms of the marginal utility/disutility relationship. So, an individual with a talent x, used to produce good b, which is exchanged for good a, which the individual consumes, can find a combination of quantities of all activities which constitute a utility maximised equilibrium for any given set of relative prices. Thus, if an individual dislikes work a lot and has a low relative level of desire to consume, then a lower level of activity in society might be expected for any combination of prices compared with an individual who likes to work and likes to consume. This unexceptionable conclusion can be complicated by assuming many individuals have a strong dislike of productive activity and a strong liking for consumption, then when wages and interest in terms of consuming power change, this could lead to significant changes in the amount of *social* productive activity. It is this kind of reasoning which partially accounts for subjective preference theorists' distaste for taxation on incomes, since they would predict that this biases the choice of individuals against participating in society which threatens to erode both levels of social interaction, that is not only the price system as an allocator of resources, but also the more fundamental acceptance of voluntary contracts as the basis of social relationships.

But why should individuals with firm tastes (an advertiser may fool them into buying once, but after that it is the experience of consumption that counts, i.e. in practice all advertising is informational) and innate talents (education can develop skills not create talents) form societies in which millions of individuals are interlinked intimately in a complex network of contracts? Whilst subjective preference theory often seems most comfortable in dealing with Robinson Crusoe, pure exchange (i.e. without production) or peasant/artisan economies, nevertheless there is the possibility of going beyond these simple models by recalling Adam Smith's discovery for economics of the productive advantages of a complex division of labour.

A complex division of tasks, where large numbers of people with highly specialised talents produce each product, and materials have to pass through a number of different processes before consumption, is obviously the condition of many societies today. Sequential organisation of production produces no problems for subjective preference models of society, as each movement of products could be seen essentially as a voluntary exchange between two individuals. However, a problem of organisation arises when many individuals are brought together at one time in one place to take advantage of high productivity, defined in terms of physical units of output per labourer. For instance, assume that one hour is effectively the minimum labour supply from an individual and there are 40 people working separately, each for an hour, producing 1 unit of output each, i.e. a total output of 40 units. If working simultaneously in one place, the same 40 people can produce a total of 50 units in an hour, then, providing the work is no more objectionable, the technically efficient method is to bring all the labourers together for a single hour. But this requires coordination and planning for all the individuals involved. If this technical efficiency involves organising many individuals, this will encourage the application of specific talents for taking such responsibility, i.e. *entrepreneurs*, to take control of production.

The word 'entrepreneur' conjures up the image of a dynamic, talented individual who takes the initiative in, and accepts the risk of, both setting up and managing a productive enterprise, the firm. For the purposes of subjective preference theory, this popular image needs some slight qualification if the theory is to be rigorously developed. Firstly, the entrepreneur (in effect 'go-between') is best separated from the provision of resources to start and enlarge the firm. Such resources come from savers who receive interest for their sacrifice of immediate consumption. Secondly, and more controversially, it is appropriate to assume a subjective preference economy is riskless.

The reasons for this assumption centre on the subjective preference view that individuals are sure what they want to consume and supply to society, given prices that are social facts for these individuals with techniques of production adjusting smoothly to meet any minor changes in tastes and talents. Residual problems of future consumption or supplies can be coped with in markets for goods in terms of future time, analogous to markets which move goods across space. Vagaries of the natural environment can be met by insurance, which turns haphazard risk into the science of probability. Risk as a crucial aspect in production decision is central to cost-of-production thinking in its Keynesian form as we shall see in Chapter 6, not to subjective preference theory, which praises dynamic entrepreneurs for recognising opportunities rather than taking risks.

For our purposes here, therefore, we can accept that in a joint stock company legal ownership lies with shareholders (i.e. savers) and management is undertaken on a bureaucratic basis (i.e. labour with special talents), not a buccaneering individual. The rewards for this organising activity being not only split between many individuals, but also analytically divided between a reward equivalent to the opportunity cost incurred in the supply of this particular type of labour service, i.e. the going wage compensating for the leisure time forgone, and occasionally also an economic rent as the return to a not easily reproducible skill for an exceptionally talented management. A crucial question for subjective preference theory can then be raised. If this organising entrepreneurial function is crucial for subjective preference theory to gain credibility as relevant to current societies, then can the entrepreneurs' powers of decision making be described logically and convincingly in such a way as to make it subordinate to the wishes of individual consumers?

3.7 The abuse of social organisation: what entrepreneurs might do

For the aspiring entrepreneur in subjective preference theory, like the individual consumer, prices of inputs and outputs exist as data. The prices of inputs provide a basis for making any combination of inputs into a single number, i.e. a total cost. Thus, many types of labour (including the opportunity cost of that particular entrepreneurial talent), raw materials and machinery can be summed for every possible combination of inputs which are *technically* efficient (i.e. lie on an isoquant in the two-input case) to find the combination for any given level of output which is *economically* efficient (i.e. gives a minimum total cost for that level of output). It is only this combination of inputs for each level of output that the potential entrepreneur need examine when deciding whether to produce or not. A simple numerical example (see Table 3.1) illustrates how costs of economically efficient combinations can be represented in a number of different forms. The example is purposely designed to show dramatically two features of costs which

Table 3.1   Cost functions for a hypothetical firm

(a) Output per time period	(b) Minimum total cost of output (assuming given input prces) (£)	(c) Average cost per unit (b/a) (£)	(d) Change in output (from a)	(e) Change in total cost (from b) (£)	(f) Marginal cost (extra cost per extra unit of output, e/d) (£)
10	100	10	—	—	—
20	100	5	10	—	—
30	120	4	10	20	2
40	200	5	10	80	8
50	500	10	10	300	30

subjective preference theory requires to produce a theory of the firm in which firms are of determinate size. The first two levels of output show the impact of technical indivisibilities on costs. That is, the firm has to be a minimum size in total cost terms before production can even be contemplated, possibly due to fixed minimum opportunity cost of the entrepreneurial function. The two highest levels of output show a dramatic increase in total costs as the firm reaches the limits of the managing skill of the entrepreneurial function and breakdowns in organisation start to appear.

The example is shown Fig. 3.10 in the form of a graph showing the relationship between average and marginal costs and level of output.

These cost curves are just mathematical deductions from total output and total cost data, but give crucial analytical insights for the theory of the firm. For instance, suppose that the entrepreneur was able to sell the output at only £3 per unit, then production would not take place because at no level of output can this entrepreneur break even; even producing the output with minimum average cost (£4 in this case) of 30 units per time period, would mean a total cost to the entrepreneur of £120, against total receipts of £90 (3 multiplied by 30), i.e. a loss of £30 per time period. Thus, the lowest point on the average cost curve (which is where the marginal cost curve is mathematically fated to cross it) shows the minimum price required if production is to be undertaken at all. Above that level the question is not whether the firm is viable, i.e. can enter into production and survive, but how much will be produced. Again take an arbitrary, but fixed, price at which all output can be sold, say £10 per unit. Production of 10 units per time period costs £100 in total and total receipts would be £100. Also production at the level of 50 units costs £500 and gives receipts of £500. At both these levels of output, the firm can continue in production indefinitely, providing input prices remain unchanged. But this is true for all levels of output between 10 and 50. Indeed, at these levels the firm is not only paying for all inputs (including a reward to the entrepreneurial function

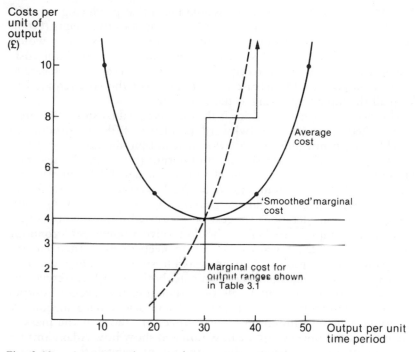

Fig. 3.10   Average and marginal cost curves

sufficient to keep it in the firm, i.e. its opportunity cost) but in addition has an economic rent available for distribution.

Within this range of possible production levels (remember that the entrepreneur in subjective preference theory chooses input combinations, line of production and level of output; prices are data, not decision variables) a number of decision principles might operate. Firstly, high levels of output might require high levels of entrepreneurial input from certain individuals, and thus cut into the leisure time of those providing that input. If leisure is highly valued, then a tendency to settle the firm at around 10 units of output might be expected. On the other hand, if the size of the firm (gauged by level of output) is itself a source of utility to the individuals performing the entrepreneurial function, then a level of production towards the higher end of the range is possible. The third decision principle puts the question of desired leisure and status to one side and argues that the entrepreneurial function is performed by individuals in search of more tangible rewards for themselves, and thus choose a level of output which maximises the 'economic rent' which they can use their position to appropriate. This rent is in addition to the reward necessary to keep them in their current activities. Such a level of output can be located mathematically by equating *marginal* cost with the price to be received (40 units per time period in the case of £10 per unit in our example). Producing less than

40 units, e.g. 20 in our example, would mean that producing an additional 10 units will add less to cost (£20) than it does to receipts (£100); producing any more than this output, e.g. 50 in our example, would mean that producing 10 less units would subtract more from costs (£300) than it would from receipts (£100). In either case, the change in level of output would increase net receipts over the cost required to keep all the inputs operating at the new output.

This decision principle, which is the one favoured by subjective preference theory, raises two awkward problems. Efficient production would suggest not only the criterion that output should be produced at minimum total cost for that level of output (built into the selection of input combination underlying the total cost schedule), but also that the chosen level of output should be the lowest average cost for all possible levels of output (in the example 30 units per time period). Also, equity considerations suggest no reason why those who happen to have an entrepreneurial talent should receive a bonus, an 'economic rent', on top of the reward necessary to keep them in their current occupation. These problems are answered in subjective preference theory by demonstrating the forces that exist both to push entrepreneurs towards choosing efficient levels of output (i.e. the levels of output associated with minimum average cost) and also reduce inequitable economic rent to a minimum. These forces are those of the market, and it is to that concept that we now turn and show how Adam Smith's fears about the non-progressive activities of capitalists (now read 'entrepreneurs') were answered in subjective preference theory.

3.8 The role of the market in ensuring efficiency and equity

In the last two sections individuals, as consumers, input suppliers and entrepreneurs were discussed as decision-makers responding to given prices which they took as social facts. Their decisions were thus about quantities and not about prices. Prices guide individual actions, but so far have no explanation. If, for instance, the government chose how goods should trade off with each other, then individuals still have the choice about how far, if at all, to participate in society and the general analytical points established so far would still apply. But the power of deciding those trade-offs would then be open to abuse by some individuals as politicians at the expense of the rest of society. In such a situation, people would become puppets of the price-makers, preserving some freedom to adjust individual activities, but with no guarantee that the social outcome is efficient, equitable or sustainable. The crux of economic analysis for the subjective preference theory of value is to show that *no* conscious agent is needed to choose a price for a good, and that the sum total of individual tastes and talents is sufficient to determine a price, and that such a price will guide resource allocation towards efficiency, equity and stability. The analytical framework which is used to demonstrate this reconciliation is called a *market*.

A market consists of two relationships which are virtually totally independent of each other, but with the common characteristic that they both link the quantity of a good with its own price. For the purposes here, the price will be treated as a money price, but readers should remember that the notion of price is primarily to do with trade-offs between goods and between goods and productive activities, not to do with money. Money is only a convenient device for representing prices, not a cause of prices. Smith put forward command over labour, many other economists have talked of weights in gold as devices for standardising measurement of value. When we use the pound sterling (£) as a standard of price below, the reader should constantly bear in mind that any resemblance to the currency of the U.K. refers to a time, past or future, when the price level was stable. That is, a time when whenever a price of one good rose, the price of another good or goods fell in money terms. For those without such a long memory or vivid imagination, we recommend you think in terms, rather like Smith, of an hour of relatively undemanding work as a domestic servant performed for the owner of the good as the standard of price, i.e. a price rise means having to work longer to acquire a unit of the good in question.

For this exposition, assume that the good is used only in final consumption and that the individuals who are involved in producing the good as workers, savers and entrepreneurs are insignificant consumers. This avoids the problems of feedback between changes in the price of the good and a *shift* in either of the relationships, i.e. we can understand changes in price as producing movements *along* curves only. Now, in section 3.3, the theory of consumer choice was shown to predict that if an individual is constrained to stay on the same iso-utility curve, then a *rise* in the price of the good (the own-price) relative to all others will lead to a *fall* in the quantity demanded, in graphical terms, a downward sloping demand curve. The theory thus suggests, although with some ambiguity, that if actual observable variables like individuals' money incomes and all other prices, are held relatively constant, then the inverse relationship between own-price and quantity will continue to hold. This conclusion will certainly not hold, by definition, if a consumer associates *higher* price with *higher* desirability (the so-called Veblen-effect), but has sufficient general appeal not to have been seriously challenged. If all consumers exhibit this relationship individually, then the sum total of responses will be in the same direction as individual responses, i.e. an inverse relationship. Fig. 3.11 illustrates this point for two consumers.

Note that this demand curve will change position if any variables are allowed to change other than the own-price. The implication is, however, that such *shifts* are likely to be relatively insignificant compared with *movements along* the curve for the purposes of this analysis.

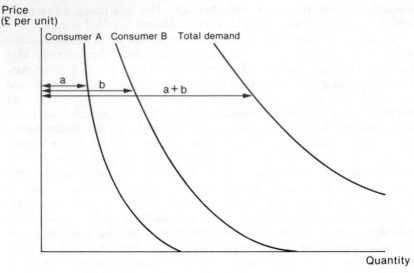

Fig. 3.11   A demand curve summed for two consumers

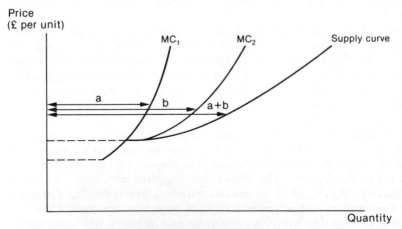

Fig.3.12   Supply curve summed for two firms

The supply relationship can be treated similarly. Each potential entrepreneur has a price of entry into production of the good, given by the minimum average cost. Above that price, entrepreneurs, in pursuit of economic rents, choose to produce at levels of output associated with their marginal cost curves, again assuming that all other variables remain constant like technology, prices of inputs and other possible outputs. As marginal cost curves are assumed to slope upwards, then the overall supply curve, if simply the sum of individual entrepreneur's decisions, will also slope upwards, as in Fig. 3.12.

These two relationships can be combined on one graph to make up a market, see Fig. 3.13.

As this market is for only one good, with restrictions on most variables, it is not surprising that the result is a very strong prediction. This prediction can be found by examining the implications of setting prices at various levels. If the price is at level a, then consumers wish to purchase more than suppliers wish to sell. Frustrated potential consumers must then find a way of expressing their frustration at not having enough, say through forming queues. Consumers will thus be willing to see prices rise, putting an upward pressure on price, which simultaneously encourages an increased quantity to be supplied and a decreased quantity to be demanded. Conversely, at price b, supply is more than demand and overstocked suppliers will reduce output and be willing to see prices fall, which will also encourage quantity demanded to increase. Only at price c will these dynamic processes no longer exist and equilibrium will prevail. Thus, the possibility now emerges that prices which each individual accepts as data are actually the outcome of the sum total of individual actions. No outside agent like the government is required to determine this market price, and all individuals are equal in powerlessness before the anonymous market.

But, having disposed of the need for government intervention in price determination, what of the entrepreneurs whose activities seemed

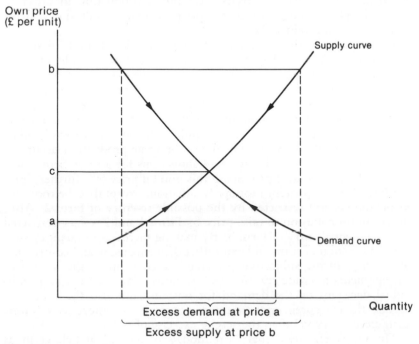

Fig. 3.13   A market

likely to offend principles of equity and efficiency in the previous section? The major constraint on their anti-social behaviour can now be seen. If existing entrepreneurs in this market are all achieving economic rents, then any equally talented entrepreneurs, who are only making just sufficient to stay in their present occupation elsewhere, will be tempted, once they have gained this information, to change occupation. They will move into the production of the good and, thus, play a role in increasing the quantity supplied, even if the existing entrepreneurs restrict their own output. Only at price c will this process stop, when, at least some firms, and possibly many, will be operating at minimum average cost and entrepreneurs will be making no economic rents. Other firms may still be operating above minimum average cost and rewards will accrue as an 'economic rent' to the entrepreneurs. However, the threat of new entry and accurate flows of information through balance sheets of firms would keep the inequitable 'economic rent' and the associated inefficiency, seen in terms of output not produced at minimum average cost, small. This condition of easy entry with low technical and social barriers to starting up production, combined with free information flows, are associated with a particular type of relationship between firms called 'perfect competition'. From the point of view of the individual entrepreneur, the effective result of perfect competition is the inability to influence prices significantly by the firm's own level of activity; restraining production in order to reduce supply and thus force up the price, will only result in new firms being set up to produce the good.

The elegance of the subjective preference model of the firm should now be clear. The U-shaped cost curves mean that a single 'efficient and equitable' size (in terms of level of output) exists for every firm. Providing there is free entry, then existing and potential competition pressures firms towards this size. Thus, whilst some firms engaged in the production of the good may end up with some entrepreneurs receiving economic rents even at equilibrium because of exceptional organisational talents, there will always be some production occurring at minimum average cost. Fig. 3.14 shows this for a three firm case.

Firm 2 will go out of producing this good if price falls further, leaving Firm 1 in an apparent monopoly situation, except that the room for manoeuvre is still restricted by the possible re-entry of Firm 2. Also, the room for collusion to raise price by Firms 1 and 2 is very restricted by the potential entry of Firm 3. By making increases in quantity supplied, a function of entry and exit rather than expansion and contraction of existing firms, subjective preference theory limits the ability of entrepreneurs to erode consumer sovereignty. Squeezed between individual decisions on the demand for outputs, and also the supply of inputs, the entrepreneurial function is experienced more as a frantic struggle for survival than the serene exercise of power.

The rather elaborate analytical models of individual behaviour as consumer and entrepreneur are thus constructed in a particular manner

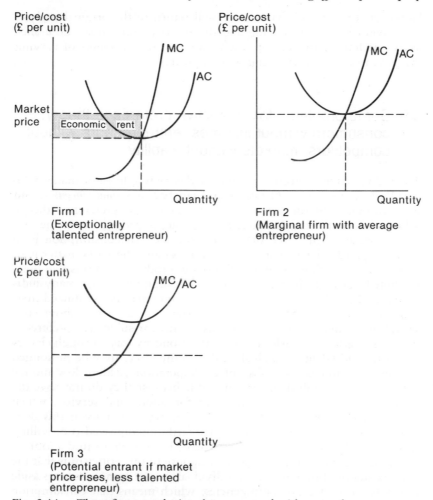

Fig. 3.14   Three firms producing the same good with unequal
entrepreneurial talent

for the purposes of subjective preference theory. Bringing them together in a single market framework shows that, given these assumptions, the free market system, where the price is determined only by the sum total of actions of individuals, is a sufficient condition for the efficient allocation of resources, within a framework of equitable liberty in which everyone chooses what to put into society in the full and accurate knowledge of what they are going to get out. Of course, this has only been demonstrated for one market with lots of restrictions on other variables (called partial equilibrium analysis) and generalising these results to many markets (general equilibrium analysis) does raise some specific problems, which will be outlined in the next chapter.

However, to end this chapter, we will return to the original analysis of individual decision-making and the single market to see how subjective preference theory copes with some of the problems of varying the assumptions underpinning its own analysis.

3.9 Some problems for subjective preference theory: consumers without incomes, entrepreneurs without competitors, markets without stability

The individual in subjective preference theory is a decision-maker who decides how to dispose of talents and satisfy tastes *simultaneously*. But in a complex interdependent society, subjective preference theory acknowledges that the decisions to play roles in production are necessarily separated from each other and from acts of consumption by a general agreed intermediary (called money) and the work patterns of such a society with many indivisibilities in production means that there is limited flexibility in type and hours of employment for many individuals. Thus, the search for a money income may be conducted first, and only then, once this income is known can decisions about consumption be made. The implications of this for subjective preference theory are serious, as dislocations of the economy (say, through changing tastes and talents) which should be temporary, may be prolonged if many individuals take jobs out of desperation yielding low money incomes. People will then consume little because they do not have the effective (money supported) demand for goods and services which could otherwise have been produced. The repercussions of this deficiency may leave other people involuntarily unemployed (i.e. willing to work at the going rate for their talent, but unable to find a job).

The subjective preference theory response to this criticism is that the very existence of money allows individuals to put some resources aside precisely to meet such contingencies, which means that consumption never has to be drastically reduced in the face of any loss of current income. Further, individuals, even if they have not had the foresight to put resources aside, can make contracts with savers for present consumption to be repaid from future income, albeit with interest, thus again relaxing the constraint of current income on current consumption. These responses suggest that subjective preference theory does not easily explicitly deal with time and uncertainty, in general tending to see time only in terms of a simple distinction between two markets (current and forward) and uncertainty as being met by suitable insurance arrangements.

The question of increasing indivisibilities in production raises a second problem for subjective preference theory. If an entrepreneur comes to control more and more resources, then the size of that firm relative to the market for a good may grow. Even with potential competition, one entrepreneur may still be able to affect the price of a good by varying output, rather than being forced to accept the price as a fact for decision-making purposes. This situation is called imperfect competition (examined in more detail in Chapter 6). It further strengthens this criticism if it is argued that firms can limit entry of new entrepreneurs by manipulating information, say through patents on production techniques or advertising to influence consumer motivation. The resulting problems of inefficiency and inequity are similar to those outlined in section 3.7 for the non-marginal entrepreneur in conditions of perfect competition not producing at minimum average cost and receiving an economic rent above opportunity cost into the bargain. The response within subjective preference theory has been to maintain that sustained imperfect competition is difficult, if not impossible for a number of reasons.

For instance, it can be argued that even the largest firms have competitors, if not in producing identical goods, certainly in producing substitutable sources of utility, e.g. desires for nutrition, heating and communication can be satisfied by a whole range of goods. Any firm may also have to raise funds for large-scale investment projects which brings them under the critical, informed eye of financial institutions who only judge a firm by its returns to savers, not to its entrepreneur. This tends to encourage the dispersal of rewards over a wider group than those playing the entrepreneurial function alone. Lastly, within the firm, managers of sub-divisions or sections will be aware of the possible advantages of alternative sources, and provide criticism of inefficient sections by reference to open market prices for inputs and outputs. Pressures, therefore, exist on even the largest firm to keep prices down, distribute any economic rents widely, and maintain productivity in line with smaller, specialist firms.

Another criticism aimed at undermining subjective preference theory, through questioning the prevalence of competition between firms in contemporary societies, rests on the assumption that firms' average cost curves will start to rise at some level of output, small relative to total market demand at the going market price. This rise ensures that firms will be determinate in size and economically unable to expand to absorb whole markets, and eliminate competition. Now the fact that examining actual cost figures for samples of firms in many industries generally does not show this rise, suggests a problem for subjective preference theory of the firm. However, subjective preference theory argues this is not the case on two counts. Firstly, the average cost may be rising for each individual firm, even if the cross-sectional locus of all these minimum average costs is a straight line (see Fig. 3.15).

Secondly, company accounts are prepared by accountants, not economists, and there are great problems in converting accountants' categories into subjective preference economics' analytical concepts. For instance, what an accountant calls 'profit' has no direct analytical significance at all, and what an accountant calls 'rent' means something

77

Average cost
(£ per unit)

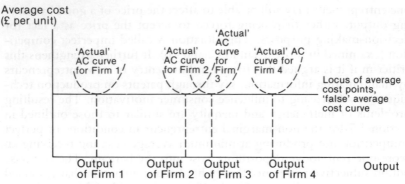

Fig. 3.15   A 'false' constant average cost curve constructed from
cross-sectional cost information on four firms

completely different. Thus, like the demand function where the prediction of a downward slope is hedged by so many qualifications that
testing is virtually impossible, analytically adequate cost curves are not
easily observable and hence the theory of the perfect competition is
virtually untestable. All too often, it would seem, the Popperian criterion for science, accepted by eminent subjective preference theorists,
that knowledge is only scientific, when pursued critically in the face
of observable falsification is honoured in principle, not in practice.

The prediction that a market is a stable equilibrium system (that is,
there is an inherent tendency for a market price to return to a central
value) can be questioned by varying underlying assumptions. Firstly, a
market may be unstable if firms expanding together produce economies
which no firm on its own could achieve, for instance creating a pool
of appropriately skilled labour. Such *economies of scale* (that is, economies that depend on the level of scale of output) are external to the
firm (every firm individually can still have a rising marginal cost curve)
and only appear at the level of the whole market as a downward sloping
supply curve. That is, the larger the total quantity of the good mar-
keted, the lower the price at which each firm will break even and be
able to meet minimum average cost. However, instability only occurs
in the case in which these economies are so large that the supply curve
slopes down faster than the demand curve (if we assume that individuals only respond in terms of quantities and accept prices as given facts)
(see Fig. 3.16).

At price a, quantity demanded (Qd_a) exceeds quantity supplied (Qs_a)
and existing entrepreneurs have reason to supply more. But in expanding production they lower the costs of production for new entrants,
and there is pressure for price to fall, thus *increasing* the gap between
supply and demand, rather than diminishing the gap. At price b supply
(Qs_b) exceeds demand (Qd_b) and thus existing entrepreneurs will contract production and in so doing will raise costs, force firms out of the

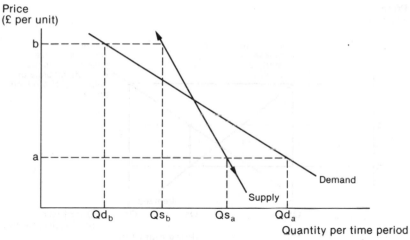

Fig. 3.16　An unstable market with increasing returns to scale external to the firm (NB: entrepreneurs can only choose quantity not price)

industry, leading to price rises and an increase in supply over demand. In this example then, individuals are all behaving rationally in line with subjective preference theory, but the market is unstable leaving the theory only able to defend itself by claiming that cases of significant external returns to scale are rare.

Even if demand and supply curves are assumed to have normal slopes, instability can still be introduced by assuming a time lag in supply response, due to a finite production period with decisions over level of output being made at the start of the period (say, an agricultural good where vital decisions have to be made at the time of sowing. This assumption gives rise to a process of adjustment over time which may be unstable, if it is assumed that the demand curve slopes more steeply than the supply curve (see Fig. 3.17).

In the first time period, starting from an initial market price a, entrepreneurs will be willing to supply a quantity Qs_a. However, consumers faced with this quantity will, from the demand function only, be willing to offer a price of b. At the beginning of the second time period, therefore, faced by the new market price of b, entrepreneurs will modify their production decisions in accordance with the supply function, and will only supply Qs_b. Consumers, now faced by a reduced amount of the good will offer the higher price of c, there now being a situation of excess demand. Consequently, in the third time period production decisions will be revised yet again. In this example, the amount that consumers are willing to pay for a given quantity and the amount that entrepreneurs are willing to supply for a given price are tending away from the market equilibrium values. For obvious visual reasons, this model is called a cobweb model. In contrast

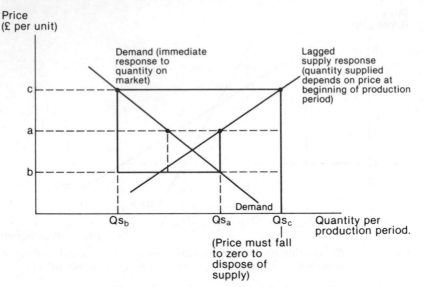

Fig. 3.17   An unstable market with quantity supplied responding to price at the beginning of the production period

to the first case, the individuals here could be considered to be behaving with a lack of foresight which comes close to irrationality. By buying the good when the price is low, storing, and selling when price is high, some enterprising individuals could act as wholesalers by 'hoarding and speculating' in everyone's interest and earn a reward into the bargain. Thus, the free pursuit of individual gain in this case will tend to reduce instability.

Even an 'observation' of prima facie instability in terms of wide variation in the price of a good, as shown in Fig. 3.18, is not conclusive evidence that the essentials of subjective preference theory are failing to meet a test of falsification.

Providing some reasons can be advanced for the demand curve or the supply curve or both to be shifting, which given the number of variables assumed fixed in order to arrive at the demand and supply relationships should not be hard to do, then, in principle, the variations can be explained. This does not dismiss the work performed by many economists in the realm of statistics. But it does throw doubt on whether their work is likely to ever fundamentally challenge subjective preference theory. Exhaustive formal empirical testing is not essential to the survival of the theory. The criterion of success within subjective preference theory, is not in statistically valid observations, but is self-evident in the relative material well-being of the citizens of those societies where governments have appeared generally to act as if subjective preference theory were true.

Price
(£ per unit)

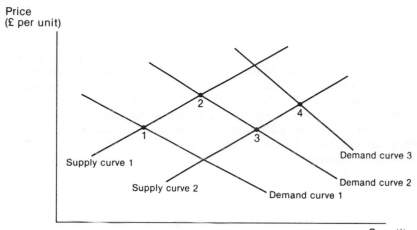

Quantity

● : observations of price and quantity combinations

Fig. 3.18   'False' observation of market instability when, in fact, there are
shifts in demand and supply curves with movement along curves

Further reading

The historical development and basic philosophy of subjective preference theory is favourably treated in the works of Friedman (1953) and
Stigler (1965) mentioned in the bibliography to Chapter 1 and in Oser
and Blanchfield's *The Evolution of Economic Thought*, Chs 12, 13, and
15. It is more critically treated in the first two articles by Dobb and
Meek in Hunt and Schwartz (eds) *A Critique of Economic Theory* and in
Routh's book again mentioned in Chapter 1. We would disagree with
many similar writings on the history of economic thought, such as Roll
(1973), in the general use of the term neo-classicism and the classification of Marshall as a neo-classicist. The use of marginal analysis,
which is central to this classification at the level of individual decision
making is not a fundamental point of disagreement between most economists, who totally disagree on the essential nature of value in society.

Analytical development of subjective preference ideas underpins
most microeconomics text books and the microeconomics section of
basic economics text books. But many, like Lipsey and Samuelson
mentioned in Chapter 1, steer an uneasy course between the full logic
of subjective preference theory and rather casual inference put in terms
of asserted common-sense. An honourable exception is Lancaster's
Introduction to Modern Microeconomics, whose chapters perhaps should be
read in the order 1, 7, 4, 5, 6 (omitting the section on monopoly), 2,
3, (with Chs 9 to 11 being useful for the issues raised in our next
chapter). Earlier editions of this book are less clouded by sophisticated
mathematics for some readers, and for those who like their economics

even more mathematical, Henderson and Quandt's *Microeconomic Theory* develops the theory in this direction.

Nobel prize winners writing broad analytical introductions to subjective preference theory include John Hicks in Part 1 of *Value and Capital* and a collection of Milton Friedman's lectures to undergraduates collected together in 1962 under the title *Price Theory*. Of the many books of readings collecting together journal articles, one worth mentioning as reflecting a strong subjective preference bias is David Kamerschen's selection *Readings in Microeconomics*, although even here there are notable criticisms of subjective preference basic tenets in the articles by Schumpeter, Mishan, Nordquist, Modigliani and Kaldor.

Freedom is the market: the subjective preference theory of value

Summary 3.1 _____

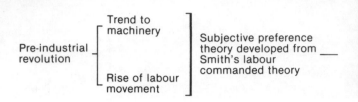

Summary 3.2 _____

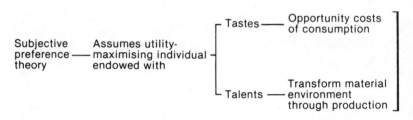

Summary 3.3 _____

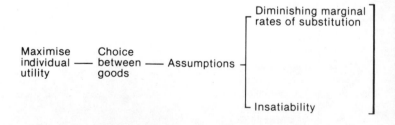

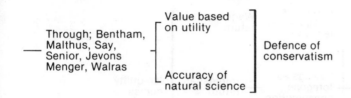

Through; Bentham, Malthus, Say, Senior, Jevons Menger, Walras — Value based on utility / Accuracy of natural science — Defence of conservatism

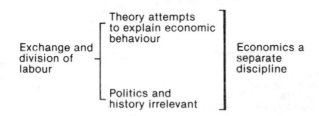

Exchange and division of labour — Theory attempts to explain economic behaviour / Politics and history irrelevant — Economics a separate discipline

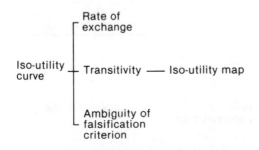

Iso-utility curve — Rate of exchange / Transitivity — Iso-utility map / Ambiguity of falsification criterion

Freedom is the market: the subjective preference theory of value

Summary 3.4 _____

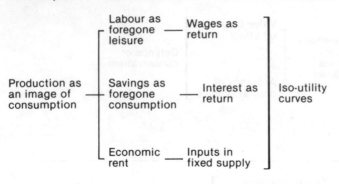

Production as an image of consumption
- Labour as foregone leisure — Wages as return
- Savings as foregone consumption — Interest as return
- Economic rent — Inputs in fixed supply

Iso-utility curves

Summary 3.5 _____

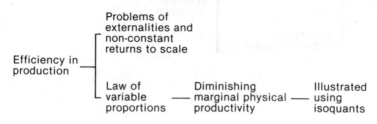

Efficiency in production
- Problems of externalities and non-constant returns to scale
- Law of variable proportions — Diminishing marginal physical productivity — Illustrated using isoquants

Summary 3.6 _____

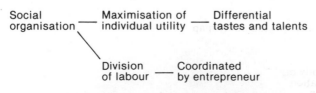

Social organisation — Maximisation of individual utility — Differential tastes and talents

Division of labour — Coordinated by entrepreneur

Summary 3.7 _____

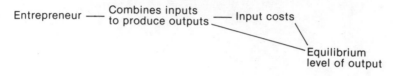

Entrepreneur — Combines inputs to produce outputs — Input costs

Equilibrium level of output

Summary 3.8

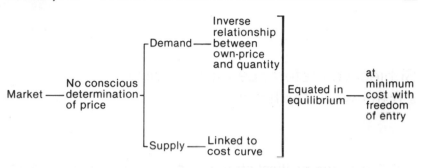

Summary 3.9

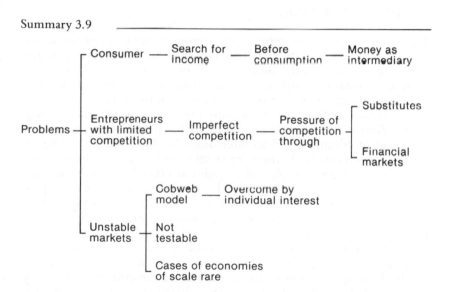

Chapter 4

Subjective preference theory policy:
a framework for liberty

4.1 The broad political strategy associated with subjective preference theory

If we look at any recent multiparty election in the western world we can invariably find a party which is advocating the reduction of government 'interference' in the domestic economy; lower taxes on higher incomes; decreasing restrictions on international movements of goods and finance; and strict control over changes in the amount of money in the economy. Also such politicians advocate a social policy resting on the family and emphasising the need for punishment rather than treatment of criminals, and an international political stance resting on national superiority and strong opposition to the USSR. In 1979 the Conservative Party was elected to political office in the UK on such a manifesto and made a determined effort to implement such a programme. This programme was highly radical by post-war British standards and in the first year every economic indicator moved in the 'wrong' direction. Pragmatism seemed to demand a reversal of some parts of policy, but appeals for a return to previous conventions of 'commonsense', 'realism' and 'rationality' were all treated with scorn by the leading members of the Conservative government. Not only did these leaders appear to be exceptionally clear and unified on their overall strategy but also they were seeing every particular policy as contributing to an overall strategy.

This exceptionally firm principled stand can be partially explained by reference to the logical power of subjective preference theory of value. In a situation of crisis (and who could doubt that the UK in the 1970s was in political crisis with four elections and effectively four changes of party/parties in government with changes from Labour to Conservative to Labour to Labour with Liberal Parliamentary support to Conservative again) the recent past ceases to be a guide to the future and strong beliefs become more important in making decisions. Strong beliefs carry greater conviction if they are logically coherent, thus a logical argument is important to encourage supporters and defuse opposition. To say someone's ideas make sense only on the basis of a particular set of assumptions is much less damning than to say they do

88

not make sense at all. Subjective preference theory is the logical under-pinning of the 1980 UK Conservative Government's policies.

The crisis situation in the UK was important in providing the back-ground in which fundamentalist ideas become politically significant. Margaret Thatcher and Keith Joseph were significant in forcing the Conservative Party to adopt a rigorous subjective preference view of the world. But the ideas themselves were readily available because many economists in ivy-clad, ivory towers in Europe and the USA between 1870 and 1980 had been developing and refining that view of the world. It might then be more accurate to call economics the 'con-servative science' rather than the 'dismal science', though for many of us in the UK in 1980 the two descriptions may be interchangeable!

At one level we could shorten this chapter considerably by referring to the previous chapter, pointing out that we have shown how utility-seeking individuals can combine through voluntary contracts in a mar-ket for a good and exchange at a price which guarantees everyone who participates some gained satisfaction. Perfect competition is pretty much guaranteed by freedom of information and pursuit of individual gain by potential entrants and thus the unrestricted market is equitable and efficient with only a few unlikely exceptions to this rule. All the components of a basic centre-right (in the political spectrum) philo-sophy are present in this model. Tough-minded individuals pursue their own ends on a world scale whilst recognising the self-interest in vol-untary contract (the first to use violence is not always the final victor) as the typical social relation. Laws of supply and demand are then shown analytically to be 'natural' laws, akin to the law of gravity operating with an anonymous, universal force on everybody and thus inevitable (in the sense that a plane flying in circles does not break the law of gravity but wastes energy in resisting that law) and fair (in the sense that the constraints on individual behaviour are not due to human agents but blind providence).

All any socially conscious agent has to do is to protect the rule of voluntary contract. For providing that service it may exact some com-pensating amount of resources as a tax from each participating indi-vidual. (There is no strong reason why the tax per individual could not be equal since all individuals would lose from the breakdown of the market and the tax would hopefully be so small as not to be significant). Undoubtedly, many voters for political parties of the right regard this argument as quite adequate as a theoretical basis for their support. From this position they could go on to argue that societies which do not allow free markets to operate are political tyrannies and that the people who live in them are socially uncivilised for permitting the tyr-anny to continue. Only societies which are moving in the direction of freer markets are seen as developing whilst those which are further restricting markets are not. But to go much beyond this point in terms of a logical subjective preference justification for nationalism (leading to a policy of strong military forces) and racism (leading to a policy of restricting migration) would be to exaggerate the case. To go this much further would need the introduction of the debate about genetics versus environment in the formation of individual personality and ethnic characteristics. Let it suffice to say that the rigidly pre-social view of economic preferences and choice in subjective preference theory is compatible with genetic determinism at the group and individual levels.

Thus at this rough and ready level we can see the connections between the essentials of the subjective preference theory of value and a widely prevalent contemporary political stance. To increase confidence in subjective preference theory (and therefore its associated politics) it helps to refine the argument by showing that the analysis of a single market can be logically developed into a theory of a whole economy. It is this project that has dominated subjective preference economics from 1870 to the present day. Before attempting to summarise that activity we will briefly rehearse the general criteria by which we can judge a theory to be correct from the perspective of subjective preference economics (and more generally the Popperian theory of knowledge).

Theorising is divided into three components: assumptions, deductions and testing. Assumptions are essentially arbitrary; to talk about assumptions in themselves being more or less acceptable is meaningless from this point of view since all assumptions are deviations from the complexity of experience and thus united by a lack of realism. Deduction is dominated by rules of logic and as such is not open to criticism, the ability to replicate a logical deduction precisely is increased by the form of the argument being mathematical. This encourages the use of mathematics and feeds back to the choice of assumption which must be amenable to mathematical formulation. This would seem to leave the only area of criticism as empirical testing, that is comparing the outcome of deductions from a set of assumptions about the observable with actual observations and, preferably evaluating the performance of this theory against predictions from the deductions deriving from some competing set of assumptions.

For subjective preference theory both ends of the process are fixed. The assumptions about utility-maximising individuals (which are amenable to mathematical representation using differential calculus) are mandatory and the goal of predicting a stable, efficient, equitable outcome is, to say the least, highly acceptable. Objections that this process seems to neglect the crucial testing stage can be met from a number of directions. Firstly, the assertion that the 'market' economies in the world today are relatively stable (yesterday's prices are relatively good guides to today's), efficient (people who live in them have high levels of consumption) and equitable (coercion is by historical standards at a low level). Secondly that the theorising process is still only at the second stage, deductions from assumptions are still crude and the project is to refine the argument by the use of more sophisticated mathematical techniques, which weaken restrictions not essential to the basic assumptions but only necessary to allow the use of our present inadequate mathematics. Thirdly, that no competing theory has been demonstrated to be better in tests where different observations are predicted. Thus methodologically, subjective preference theory is able to defend itself against much criticism.

The next three sections of this chapter summarise the attempts by economists to validate the subjective preference view of the world rigorously. They also show how the theory re-emerged from set-backs in the 1950s and 1960s to become the dominant theory of economics again in the 1970s in many universities, government departments and international institutions. The last section of this chapter moves towards an assessment of the political support for subjective preference economics and concludes that its place in the economics pantheon of capitalist societies is assured.

4.2 The economy as a single market: the capital controversy

The experience of the 1930s in the USA greatly eroded the inherent conservative complacency in mainstream economics as unemployment rose dramatically and failed to fall significantly for a decade. The first defence of subjective preference theory that relative stability, efficiency and equity were self-evidently the properties of free-market economies looked rather shaky in the face of that experience. And, if that were true for the USA, then in the UK the lessons were even harsher as registered unemployment remained over the million mark for virtually the entire inter-war period. This erosion was compounded by the emergence of an alternative theory associated with the name of Keynes, whose position in the elite of society and economics was well-established, despite a rather maverick image. Up to that time subjective preference theory had not been particularly concerned with the determination of the level of aggregate activity, seeing that level as the unpredictable outcome of millions of individual decisions in thousands of markets. To be unemployed meant to choose not to participate in the markets for your talents because the extra satisfaction from leisure as opposed to work was more highly valued than the additional commodities that could be obtained with the wages currently offered. Keynes claimed to explain the aggregate level of activity in the economy and predict true unemployment where individuals desiring to work at the going wage could not get jobs. This ex-post prediction of the 1930s 'Depression' appeared to make the theories associated with Keynes superior by Popperian standards. A challenge which had to be met if subjective preference theory was to regain its dominance.

If the answer were to meet the Keynesian heretics on their own ground, then predictions about general economic growth and fluctuations in overall employment levels would be necessary. The deduction of such predictions from subjective preference assumptions is apparently a relatively simple matter if the economy could be treated as a single market with the level of employment as an explicit variable. A single market involves assuming a single good being produced and consumed. The level of employment as a variable suggests assuming a single talent if unmanageable graphical complications are to be avoided. But if the one good is simply the product of a single type of labour then all that can be predicted is that the efficient level of employment will fall as output of the good falls. Not a very interesting, indeed rather trivial, prediction, namely that if people value leisure more than employment, then the output of the good will decrease, if people are allowed to express that preference through the market.

Figure 4.1 illustrates this case and shows how the increased desire for leisure can be represented as a shift in the supply curve, which then cuts the horizontal demand for labour time curve (assuming overall constant returns to scale in production) at a lower level of employment. This simple formulation is useful to explain what in subjective preference theory is called the 'natural' level of employment. 'Natural' in this context means the overall level resulting from the decisions of individuals choosing freely whether to work or not at the going rate of reward. This concept has the effect of diminishing the ability to criticise an economic system for having large numbers of people registered as unemployed as it is almost impossible to establish with certainty whether an individual registered as unemployed is actively seeking work or content to live off welfare payments and merely go through

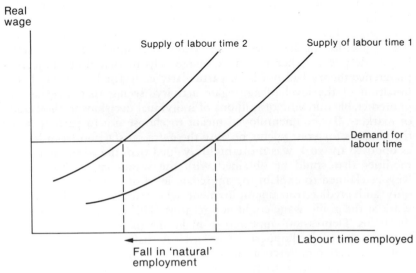

Fig. 4.1   A simple aggregate labour market

the motions of seeking work to satisfy the welfare authorities. Unemployment for subjective preference theory is a state of mind not a state statistic.

To go beyond this argument that removes unemployment as a problem by definition rather than by policy action simply requires a revision of Fig. 4.1 to look more like an orthodox market diagram. In Fig. 4.2 the demand curve slopes downward and the possibility of 'involuntary' unemployment is introduced when the wage rate is above the equilibrium level. For subjective preference theory such a situation can only continue to exist if some human agency is unfairly exercising power against the interests of those who are willing to work more at that wage or indeed for a lower wage. It will surprise few readers that the agency singled out in subjective preference circles is trade unionism. Greedy workers are responsible for the frustrated unemployed, trade union power only works by excluding the involuntary unemployed, not by attacking employers. The market is on the side of the unemployed.

But to get this conclusion we must have asserted something additional to that of Fig. 4.1, i.e. a downward sloping demand relationship. One assumption to give this result could be that as more labour is employed physical productivity per labourer falls. This implies overall decreasing returns to scale in the case of only one input, i.e. a standard type of labour. Decreasing returns to scale is not an assumption that subjective preference theory makes easily, preferring to assume constant returns to scale as we saw in Chapter 3. An alternative assumption is to introduce at least one other input which can be substituted for labour as the wage rises with the possibility of off-setting the fall in output. The simplest input to introduce as a competing substitute input

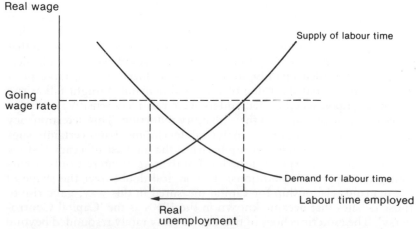

Fig. 4.2   An aggregate labour market with downward sloping demand relationship

for homogeneous labour appears to be something called capital, with its own reward, interest. This assumption is doubly attractive because it is both apparently simple analytically and powerful in the range of questions it allows to be examined. Capital as a collection of machines leads towards growth theory, capital as a source of a form of reward called interest leads towards aggregate distribution theory, capital as a result of technical knowledge and natural resources leads towards international trade theory as an expression of unequal endowments.

All these questions could thus be discussed in a simple model which incorporates amounts of uniform labour earning a wage and a measure of capital stock earning a rate of interest. This seemed to permit subjective preference theory to say something rigorous but intelligible to non-economists on all the issues where Keynesians were virtually unchallenged in the 1950s. The model predicted that as interest rates fell relative to wages then the effective capital stock used would increase as employers were forced by competition to economise on relatively expensive labour time and increase the use of capital, i.e. the demand curve for labour would slope down. If this could be shown to be the case, then natural laws for unemployment, economic growth, international trade and income distribution between inputs could be shown to exist at the aggregate level in parallel with the laws of any single market. Unfortunately for subjective preference theory this did not turn out to be as simple as it at first seems.

The critical problem is the measurement of the stock of capital in an economy. To add capstan lathes to warehouse space without some common index is impossible. The index for subjective preference theory which reflects accurately the value of commodities is the system of relative prices. But relative prices already include interest being paid out as part of the cost of goods included in the capital stock. Thus as the rate of interest changes, relative prices of all non-labour inputs change and the total size of the 'capital stock' measured in terms of those prices also changes. It is rather like the value of a good rather than its physical quantity being used in a single market analysis. In that situation if the price of the good rises then we would expect the physical quantity demanded unambiguously to be reduced in subjective preference analysis, but the value of the good demanded might fall *or* rise depending upon whether demanders were relatively sensitive or insensitive to the price change in their quantity reduction. This determinancy is not conducive to rigorous analytical development and certainly suggests that an inverse relationship between the total use of a capital stock measured in price terms and the level of the rate of interest only occurs under well-specified conditions. This logical doubt over the shape of the demand relationship for capital measured in this way, gave rise to those debates that became known in the 1960s as the 'Capital Controversy'. The esoteric echoes of this controversy rarely resounded beyond economic departments of universities but do have significance in understanding how a revitalised subjective preference theory grew out of an apparent defeat in the late 1960s.

This controversy concluded that it is impossible to deduce an unambiguous prediction of any crucial variables from aggregate capital models where capital is measured by using prices to add up all types of manufactured inputs and raw materials. To get an unambiguous prediction required the assumption of either a zero rate of interest (in effect a labour only economy) or a rigidly fixed relative price between a unit of the capital input good and a unit of the final output good. This latter condition removes the *economic* difference between the two goods and is effectively a world in which a single good is consumable, storable, and capable of being used with any amount of labour to produce more of itself. A world entirely lacking in economic interest but possibly useful for science fiction writers.

The responses to this defeat by economists loyal to subjective preference theory were twofold. The first, which most students still experience, is to assert that the perverse cases do not empirically exist, or are rare, and that, in general, we can treat the whole economy as if the price of an input was inversely related to its degree of use. Capital is put on one axis of graphs in textbooks, often without even suggesting this might be a problem, and logical conclusions are drawn as if they were rigorously unambiguous. Mysterious and enigmatic, this capital exists only in economics texts, justifying inequality to generation after generation of students of economics, not admitting that belief in capital so defined is faith which only masquerades as fact. The second response has returned to the roots of subjective preference theory and accepted the need to prune totally all the single market models of the whole economy. The questions that these models tried to answer about unemployment, economic growth, international trade and aggregate income distribution are thus declared to be either inaccessible or uninteresting to truly scientific economics. This is justified by the argument that these aggregate social phenomena are analytically the outcomes of many individual decisions and, therefore, cannot be directly analysed.

In effect this has led to other schools of economic thought dominating many topics of economic policy. Concepts like monopoly, poverty and exploitation have no place in subjective preference theory. This may help explain the unpopularity of subjective preference theory formulations among economics students. It is not so much that subjective preference theory gives unpalatable answers but that it refuses even to ask certain questions at the basic level of principles. However, for those who nevertheless persist in studying economics (and develop the necessary mathematical skills) within a university degree there is a higher state of mind achievable, which can conceive of a 'general equilibrium' where the positive properties of a single market do exist for the whole economy. In the next section we will take a quick look at this conceptualisation to avoid the impression that subjective preference theory can only discuss the United Kingdom economy as if it were Robinson Crusoe living off coconuts on a slightly larger island.

4.3 The economy as many markets: general equilibrium analysis

The integration of economics and mathematics has reached one of its highest points in examining the properties of a multi-market economy from a subjective preference standpoint. The concern in this section, however, is with the principles involved and so a mathematical formulation is not used which means that the aesthetic properties of mathematics are lost. This loss is not trivial since as economics has ascended into ivory towers the criterion of success and excellence has changed for many economists from social relevance to mathematical elegance. This potential which existed in the flirtations with mathematical formulations by economists like Jevons, Menger and Walras in the late nineteenth century has now achieved full consummation. This is probably to the horror of many of our readers who may see the marriage as the work of a mathematical Frankenstein who constructs the economics bride to suit his needs.

Subjective preference theory starts from the individual with inherent tastes and talents expressing preferences through freely entered into contracts to maximise utility. The decisions of the individual can be divided into two interconnected groups, those which involve a net inflow of utility and those which involve a net outflow. The questions of whether a particular good or service will be in one group or the other for an individual depends only upon its relative price. For instance, if a good has a relatively high price in terms of others and the individual does not value the good particularly highly then a net sale of that good might be expected. Thus goods and services cannot be classified into necessities or luxuries, since all individual decisions are sensitive to prices within a structure of specific, individual, and inherent tastes and talents. The possibility of continuing widespread trade exists due to varying tastes and talents, although the specific transactions involved will vary enormously in response to price changes.

The first prediction that general equilibrium theory makes is that there exists a set of prices in all markets under which everyone will be satisfied to the extent that nobody wishes to exchange further at those prices. That is starting from individuals who respond to price changes in the systematic fashion described in Chapter 3 it is possible to logically deduce that there is always a set of non-negative prices where nobody sees it in their interest to trade further. This also assumes there are constant returns to scale and competition in production. Mathematically this equilibrium is a situation where the desired net inflows and outflows have all gone to zero for all individuals and all goods and services, unless a good is still so plentiful when its price has dropped to zero, that no one wishes for more. In that case those who possess that good may still be willing to dispose of it but cannot even give it away. Such a case of excess supply at zero price is treated as unusual and in general it is assumed that for most goods at least some people will be willing to hold the total available quantity of the good once its price has fallen sufficiently.

This type of equilibrium can be shown to exist for any number of individuals and any number of goods and services including as many types of labour and machinery as it is wished to economically distinguish. The importance of this demonstration is not that it describes any particular economy or enables us to measure the price at which one good or service will exchange for another but that it shows qualitatively that prices exist which will satisfy everybody, including those who possess a chosen amount of a good, those who have given up possessing some amount of the good to obtain another, and all those who never possessed the good or wanted any amount of that good at that price. For obvious reasons the mathematical proofs of this prediction are called existence theorems and jobs in several famous universities are available to those who wish to try to simplify the assumptions necessary for this prediction. Only those with degrees in mathematics need apply.

This mathematical achievement of demonstrating existence is not considered further here, rather the important ideological significance in this exercise is raised. Thus, if the underlying assumptions about the nature of human existence are accepted both descriptively and morally then a remorseless logic apparently draws us to the unavoidable conclusion that a society always has a possible situation in which a set of numbers, called 'prices' exist. These prices will link all society's members through voluntary contracts in a complex fashion so that everyone is relatively content. Everybody would prefer more of everything (except those few foods in excess supply) but can only gain more if someone else is *forced* to give up something. The fundamental principle of individual liberty is offended unless all exchange is on the basis of voluntary contract. It is this that determines the welfare (and the civilisation or development) of society. Therefore a society has achieved a desirable state when nobody can become better off without somebody else becoming worse off. This state of society is technically known as *Pareto superiority* and is implied in any general equilibrium and thus links the mathematical existence of equilibrium with an equity criterion that any such equilibrium is desirable.

Subjective preference supporters accept an equity criterion which assesses a state of society in which one person being immensely rich and everybody else being destitute as no different in welfare terms from a state in which everybody consumes equally. They are unable to choose who is to decide if an attack upon the liberty of the rich to use their resources and satisfy their tastes is justified, as not to accept the inequality of the market means to accept the tyranny of some other person. The core strength of subjective preference theory can now be seen. Starting from plausible assumptions about human nature, a whole economy is logically constructed which proves to have desirable properties in harmony with the original image of human nature. This 'natural' harmony of strong individuals and a society organised on market principles is underpinned by appeal to the liberal virtues of voluntary contract and equality before the law.

But ever since the formal development of general equilibrium analysis in the nineteenth century there have existed doubts about the stability of the system. Even accepting that general equilibrium can exist there is still uncertainty that after a shock which displaces the system from one equilibrium there will be forces to move the system towards a new equilibrium. The analytical crux of this doubt is that when individuals trade at non-equilibrium prices then they are unable to retrieve the original situation as prices change. For instance, if my talent to produce is contracted to be sold at a low price despite my general tastes for high consumption because I do not believe prices will change in the future, then those who would have been willing to buy my talent at a high price or sell me consumption goods at a lower price at equilibrium, or both, will be frustrated if prices change. They will then be forced to change their decisions, which then feed back to my next decisions and so on, with no guarantee that the system will settle down at all to our mutual satisfaction. Various behavioural conditions have been suggested to ensure that such stability can be mathematically guaranteed.

The best known of these conditions is one called 'tâtonnement' which does not allow any non-equilibrium trading, but instead draws on the image of an auction in which prices are called, bids are collected and compared from all the individual participants, and prices then raised for goods in excess demand and reduced for those in excess supply. No actual transactions are permitted to take place until all the bids balance out. Obviously this device is behaviourally very artificial and a great deal of effort has gone into weakening this condition. The greatest advance has been locating the major cause of instability in situations where a rise of price for a good is met by a strong preference by many individuals to maintain the level of consumption of that good and thus reduce consumption of other goods and services. The future will see further efforts in this direction to reduce the dependency of the stability of general equilibrium on processes as artificial as 'tâtonnement' by theorists of the subjective preference persuasion.

Other problems of general equilibrium theory are less threatening. For instance, jointly consumed or produced goods do face general equilibrium analysis with problems. Some goods and services are not used up in consumption by identifiable individuals but are 'public goods' in that they become accessible to others as soon as they are available to one and thus allocating the costs to individual consumers becomes difficult. National defence and non–cable television transmissions are two possible cases. Products jointly produced in one process also throw up similar problems in attributing costs. For instance, beef and leather come in relatively fixed proportions as do various oil products. Economists supporting the subjective preference school are willing to assume these cases are not widespread in practice and exclude them by assumption. Their critics have paid much attention to hypothetical cases, arguing that public and jointly produced goods are a strong reason for government intervention. The impact of this criticism has been very limited as the general principle that market prices do reflect the real scarcity or abundance of goods and services is not fundamentally challenged.

It is this lack of fundamental theoretical challenge on its own terms that ensures the central place of subjective preference questions in academic journals. Certainly general equilibrium analysis still involves making assumptions which are very strong, for example contracts for future transactions being made with perfect foresight and all goods and services being overall substitutes for each other. But this situation simply gives subjective preference theory a continuing research programme. This academic project has continued independently of political favour continuously for a hundred years. Periodically however, political and economic conditions emerge which bring subjective preference theory in a relatively pure form to the centre of the political stage. Such general conditions came into being in the 1970s and found subjective preference both consolidated in theory and militant in policy recommendations. No longer content to sit in the royal box barracking the new plays, subjective preference theory found some influential backers, an appreciative audience, and a superstar in Milton Friedman from Chicago.

4.4 Economic policy and subjective preference theory: monetarism

The paradox of subjective preference policy is that, whilst the whole theoretical discussion on 'general equilibrium' can be conducted with no mention of 'money' (all prices could be barter rates of exchange), when we come to policy very little else but money is discussed. This paradox can give the impression that the policy package called 'monetarism' has no firm roots in value theory, being the product of a few fanatics unable to hear the truth for the rustle of banknotes and blinded to reality by the glitter of gold. We can now see that this need not be the case. If a market economy is assumed to rest on the bedrock of general equilibrium with thousands of markets efficiently interconnected by prices reflecting the stable tastes and talents of millions of individuals, then it is unlikely that a change in any particular market or modified individual choice will produce significant disruption of the economy. The shock waves of such change would run through the whole economy, through long chains of substitutes only requiring infinitesimally small alterations by the mass of individuals to restore equilibrium, like dropping a stone in the middle of the Pacific.

The only exception to this rule is the market for any good that enters into many transactions because it has the property of being widely acceptable for exchange purposes, i.e. money in any of its multifarious forms. Disruption in that market affects directly every individual's confidence in being able to move between markets where he or she wishes to sell to markets where he or she wishes to buy. It is not that the ends of individuals become uncertain but that the confidence in the means to those ends is eroded. Monetary policy is important because money is the lubricant for the general equilibrium engine, the engine can tolerate some variations in the amount of lubricant and still run but it is vulnerable to sudden large changes. To analyse the detailed policy implication of this broad position we can again use the analytical framework of the single market we developed in Chapter 3. As a first step this involves dividing influences on the quantity of money in an economy into those that determine supply and those that determine demand. Some critics would object to this preliminary step in organising influences, claiming that if sufficient money does not exist then more would and could be created or invented to satisfy the excess demand, i.e. supply is not independent of demand but determined by demand. But having noted that criticism here which will be returned to in Chapter 10, we will develop now the pure subjective preference case, starting with the supply side.

If we lived in the UK in the nineteenth century, we probably would be extolling the virtues of the gold standard, as did the French authorities in the 1960s. The argument would go as follows. As market exchange extended over space and time involving more and more people who never met face to face then the need grew for some convenient, universally accepted medium of exchange. Gold as an easily divisible, durable commodity, available in a fairly restricted quantity with various other uses and thus valuable in its own right, has obvious advantages as such a medium. Provided everyone accepts some basic rules in terms of not issuing notes, which promise to pay gold on demand, much beyond their immediate stock then trade can occur throughout a large economy without the gold itself having to circulate. Even if confidence in notes is diminished then the gold itself can be used and trade can continue. This suggests the government will have no need to intervene in monetary matters unless there is widespread fraudulent issue of notes not backed by sufficient stocks of gold.

Internationally the use of gold as money provides an automatic mechanism for correcting national trading imbalances. The mechanism works as follows. A nation in overall trading deficit, i.e. buying more from abroad than selling in terms of gold prices, would suffer an outflow of gold to pay for imports not matched by exports, people losing gold would have to reduce the number of notes in their names in circulation to match this loss. Fewer notes would thus be matched against an undiminished supply of commodities and the value of each remaining standard note in what it could purchase would rise. For instance, a note redeemable for a gram of gold would now be exchangeable for a greater weight of flour than before. This is equivalent to a decrease in the gold price of goods in the national economy. Foreigners with gold would find themselves able to buy greater amounts of goods and total exports would tend to increase; conversely, imports would fall as locally produced goods would appear more competitive in terms of gold compared with foreign substitutes.

The problems with the gold standard are twofold. Firstly, sudden changes in supply could be brought about by private companies and governments with control over gold stocks, either in the ground or in vaults. Such changes could produce highly undesirable disruption if large adjustments were entailed. Secondly, it is difficult to ensure that individuals, companies and governments obey the rules that notes should only be issued against actual gold stocks. Governments have often proved unwilling and unable to enforce these rules on others and, where they have legislated to themselves the virtual monopoly over the issue of notes, they have almost invariably broken the rules.

A radical alternative to the gold standard system has been advocated by the toughest-minded supporters of the subjective preference view of the world. Arguing that it is always in the government's interest and against the general interest to expand the supply of money to increase the government's ability to purchase goods, some writers, like Hayek, recommend that the only solution can be virtually unregulated private banks issuing their own notes up to whatever level each bank owner wished. This solution is totally in line with subjective preference principles as it puts responsibility for their actions squarely on the shoulders of individuals, removing the illusions that the gold standard protects them from the avarice of their fellow citizens in their role as bankers and that politicians are protectors of any interest, other than their own. Despite being admirable in its consistency to subjective preference principles, this alternative is too heady even for Milton Friedman. In analytical terms it could be argued that entry into, and exit from, banking under such conditions would be so easy that the money market would be chronically liable to cumulative expansion and contraction again producing risks of disruption of the supply of money and dislocation of the whole economy. Such a cumulative contraction could form a monetarist causal explanation of the 1930s economic depression in the USA.

Today, the mainstream view of subjective preference theorists on the money supply is that the government does and should exert considerable influence on the domestic money supply. To aim for complete control is impossible as the government can only directly control the base and not the height of a pyramid of money creation in any economy where cheques drawn on private banks are widely used. Government influence should be used to limit rapid expansion or contraction of money supply by acting on the monetary base in a decisive manner by providing money to the banking system at times of contraction and refusing to provide money for rapid expansion, even though this must almost inevitably involve accepting an unpopular rise in interest rates. It is this strong policy guideline that has given the name 'monetarism' to the economic policy of the subjective preference school of thought. But it must be remembered that, firstly, 'monetarism' is a policy which expresses a deep confidence in the free market system and, secondly, even that policy does not extend to the international monetary sphere.

Internationally, there is no reason for the government to intervene in the free working of the markets for national currencies. In such markets each country's monetary unit is quoted in terms of other countries' monetary units. These markets correct imbalances in national trading positions by pushing up the value of those monetary units which are scarce (currencies of countries which are exporting a higher value of goods and services than they are importing) relative to monetary units which are abundant (currencies of countries which are purchasing a higher value of goods and services from abroad than they are selling) and thus tend to redress imbalances. The activity of the government is limited to the national level and, even at that level, policy need only be concerned with relatively wide targets, not precise fine-tuning of a rigorously defined variable. Thus monetarists could admit that it is difficult precisely to define what money is for any particular economy and still claim that if the money supply by any definition rose or fell by more than ten per cent in a year then the government is neglecting its duty compared with the situation in which money supply by that same definition rose or fell by five per cent or less.

Given that a free market society tends to achieve general equilibrium states and can smoothly adjust to piecemeal changes in the tastes and talents of its individual members providing the government offsets substantial fluctuations in the supply of money, then it might appear unnecessary to go on to discuss the demand for money. Yet the demand for money relationship has been the centre of much debate in its own right. The reason for this interest does not lie in the internal logic of subjective preference theory but in a proposition advanced in the development of Keynesian ideas that at certain crucial times large amounts of money would cease to be used as a means of exchange. At such times holding the money supply steady would mean accepting a substantial fall in the effective amount of money in the economy with a consequent disruptive impact on many individual decisions. This theoretical situation was given the name *liquidity trap* and has the distinction that it has been carefully taught to students of economics for around thirty years without ever being observed. A rather cruel parallel would be if dragon anatomy appeared on the current biology syllabus.

With monotonous regularity economists have observed that the total values of activity in an economy are strongly statistically correlated with the supplies of money over the same period. But the theoretical criticism of the liquidity trap put forward by Milton Friedman does give insights into the currently best-known subjective preference economist in action and, more specifically, shows the mechanism of monetarism as a set of policies.

Friedman treats the demand for money relationship as just another demand relationship. Individuals demand money because it has a use for them, i.e. it possesses utility. Money's main use is to facilitate current purchases of goods and services. In this role it is very difficult to substitute anything else for money. Techniques of exchange and individual tastes for holding money will change but such changes are likely to be systematic and piecemeal respectively. To discard the concept of a money demand function because these kind of changes occur would mean discarding all demand functions not just the one for money. However, money does have a second role which is to store up purchasing power for the future. In this role, money has many substitutes which can be grouped into three main categories, physical goods, financial assets and training. Physical goods are attractive substitutes for money as a store for purchasing power because any general price rises will mean that fewer goods will be able to be purchased in the future. Financial assets are attractive because either interest is paid, e.g. government bonds, or in the case of company shares there is a probability of profits enhancing their value. Training to enhance a natural talent is attractive because it can yield an increased flow of purchasing power over the rest of a working life.

Friedman was able to argue on this basis that the demand for money as a store of value is theoretically the same as any other demand relationship. There are close substitutes with different advantages which will take much of the strain of any adjustment to changed circumstances and there is no reason to expect the quantity of money demanded to be drastically affected. Having deduced this prediction from standard subjective preference assumptions, Friedman then sets out to test this prediction statistically and fails to falsify the hypothesis that the total demand for money is almost entirely dependent on the total value of current economic activity. This piece of work can be seen as a classic example of subjective preference theorising meeting all the criteria we set out in section 4.1. Since there is therefore good reason to assume that the main use of money is for financing current transactions, we will now make this assumption and combine it with the dominant subjective preference views on the money supply to examine the mechanics of monetarism.

Any government wishing to increase its type and levels of activity is unwilling to increase taxes to finance them because of resulting political unpopularity and unwilling to borrow because this may directly draw resources away from investment. This produces a tendency to expand the money supply, say, through cash and cheque payments to new employees and private suppliers; an increase not matched by removal of money elsewhere. The new employees and suppliers find themselves holding more money than they desire and go into various markets to purchase the goods and services they prefer to have instead of those sums of money. But the economy is already in a state of general equilibrium and people are not willing to sell those goods and services unless they are offered higher prices. Therefore, a tendency will exist for all prices to rise, a condition called *inflation*. That is the value of total activity will rise roughly proportionally to the increase in the money supply because prices have risen, not because real economic activity has increased, and only in this situation will individuals stop trying to dispose of excess money balances. It is the unexpected change in prices that directly erodes individuals' confidence in contracts and, for subjective preference theory, loss of confidence in contract means loss of confidence in civilised society. The extreme alternatives to the natural law of markets are political tyranny and the natural law of the jungle.

For a government that wishes to avoid these alternatives there are three paths, two of which are rejected by subjective preference theory. Firstly, increasing taxes or borrowing to finance any increased government economic activity is undesirable because it erodes that freedom of individual choice which is at the core of subjective preference ethics. Secondly, building in general price increases into contracts involving future payments is undesirable because such indexing is unlikely precisely to anticipate specific price changes and the arbitrary distributional effects of this unpredictability still threaten confidence. Thirdly and desirably, the government drives out inflation by reducing its contribution to the rate of growth of the money supply directly, assisted by reducing its own economic activity. Unfortunately, whilst putting inflation into an economy is easy, taking it out is difficult. Many individuals who have entered into speculative contracts which anticipated borrowing money in the expectation of repaying out of future money incomes increased by future price rises will find they cannot meet those contracts out of the decreased money supply, bankruptcies will result and real economic activity fall. Only after this process is complete, inevitably involving unemployment, will the rise in prices abate and the dominant relationship between changes in the supply of money and changes in prices reassert itself. Without this painful process, which could take years, general price rises are likely to accelerate and the threat to the thin fabric of civilisation grow. Subjective preference theory allows for the possibility of collapse of civilisation, experienced as a general loss of individual liberty and the rise of political tyranny. Continuing unpredictable rises in prices due to irresponsible government expansion of the money supply is a possible road to this collapse.

4.5 Conclusion: towards a critique of subjective preference theory

Subjective preference theory in its present form appears formidable. The loss of theoretical face in the capital controversy resulted in a shift back towards the more rigorous statements of general equilibrium theory. The rather abstract conclusions of general equilibrium have been more than compensated by the straightforward policy recommendations of monetarism. Thus, by combining complex theory and simple policy, the subjective preference school of economic thought seems powerful in its appeal to both faith and reason. The faith lies in the assumption of self-assertive individualism as the essence of human nature. Like all doctrines of immutable human nature there is an element of circularity in the argument. The statement that all our actions are in pursuit of gaining individual utility is unquestionable if we accept the assumption that maximum individual utility is what we seek. Why this hunger for personal gain should stop at mutually agreed contracts is a difficult question. Another awkward question is whether all those people who refuse to accept that subjective preference theory describes the world, and can only be explained in terms of criminality and insanity, deserve to lose their liberty.

Thus, if all human beings are by their very nature doomed to seek their own individual interest and, under favourable social circumstances, are willing to accept the discipline of contract, then what kind of creature will object to such a state of society? Obviously the answer is a creature which is not altogether human. Not accepting contract is evidence of a criminal personality, whether the non-acceptance takes the form of burglary or striking. Not seeking self-interest, including some moderate self-gratifying altruism, is prima facie evidence of insanity, whether the label be saint or lunatic. Such deviance can only be met in a civilised society with force before it threatens the very fabric of civilisation, since, like inflation, it diminishes general confidence in contracts. When the deviants are whole societies then the subjective preference approach to international politics can legitimate imperialism, as a civilising mission to those individuals willing to accept the principles of civilisation, and also justify repression of any remaining barbarians.

Inside civilised society, politicians are a major problem. In courting popularity for their self-advancement, politicians almost invariably break the rules of contract by offering what they do not own at a price which does not reflect the real opportunity cost of the resources. Thus the less resources they have to use the better in subjective preference theory. But if it is accepted that sovereignty has to reside in political institutions in order to guarantee contracts under the law then it is difficult to set binding limitations on politicians as a group. Appropriate limitations might include written constitutions; separation of powers between executive, legislature and judiciary; and low payment of politicians forcing them to have economic goals other than political office. These formal limitations are important but even more significant has been the shift in subjective preference politics from such formal (and often elitist) views of a desirable political system towards a much more populist position.

Mass suffrage, in this latter position, becomes desirable as the most effective check on political ambition, as the 'ordinary citizen' knows the reality of the subjective preference view of the world and, in the end, will exercise choice in favour of those politicians who talk in terms of that reality. Less scrupulous politicians may try to make their particular brands of politics attractive by advertising and using bright packaging but, like all false claims, the discerning consumer will only try it once. Universal suffrage combined with the right to form pressure groups to inform fellow-citizens and politicians better on particular issues is a concept of democracy totally compatible with much in subjective preference theory. However, this espousal of democracy sits uncomfortably with the more repressive attitude towards political opposition entailed in the restrictive definitions of human nature and civilisation. An emphasis on strong law and order and national defence in the interests of civilisation coexists uncomfortably with the proclamation of fundamental human liberty. At times of stress, intolerance of opposition may not just remain confined to criminals and aliens. The political economic critique of subjective preference theory can start from examining this contradiction between the denial of reasonable opposition and the proclamation of individual liberty. But that critique must also explain the current ascendancy of subjective preference economics as the basis for economic policy making in many countries in 1980.

The basis for this success will only be suggested here. Firstly support of political parties which adopt the rationale of subjective preference economics by those receiving significant incomes in the forms of rent, interests and dividends is long-standing. At the very beginning of the twentieth century, economists like Irving Fisher and J.B. Clark in the USA were using the concept of utility to justify such forms of payment. These justifications acknowledged that such rewards were not directly associated with acts of labour or taking risks of losing resources, the latter element being greatly reduced by the ability to hold a portfolio of assets representing stakes in large numbers of enterprises through stock markets.

The argument was that in a world of competitive individuals pursuing their own interests within the rules of free contract, such payments would only be made by entrepreneurs if in general there was a reluctance to put aside resources for the future, notwithstanding that production processes which took longer might produce more or better commodities (the obvious examples are trees growing for timber and wine maturing). Thus, productive improvements which required time for implementation, i.e. greater 'roundaboutness' in production, would only be undertaken if some people were willing to sacrifice something which most people valued highly, that is immediate gratification through consumption. Analytically, the payment of interest is the natural reward for this deferment. Thus, those who receive interest, rent and dividends as income can claim justification for their position in subjective preference theory, and only in that theory. This argument can be extended from the self-interest of individuals in distribution to the whole financial sector when this sector is seen as the vital agency for linking whole groups of transactions. This includes linking the present to the future through life assurance and pension schemes, smoothly transferring control over resources into the hands of new entrepreneurs, and reinforcing competitive pressures by continually threatening complacent managements with replacement if they neglect their shareholders. Stockbrokers, insurance underwriters, and bankers might therefore view requests for political donations to parties espousing subjective preference views very sympathetically.

Beyond such obvious individual and corporate self-interest is a much wider but less-certain appeal. Any success in obtaining a higher real income is a sign of social merit in subjective preference theory. General usefulness is reflected in prices. Therefore to be paid well gives not only material security but also social prestige. In an expanding economy, those people who are gaining higher incomes can associate those gains with individual achievement and accept the liberal subjective preference view of the world as fitting with their experience. In times of depression those most directly suffering can be as easily attracted by the repressive side of subjective preference politics, as scapegoats are found for the failure of the economy to be in its natural general equilibrium. In the belief that when such 'wreckers' are removed then society will regain its stolen equilibrium. 'I am responsible for success, someone else is responsible for failure' is a statement which has much appeal, unless you stop being 'I' and become 'someone else' in the eyes of a government.

For instance in dramatic terms 'I' withdraw my labour as an expression of personal liberty, 'someone else' is a mindless striker. 'I' lobby my representative in Parliament, 'someone else' attempts to bully his or her way to power. Thus, we return to the contradiction that subjective preference economics seems finally unable to take responsibility for its own self-proclaimed belief that its natural political expression is an open liberalism. Its undoubted logicality is too easily harnessed to the politics of intolerance and the brutal defence of private property against those with little or none. But the ideas of subjective preference economics have never been unchallenged as the views they dismiss have also found influential spokespeople. The first spokesman for this opposition who is acknowledged as a great economist was David Ricardo, whose ideas we will examine in the next chapter.

Further reading

For basic subjective preference theory we refer you again to Chapter 3 and to the annotated bibliography at the end of the chapter. With regard to the underlying theory of science the best reference is still Milton Friedman's (1953) *Essays in Positive Economics*. There are many references for the 'capital controversy' but the most comprehensive is Harcourt's (1972) blow by blow account in *Some Cambridge Controversies in the Theory of Capital*. For subjective preference theory Blaug (1975) judges such an assault to be misplaced in *The Cambridge Revolution: success or failure?* and this has the advantage over Harcourt in being short and to the point. The subject of general equilibrium has many possible references, including the relevant sections of Lancaster's (1974) *Microeconomics* and Hicks's (1946) *Value and Capital* mentioned in the Chapter 3 bibliography, but any treatment of this subject very quickly rises into the realms of advanced mathematics. As an introduction see Bator's classical 1957 article in American Economic Review or the first three chapters of M. C. Howard's (1979) *Modern Theories of Income Distribution*. But be careful, because Howard, like in Simpson's (1975) otherwise excellent book *General Equilibrium Analysis*, does not try to understand the theory as an expression of the principles of individual choice at the level of the economy, but rather as a technique which can be applied to any school of thought. In this regard Wientraub (1974) in his book *General Equilibrium Theory* is more solidly in the subjective preference mould. On monetarism as the logical policy consequence of subjective preference theory the best source is Friedman, especially his *The Quantity Theory of Theory – a restatement* (1956), *The Counter Revolution in Monetary Theory* (1970) and *Inflation and Unemployment: the new dimension in politics* (1977 – his Nobel Prize acceptance speech). Virtually every economy had a demand for money function estimated at some time in the 1970s. The results are reported in economic journals and central bank bulletins, a useful summary of US results is contained in Laidler (1969) *The Demand for Money: Theories and Evidence.*

The practical political implications of monetarism are found in much of Friedman's writing and came out well in his 1969 debate with Walter Heller *Monetary vs Fiscal Policy*. More recently the focus of monetarist interest has shifted to the UK, although earlier writings such as Dow's (1965) *The Management of the British Economy 1954–60* contains the essential arguments against Keynesian inspired government intervention. This criticism flowered into the dominant school of political economy in the mid-1970s, expressed polemically in the publications of the Centre for Policy Studies (especially Thatcher, Joseph and Biffen) and the Institute for Economic Affairs (notably Samuel Brittan's (1975) *Participation without Politics*). Finally, looking towards the world scale, it is worth mentioning the works of Harry Johnson on international money and development (1975, especially Part 5) and Bauer's (1976) *Dissent on Development*.

Subjective preference theory policy: a framework for liberty

Summary 4.1 _____

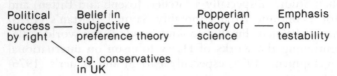

Political success by right — Belief in subjective preference theory — Popperian theory of science — Emphasis on testability

e.g. conservatives in UK

Summary 4.2 _____

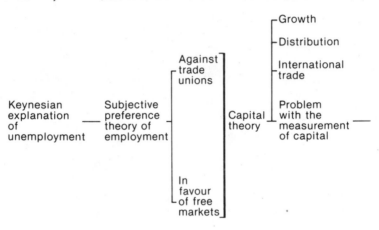

Keynesian explanation of unemployment — Subjective preference theory of employment —

Against trade unions

In favour of free markets

Capital theory

Growth

Distribution

International trade

Problem with the measurement of capital —

Summary 4.3 _____

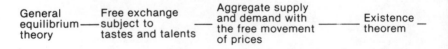

General equilibrium theory — Free exchange subject to tastes and talents — Aggregate supply and demand with the free movement of prices — Existence theorem _

110

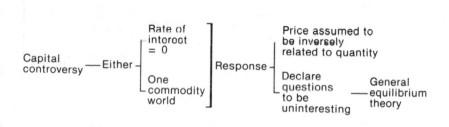

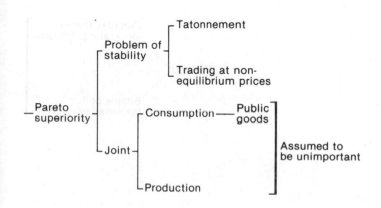

Summary 4.4 _____

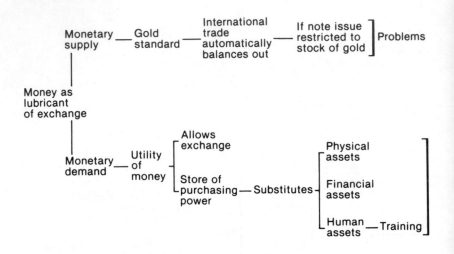

Summary 4.5 _____

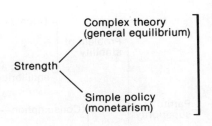

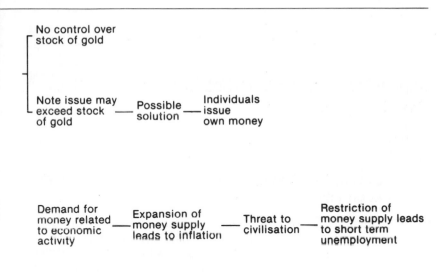

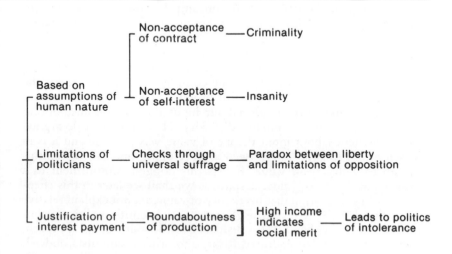

Chapter 5

Capitalists, landlords and stagnation: David Ricardo

5.1 The legacy of Adam Smith and Ricardo's experience of economic depression

Chapter 2 emphasised the importance of Adam Smith in the development of the three schools of economic thought which have developed in the two centuries since the publication of the *Wealth of Nations*. Chapters 3 and 4 then described the theory of value and policies of one of the schools – that of the subjective preference theorists – and showed how their ideas originated in Smith's theory that the value of a commodity was equal to the amount of labour commanded by it or, in other words, for which it can be exchanged. From this 'labour commanded' theoretical perspective, the subjective preference school developed and refined the notions that consumption must be the starting point of economic analysis, and that the source of value can be characterised as utility.

However, we can see in the work of David Ricardo, writing in the early nineteenth century, a very different development of Smith's writings. Smith had noted that with the coming of civilised society the labourer no longer received the full product of his work. He consequently abandoned any simple labour input theory of value, opting instead for the 'labour commanded' theory. However, Ricardo argued that a consistent labour input theory of value was possible and it is in this sense that Ricardo can be seen as developing one half of Smith's contradictory theory of value. It was this dogged commitment to a labour input theory of value, despite, as we shall see later in this chapter, Ricardo's realisation that his theory of value did not explain relative prices, that led Marx to praise Ricardo as a scientific political economist. On the other hand, Marx disliked Ricardo's ahistorical approach, an approach which has endeared Ricardo to other economists, indeed, the contradictions in Ricardo's theory can be seen as giving rise to two schools of thought. As with Smith's theory, different theorists developed different lines of argument, leading on the one hand to cost-of-production theory (see Chs 6 and 7) and on the other hand to abstract labour theory (see Chs 8 and 9).

David Ricardo lived from 1772 to 1823. From 1792 to 1815 England was almost continuously engaged in wars with France, with the result that Government expenditure rose rapidly, largely financed through a rising national debt. In 1797, partly to finance this debt, the Government had passed the Bank Restriction Act, which allowed for the circulation of paper money, not fully backed by gold. This was a period in which the general level of prices was rising and it was this inflation, and the financing of the Government's national debt, which was the first set of problems to which Ricardo addressed himself. Ricardo, a stockbroker and underwriter and the son of a stockbroker, was well placed to comment on these questions, but it was the economic depression, the protectionism and the poverty which accompanied the end of the war in 1815 which forced Ricardo to focus on different problems.

The historically high rate of growth in population in the period from 1811 to 1821 was associated with a growing labour surplus. Alongside a small group of skilled workers who probably managed to increase their real wages between 1790 and 1840, there was a growing group of workers who were underemployed, or unemployed, increasingly poor and very insecure. This insecurity revealed itself in desperate acts after the end of the Napoleonic Wars in 1815, as thousands of disbanded soldiers and sailors returned to find no work, or only lowly-paid work in their villages. During the passing of the Corn Laws in 1815 to protect domestic corn prices from foreign competition, the Houses of Parliament had to be defended by troops from menacing crowds and riots were common from 1815 through to the 1840s (Hobsbawm 1968: Ch. 4). As a leading historian of the period puts it 'in the years between 1780 and 1832, most English working people came to feel an identity of interests as between themselves, and as against their rulers and employers', (Thompson 1968:12). It is hardly surprising that Ricardo's *Principles of Political Economy and Taxation*, published in 1817 at the beginning of this turbulent period, reflected the concern about the popular discontent. In the *Principles*, Ricardo was primarily concerned with the distribution of income between rent, profits and wages, and the effects of changes in size of population, unlike Smith for whom distribution had been of lesser importance than total wealth.

But Ricardo felt that the key to analysing distribution lay in correcting Smith's theory of value. In a letter to Malthus in 1816, Ricardo wrote: 'If I could overcome the obstacles in the way of giving clear insight into the origin and law of relative or exchangeable value, I should have gained half the battle' (quoted in Sraffa, 1962: xv). Such was the purpose of his *Principles of Political Economy and Taxation*.

5.2 Ricardo's rejection of Smith's labour commanded theory of value

Ricardo was consistent throughout the *Principles* in arguing that the total labour time required for the production of a commodity determined the value of that commodity. Within this labour time he included both direct labour, that is labourers employed for a specific time and paid a wage, and indirect labour, or raw materials and tools, which were themselves products of labour. Thus, if a particular input was itself the product of four hours labour and was completely expended in production, then this four hours would be embodied in the final product. He, therefore, explicitly rejected Smith's labour commanded theory (see Ricardo 1971: 60).

The labour commanded theory implies that the value of a commodity is determined by what people are prepared to pay for it (i.e. how much labour the commodity can command) and, therefore, by the relative scarcity of the commodity. However, Ricardo argued that in industrial society, most goods are reproducible, that is they are produced again and again by labour. Therefore, the relative scarcity and value of most commodities is not accidental, but determined by their labour inputs. As a result, Ricardo maintained a clear differentiation between value and wealth. Whereas the former referred to the (labour) costs of production, the latter referred to the usefulness of the commodity in consumption. Thus, wealth and value might both rise if more labour was used to produce more commodities. However, if the productivity of labour were to increase so that more commodities were produced with *less* labour, wealth would rise with the volume of commodities, while value would fall with the reduction in labour time.

Thus, for Ricardo, the distinction between the use of a commodity in consumption and its value in production was an important one, as it was to be for Marx, as we shall see in Chapter 8. But, for Ricardo, the important reason for having confidence in the labour input theory of value was because it seemed to provide a good basis for an explanation of the distribution of the total product between wages, profit and rent. It is to his analysis of distribution that we now turn.

The natural price of labour

In analysing distribution, Ricardo first asked what determines the value of labour time? This, he argued, was equal to the wage which, in general, was regulated by subsistence. That is, it was equal to the labour time required to produce the food and other commodities necessary for the support of the labourer and the family. The wage rate tended towards subsistence level because Ricardo agreed with Malthus in arguing that the supply of labourers always increased in proportion to the means of supporting them. If the wage rate increased, then labourers could afford to support larger families, so that in the process of time the supply of labour increased, thereby reducing the wage rate to the subsistence minimum. Ricardo accepted that this tendency for the population to increase with increases in the output of necessaries was a slow process and, as a result, the market or short-run price of labour might be above the natural or long-run price of labour for relatively long periods but, in general, this Malthusian tendency would operate.

Profit and rent

Ricardo observed that, in manufacturing, the profits received by the employer were equal to the value of the produced commodity less the amounts paid to both direct and indirect labour. And Ricardo, like Smith, also noted that the rate of profit tended to be equated throughout the economy by the movement of capital from one employment to another. But where Ricardo differed from Smith was over the determination of the *prevailing* rate of profit, or in Smith's terms, the determination of the natural price of stock.

Ricardo's explanation of this average or prevailing rate of profit relied heavily on a natural rate of profit, or surplus derived from the agricultural sector. If the economic surplus was not the result of 'exploitation', of labour being paid less than it produced, then, using a labour input theory of value, it had to be the product of 'nature', hence the importance of the agricultural sector.

A numerical example helps to explain this as well as Ricardo's analysis of rent. Envisage an economy in which there are three units of land, each of ten acres. Each of these 10-acre units of land has a different natural fertility so that with the same quantity of labour and the same input of seed (that is, the same economic technique) different quantities of output are produced. Thus, with 100 days of labour time and 50 kg of seed applied to each of the three plots, the 10 most fertile acres – land A – might produce 600 kg of corn; the next most fertile piece of land – land B – might produce 500 kg, and the least fertile land – land C – might produce only 400 kg. The situation is summarised in Table 5.1 below.

In Table 5.1 the subsistence wage for 100 labour days is assumed to be 150 kg of corn, or 1.5 kg of corn per labour day. Thus, the surplus on the least fertile or marginal piece of land – land C – is 200 kg (output minus seed and labour inputs). Thus, the rate of profit calculated on the seed and wages advanced is 200 kg on 200 kg, or exactly 100 per cent.

But what about the surplus produced on plots A and B, where it

Table 5.1   Value of output and distribution (in kilos of corn)

	Production specification			Distribution (kg of corn)		
	Land (acres)	Labour (days)	Output (kg of corn)	Seed and labour	Profit (at the same rate)	Unallocated surplus
	A (10)	100	600	200	200	200
	B (10)	100	500	200	200	100
	C (10)	100	400	200	200	—
Total	(30)	300	1500	600	600	300

would seem that the potential rate of profit is much higher? The owners of these more fertile plots would be aware of the profitability of the least fertile or marginal plot of land currently in production. Therefore, they would be able to offer their land to tenant farmers at a rent which would just allow the farmers to obtain the rate of profit achievable from the next best land, that is, land at the margin. Thus, much of the surplus on the relatively fertile plots of land accrues to the landowner as rent, which Ricardo, therefore, saw as a return to the monopoly control of a natural resource in fixed supply. Returning to Table 5.1 again, we can see that because the investment in each plot of land is the same (seed + labour = 200 kg of corn), then a constant amount of profit (200 kg) results in a constant rate of profit (100%).

This in turn means that the rent for the very fertile Plot A can be as high as 200 kg or 20 kg per acre. Ricardo's analysis of profit and rent shown in our example in Table 5.1 may be easier to understand in diagram form (see Fig. 5.1).

From this diagram it is clear that the rate of profit on the marginal land sets the average, and that any differential surplus above this average is creamed off by landlords in the form of rent.

Thus, Ricardo implied that capitalists in both agriculture and manufacturing would have to be content with the rate of profit determined at the margin of cultivation in agriculture. Nowhere in his short chapter *On Profits* is this point made explicit, but as Marx and Marshall were

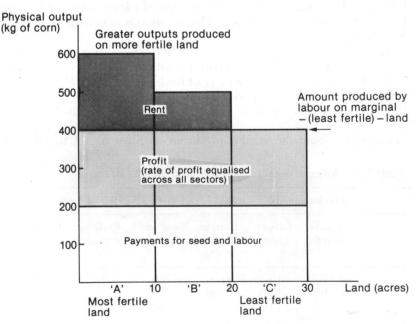

Fig. 5.1   Value of output and distribution (in kg of corn)

later to note, this was a reasonable assumption to make, since the transformation of agriculture in England had freed it from feudal restrictions
and capital was free to move into agriculture (Marx 1969: Ch. XI and
Marshall 1947: App. A).

5.3 Ricardo's theory of crisis

Ricardo's conclusions about changes in the rate of profit and the pace
of capital accumulation can, perhaps, be most easily understood by
developing the above example. We first assume that at a particular time
the agriculture sector of the economy is as depicted in Table 5.1 and
Fig. 5.1. Thus, the total output of corn in the economy is 1500 kg. But
now assume that the corn supply increases, as a result of either an
increase in population (due to, say, immigration), or a rise in the subsistence wage, for in his chapter *On Wages*, Ricardo argues that 'the
natural price of labour . . . varies at different times in the same country, and very materially differs in different countries. It essentially
depends on the habits and customs of the people' (Ricardo 1971: 118).

Here, for ease of presentation, we assume that there is an increase
in population due, say, to troops returning from the Napoleonic wars.
However, because of restrictions on imports of corn, the increase in
supply has to be met from an increase in domestic production. And,
we assume as did Ricardo, that if domestic production had to be
expanded, it would have to come from less fertile land, from, say, 10
acres of land 'D' requiring 50 kg of seed and 100 labour days to produce
300 kg of corn. This new situation is shown in Table 5.2.

This expansion of production to less fertile land, with the subsistence
wage remaining the same, has reduced both the rate of profit and the
share of total output paid in the form of profits. In addition, the absolute amount of profit paid to capitalists has been reduced; total profits
in Table 5.1 were 600 kg of corn, whereas in Table 5.2 they are only

Table 5.2   Value of output and distribution – after expansion

	Production specification			Distribution (kg of corn)		
	Land (acres)	Labour (days)	Output (kg of corn)	Seed and labour	Profit (at the same rate)	Rent
	A (10)	100	600	200	100	300
	B (10)	100	500	200	100	200
	C (10)	100	400	200	100	100
	D (10)	100	300	200	100	—
Total	(40)	400	1800	800	400	600

400 kg. The subsistence wage is still the same 1.5 kg of corn per labour day – but the labour time required at the margin to produce the subsistence wage has risen. Thus, the *rate* of profit was bound to fall, the *share* of profit in total output was likely to fall, and the *absolute* payment in the form of profits might fall. Whether the share of profits and the absolute profits fall depends on the reduction in the fertility of the land as the margin of cultivation is extended. But the rate of profit is bound to fall. Not only did Ricardo assume this, but he also assumed that it would fall to a very low level, and that once it did, the economy would stagnate. This, in essence, is Ricardo's theory of long-run stagnation or crisis. As the domestic supply of corn increases, so increasingly infertile land has to be resorted to, and the cost of production at the margin rises. Thus, the value of labour time – the subsistence wage – rises, and as this rises, so the rate of profit falls. This process can be seen more dramatically by representing Table 5.1 and 5.2 in graphical form, as in Fig. 5.2.

With a falling rate of profit, the motive for the manufacturer and the farmer to invest would cease when profits fell to so low a level as not to compensate them for their trouble and risk. The economy would stagnate, since the farmer and manufacturer were the only groups in society who would invest. Labour was paid a subsistence wage and clearly could not be a source of investment, and landlords were assumed to prefer immediate consumption to productive investment. This latter assumption generated a correspondence between Ricardo and Malthus, with the latter defending landlords in their role as consumers stimulating production through their insatiable demands. But, for Ricardo, the landlords were a class enemy, since the increases in rent merely meant that the landlords profited at the expense of the agricultural capitalists (Ricardo 1971: 100). Thus, Ricardo argued, the

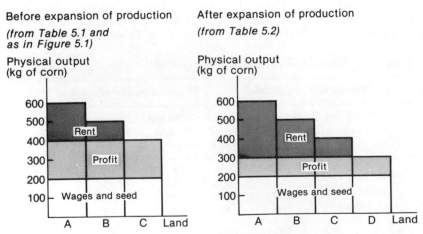

Fig. 5.2   Agricultural expansion and the declining rate of profit

landlords were an unproductive class, in terms of creating value, and their affluence was at the expense of progress.

But although Ricardo disagreed with Malthus on the role of land-lords in the economy, they found common cause in asserting that labourers were not progressive in their struggles. Wrong-headed in opposing mechanisation and producing excessive children, their actions only speeded the onset of stagnation. It was with a Malthusian popu-lation theory in mind that Ricardo opposed the Poor Laws, as had Malthus. The Poor Laws had originated in an Act of 1536 in the reign of Henry VIII, requiring the head officers of every city, parish, etc. charitably to support the poor, whilst ruthlessly putting the fit to work where possible. By the late eighteenth and early nineteenth centuries the Poor Laws were becoming a substantial burden on taxes, and it was convenient for the taxed to agree with Malthus and Ricardo in arguing that the Poor Laws, by immediately increasing the resources available to labourers, simply led to a longer-run increase in population. They claimed that the result of the Poor Laws was not, as the legislature benevolently intended, to make the poor rich, but simply made the rich poor. In 1834 payments under the Poor Laws were reduced quite drastically following the Poor Law Amendment Act (Hobsbawm) 1968: Ch. 12). Thus, Ricardo was hardly a revolutionary by the stan-dards of his own time, and yet even his mild worry about the future of capitalism left him open to vilification by the more frantic apologists for the status quo like Carey: 'Mr Ricardo's system is one of dis-cords...its whole tends to the production of hostility among classes and nations... His book is the true manual of the demagogue, who seeks power by means of agrarianism, war and plunder' (Carey 1848: 74–5)

5.4 Ricardo's free-trade policy

Like Smith, Ricardo approved of capitalism, but unlike Smith, Ricardo was pessimistic about its future. Squeezed between landlords and labourers, the best the capitalists could hope for was a postponement of the decline in the rate of profit. Ricardo conceived of a number of ways in which this decline might be postponed. Firstly, by the appli-cation of new knowledge to agriculture, but he thought of this as an unpredictable process and not amenable to political action. The alter-native method of raising labour productivity, namely by making labourers work harder, was hardly compatible with the assumption of a subsistence wage.

With improvements in the productivity of British agriculture ruled out, Ricardo realised that the only way in which the decline in the rate of profit could be postponed was by importing cheap food. And free trade, particularly for food grains, was a major issue in British politics in the first half of the nineteenth century. The money price of wheat in England had been steady for a period of about 150 years from 1640 but then, at the end of the eighteenth century, it was raised by restrictions on corn trade. The price was high through the first decade of the nineteenth century, but then with a series of good harvests, the price began to fall sharply. It was in reaction to this sharp fall in price that in 1815, restrictions on wheat imports (the so-called 'Corn Laws') were tightened.

Ricardo used his analysis in terms of labour time to show that cheap imports of wage goods lowered the labour time embodied in the subsistence wage and thus could permit the rate of profit to be maintained. Furthermore, he suggested that both trading countries would gain from free trade even if *both* commodities could be produced in one country with less labour. The example that he used to illustrate this comparative advantage theory of free trade was of potential trade between Portugal and England. The figures used in his example are summarised in Table 5.3.

Thus, with Ricardo's assumptions of the immobility of labour and capital between the two countries, the pre-trade 'price' ratios of the two commodities differ in the two countries. There is an obvious incentive for merchants to trade between the two countries. Transport costs would reduce this incentive but, ignoring these for simplicity, merchants could profit by buying wine in Portugal for sale in England, since wine costs only 80/90 of a unit of cloth in Portugal, compared with 120/100 units in England. Conversely, merchants will buy cloth in England for sale in Portugal since cloth in England costs only 100/120 units of wine compared with 90/80 units in Portugal. Thus, England will tend to specialise in cloth production and Portugal in wine production, with cloth being imported into Portugal and wine being imported into England. This trade will then set the following limits to the international price ratio, again ignoring transport costs:

in Portugal – 1 of cloth = 0.89 of wine
in England – 1 of cloth = 0.83 of wine

Ricardo was not particularly concerned with where the price would finally settle, and it was left to later economists, such as John Stuart

Table 5.3   Ricardo's trade example

| | Man-days per unit of output | |
	Portugal	England
Wine	80	120
Cloth	90	100
Ratio of labour times (prices) in terms of cloth	0.9	1.2

Mill, to argue that the relative sizes of markets in the two countries would determine where, within this Ricardian region, the rate of exchange would settle. And more recently still, writers within the Ricardian tradition, the so-called neo-Ricardians, have argued by relaxing certain of Ricardo's assumptions, such as the subsistence wage, that free trade will not necessarily benefit both countries.

But Ricardo was less concerned with precise measurements of the gains from trade, and more concerned with arguing that with the abolition of the Corn Laws, a fall in the rate of profit in England might be postponed.

In this example, Ricardo seems to be following Smith in campaigning for free trade. But, whereas Smith's concern was to free the economy of restrictions emanating from monopolies established by guilds and conspiring manufacturers, Ricardo was much more concerned with the damage arising from restrictions – such as the Corn Laws – imposed in the interest of landed property. And whilst Smith looked forward to continuing progress as capitalism developed, Ricardo only saw government policies as expedients to postpone a decline in the rate of profit.

5.5 The value price problem and the Ricardian Inheritance

In his analysis of the effects of growth in agricultural output and of changes in distribution on the rate of profit, Ricardo came across a problem which he was unable to solve. This problem is fundamental to the nature of value and economic measurement, and it is a problem which is still hotly debated today. Its importance is considerable, for it has given rise to the development of two schools of economic thought, both of which can be said, as we shall see, to have Ricardian roots.

The basic problem is that to assert that exchange value originates in the amounts of labour put into a commodity does not mean that there will exist a set of money prices which simply correspond to the ratios of labour inputs. They will so correspond where the rate of profit is zero, but the simple case of long-run stagnation in which the rate of profit has fallen to zero is hardly convincing as a general rule. The second case which does allow for changing distribution between classes, but where value is not affected, is the case of a one-commodity economy. In this case, where all farmers compete to earn the same rate of profit, the value of corn will be measured by the input of labour and this value will be unaffected by changes in corn distribution between labourers and capitalist farmers. But again, this example where the only commodity in the world is corn is hardly realistic.

But this problem is not unique to the schools which emerge from Ricardo, as we saw in the previous chapter. It was a problem that confronted those within the subjective preference school who attempted to explain the distribution of income between groups in society through marginal productivity theory. The problem for them was essentially the same as that which confronted Ricardo, namely that the prices of commodities are likely to change with changes in distribution between, say, wages and profits. And so, Ricardo realised, if relative prices shift with changes in distribution, but total labour inputs and hence values remain unchanged, then how can we say that labour inputs alone determine the rate of exchange between commodities?

We can illustrate this problem by adapting Ricardo's own example in his first chapter of the *Principles*:

Assume that a capitalist (A) employs one hundred labourers for a period of, say, one day to make one machine, while another (B) employs one hundred labourers for a day to produce four hundred kg of corn. The machine and the corn will have an equal value at the end of the day.

Thus, we have:

A: 100 labour days — 1 machine   : value of the machine
B: 100 labour days — 400 kg of corn : value of the corn.

But now assume that during the next day A employs the machine, together with the 100 labourers to produce 100 yd of cotton cloth, while B simply employs 100 labourers to produce 400 kg of corn again. During the second day they will each have employed the same quantity of direct labour but the cotton cloth will have used a machine in which 100 labour days are embodied. If we assume that the machine is completely worn out at the end of the day, then it seems that a labour input theory of the determination of prices would predict that the cotton cloth will be worth twice the day's corn production, since we have:

A: 100 direct labour days + 100 labour days embodied in the machine = 200 labour days — 100 yd of cotton cloth
B: 100 labour days — 400 kg of corn.

That is, exactly twice as much labour has gone into the cotton cloth as has been embodied in the corn. Unfortunately, Ricardo realised, the price ratio would almost certainly not be the same as the labour:time ratio.

If profits and money are introduced into the above example, we can immediately see why. Assume that gold is the money commodity, that one ounce of gold is called a pound, and that one labour day is required to produce one ounce of gold, that is, one pound. Then the machine and the 400 kg of corn which each require 100 labour days to produce will each have a price of £100. If we further assume that the subsistence wage is 2 kg of corn per day, then since 2 kg of corn require half a labour day to produce and one labour day has the price of £1, then the daily subsistence wage of one labourer will be fifty pence (half of £1).

Thus, on the first day, the 100 labour days will cost £50 but the price of the machine will be £100, thereby giving a surplus or profit of £50. Similarly, there will be a profit of £50 from the production of the 400 kg of corn. The price ratio of the machine to that of the 400 kg of corn is 1:1, which is the same as the labour: time ratio. So far, so good. But in the second period the price ratio will differ from that of the labour:time ratio. The figures are summarised in Table 5.4.

From Table 5.4 we can see that in the second period the price ratio (3: 1)differs from the labour:time ratio (2: 1), whereas in the first period the labour:time and price ratios coincide (1: 1). The problem arises from the timing of the labour inputs. In the second period the clothier (capitalist B) expects to earn the average rate of profit on his capital invested in the machine, as well as on the labour directly employed. If he cannot expect to earn the same rate of profit, then he might well prefer to produce corn in the first period instead of the machine, and consume the surplus. In the second period, profit is being required on the profit made from the production of the machine in the first period, and embodied in its price. Thus, the value-price divergence arises from the

Table 5.4   Ricardo's value-price problem

		day 1	day 2
(i) *Labour time ratios*			
Labour inputs (days)			
A Machine		100	—
A 100 yd of cotton cloth		—	100 + 100
B 400 kg of corn		100	100
Labour time ratios (values)		1:1	2:1
(ii) *Money price ratios*			
Money value (£)			
A Machine			Used to
subsistence wage		50	produce
profit (100%)		50	cotton
	total	100	*cloth*
A Cotton cloth			
subsistence wage		—	50
machine		—	100
profit (100% on *all* capital)		—	150
	total	—	300
B Corn			
subsistence wage		50	50
profit (100%)		50	50
	total	100	100
Price ratios		1:1	3:1

compounding of profits made on labour used in the commodities at different periods. And so, varying either the relative proportions of labour applied in the first and second periods (say 150 labour days in period one to produce the machine, combined with 50 labour days in the second to produce cotton cloth) or changing the wage rate to, say 3 kg of corn per day, will change the price ratio in the second period, even though the total labour inputs have remained unchanged. Plug in the figures and see.

Ricardo was aware of this problem of price ratios not coinciding with value ratios, but attempted to dismiss it by *ad hoc* generalisations. He finished Ch. 1 arguing that variations in the prices of commodities due to changes in profit rates are small, and that by far the most important effects are produced by varying the total quantities of labour required for production. He also argued that changes in the labour time required for the production of a unit of gold are small, that gold is an average commodity in terms of the mix of direct and indirect labour required to produce it, and thus, that gold is 'as near an approximation to a standard measure of value as can be theoretically conceived' (Ricardo 1971: 85). Thus, the relative price of a commodity in terms of gold is also a good measure of the relative labour time (value) embodied in the commodity.

Ricardo persisted in identifying the value of a commodity with its labour input, though he realised that differences in the 'machine intensities' of products and the existence of profits challenged this identification. For instance, in a footnote in the *Principles*, he wrote defensively, and rather unconvincingly, that 'Mr Malthus appears to think that it is part of my doctrine that the cost and value of a thing should be the same: it is, if he means by cost, 'cost of production' including profits' (Ricardo 1971: 87).

The future attempts to resolve Ricardo's logical problems were to take two different paths, leading to two different schools of thought, but both paths shared his disquiet about the future of capitalism, seeing in its development the seeds of stagnation, breakdown or crisis. At the very historical moment that capitalism was developing immense productive powers, its own critique was taking root. Ricardo 'discovered' this critique by the honest application of logic, but was inhibited from accepting the full implications of his discovery. Others, like Marshall, Veblen, Keynes, Sraffa and Galbraith were to follow him in this dilemma. Politically radical, although often denying the 'socialist' label, their economics, like those of Ricardo, started at production, but saw the 'principal problem' as arising from conflicts over distribution. Never quite believing that profits and interest are justified, the search to explain them adequately has included imperfect competition, the roundaboutness of production, or the uncertainty of outcome. Accepting the technical conditions of production as given, this search to find a source of profits independent of the exploitation of labour, we have called the 'cost of production' theory of value, and this is discussed in the next two chapters. The proposition that technical conditions plus distribution equal value, and thus abolishing Ricardo's distinction between values and prices, is the simplest starting point for this theory. In so far as such theorists in searching for the source of profits tend to deny their existence, they have come close to the socialists in political perspective but, in our view, have always failed to close the gap. Put in boldest terms, the suspicion that profits (and rent and interest) are not morally justified has not proved sufficient to go beyond a pessimistic reformism, changing its content but not its essence, since Ricardo's time.

The alternative stream from Ricardo still held to the labour input theory of value, discovered an integrated theory of profit, rent and interest *within* that theory, and showed how observed prices differed from, but were related to, value. The implications of this approach were intentionally revolutionary. It was aimed to reveal the concealed nature of capitalism and how it is centred on the exploitation of labour power, in order to overthrow it. Writers like Marx and political leaders like Lenin, Gramsci and Mao have all made a modified labour input theory of value the cornerstone of their analysis of social change, as we shall see in Chapters 8 and 9. Ricardo attempted to follow through the implications of a labour input theory, but failed to achieve a logically complete system. Whether he failed because the implications were too uncomfortable, or because he was distracted by attacks on his position from opponents like Malthus, is open to question, but his persistence in pursuing ideas not altogether comfortable to his own interests deserves great credit.

Further reading

As we persistently argue in this book, there is generally no substitute for going to original texts. Thus, for Ricardo's theory of value, the first chapter of Ricardo's *Principles of Political Economy and Taxation* (1971) is indispensible. The 1971 Pelican edition of the *Principles* has an introduction by Hartwell, which is useful for biographical details, but is inadequate (as is this chapter) on the historical setting. An excellent first source for the historical setting of the British Isles during the fifty years of Ricardo's life is provided by the first three chapters of Hobsbawm's *Industry and Empire* (1968). More detailed accounts of the period which the reader is likely to find interesting are E. P. Thompson's *The Making of the English Working Class* (1968) and *Captain Swing* by E. Hobsbawm and G. Rude (1973). Anyone who really wants to get into Ricardo's work in detail should go to the ten volumes of *The Works and Correspondence of David Ricardo*, edited by P. Sraffa, 1962. But although they might find Sraffa's introduction of some use, it is hardly exciting. Nor is Blaug's *Ricardian Economics: A Historical Study* (1958) likely to be helpful. Marx's discussion of Ricardo in *Theories of Surplus Value* (1969) is repetitive, dry, but parts are very useful; the reader is likely to find Ch. X (particularly sect 2–4) and Ch. XV (sect. B) most helpful. Chapter 3 of Guy Routh's *The Origin of Economic Ideas* (1975) is written with great clarity and humour, and is strongly recommended.

The third chapter of Dobb's *Theories of Value and Distribution Since Adam Smith* (1973) and of Barber's *A History of Economic Thought* (1967) are likely to be of interest, as is Appx I of Marshall's otherwise tedious *Principles of Economics* (1947), but the third chapter of Howard and King's *The Political Economy of Marx* (1975) is far from clear.

Capitalists, landlords and stagnation: David Ricardo

Summary 5.1 ──────────────────────────────

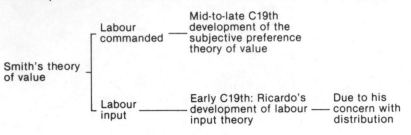

Smith's theory of value
- Labour commanded ── Mid-to-late C19th development of the subjective preference theory of value
- Labour input ── Early C19th: Ricardo's development of labour input theory ── Due to his concern with distribution

Summary 5.2 ──────────────────────────────

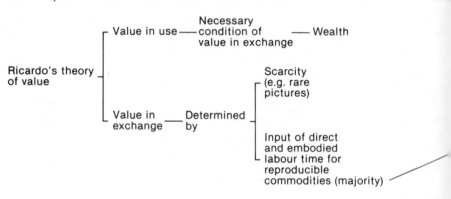

Ricardo's theory of value
- Value in use ── Necessary condition of value in exchange ── Wealth
- Value in exchange ── Determined by
  - Scarcity (e.g. rare pictures)
  - Input of direct and embodied labour time for reproducible commodities (majority)

Summary 5.3 ──────────────────────────────

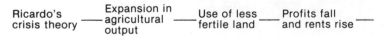

Ricardo's crisis theory ── Expansion in agricultural output ── Use of less fertile land ── Profits fall and rents rise ──

130

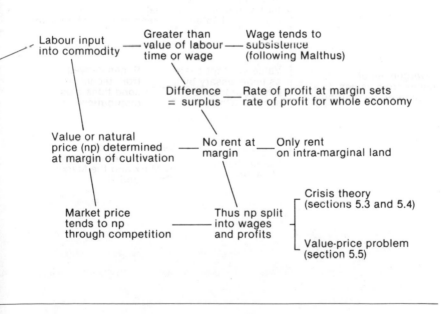

Summary 5.4

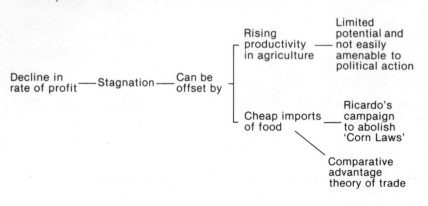

Summary 5.5

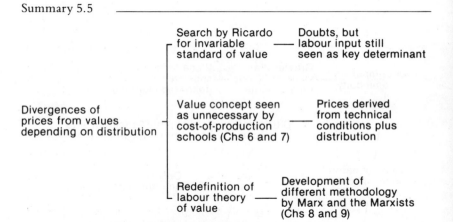

Chapter 6

Technology rules:
the cost-of-production theory of value

6.1 The foundations of cost-of-production theory (we think)

David Ricardo's work includes all the aspects that distinguish the cost-of-production theory of value as the basis of a distinctive school of economic thought. The essence of the theory is that the natural environment provides strong limitations on production possibilities; in Ricardo's theory these limitations were at the margin in agriculture. Production decisions are then made subject to those limitations by members of one key group in society; in Ricardo's theory it is capitalists who are this dynamic element. But the product is then distributed between various groups on lines not decided by the production decision makers alone; for Ricardo the product is divided between landlords, capitalists and labourers in a manner dependent on labour productivity at the margin of agriculture and the subsistence consumption requirements of labourers. Finally the whole economy shows a tendency to depression if left to market forces alone; in Ricardo's work this was total stagnation at a bare subsistence level for the mass of the population. The precise specification of these aspects has changed through time but all are present in those economists who we identify as cost of productionist.

These common assumptions as to the basic nature of the economy are accompanied within the cost-of-production school by a common methodology. Unlike subjective preference economics with its Popperian methodology aimed at discovering universal, natural laws for all people for all time, the emphasis of the cost-of-production school is a biological, evolutionary one, with economic ideas, like physical species, being seen as evolving through a series of models which must be prepared to adjust sensitively to a changing physical environment.

Two quotes from Keynes, one of the most eminent economists who we would call fundamentally cost-of-productionist, illustrate this approach perfectly. 'Economics is a science of thinking in terms of models joined to the art of choosing models which are relevant to the contemporary world. It is compelled to be this because unlike the typical natural science, the material to which it is applied is, in too many respects, not homogeneous through time' and 'Good economists are scarce because the gift for using "vigilant observation" to choose good models, although it does not require a highly specialised intellectual technique, appears to be a very rare one' (both these quotes from Keynes are in Moggridge 1976: 26).

We associate this approach to knowledge with the concept of paradigms advanced by Thomas Kuhn. Put simply a paradigm is a core logical model surrounded by a host of related ideas about many parts of experience. As new experience is gained it is viewed from the perspectives of the dominant paradigm, which is based on older out-dated experience, and resulting contradictions between experience and theory are met by denying the experience, or adjusting minor peripheral ideas, not by changing the core theory. This process continues until a crisis of knowledge occurs when an emerging new core theory, more compatible with experience, breaks through into dominance, overthrowing the old core theory or absorbing it as a special case. That is, knowledge advances through periodic revolutions, not through a research programme refining an original good idea as subjective preference theory advocates. This paradigm theory of knowledge is consistent with the general approach of cost-of-production economics, when we define new experience as a change in technology which forces adaptation on rather reluctant human beings of their economic ideas.

But the nature of this methodology produces a difficulty for our discussion here. Many economists who we describe as strongly influenced by the cost-of-production theory would, by definition, immediately claim to belong to no school of thought but to be 'realists' who carefully observe the world and then use 'commonsense' to organise those observations for policy-making purposes. Our problem with cost-of-production theory is rather like a manager of a national football team who finds that all the star players insist on playing in their club colours. It is this difficulty which makes Chapters 6 and 7 even more controversial than the others in the book. There is one consoling figure for us who exemplifies our case for the existence of a coherent cost-of-production theory of value. Piero Sraffa was writing on imperfect competition in the 1920s, was with Keynes at Cambridge in the 1930s and 1940s when Keynes produced a theory of general disequilibrium, and in 1960 published the book *Production of Commodities by Means of Commodities* which inspired the revival of Ricardian economics as neo-Ricardianism. If there has to be an equivalent figure in cost-of-production theory for Milton Friedman in subjective preference theory, then Sraffa is a leading candidate.

However, our claim that there is a cost-of-production theory of value must depend on whether readers are generally convinced by the overall coherence of this and the next chapter, not on one individual. In addition though, we urge sceptical readers to look at the unedited major writings of the economists we call cost-of-productionist. For instance we ourselves were surprised on re-reading from a cost-of-productionist viewpoint Alfred Marshall's *Principles of Economics* and Keynes's *The General Theory of Employment, Interest and Money*, at the highly selective interpretations that these writers have received in best-selling introductory economics textbooks such as Samuelson (1967) and Lipsey (1971). In these 'grand neo-classical syntheses' (the phrase is Samuelson's), Alfred Marshall is treated as largely endorsing the ideas of Jevons, which completely ignores the total rejection of Jevons's ideas as contained in Appendix I of Marshall's *Principles*; and the vital (in a cost-of-productionist reading) 'micro' theoretical foundations at the beginning of Keynes's *General Theory* are invariably totally ignored as well as his more radical prescriptions about the need for long-term, large-scale, state intervention in the economy, at the end of the book.

6.2 Technological determinism: the quality of life in industrial society

The term Industrial Revolution has a highly significant place in cost-of-production theory, parallel to that of the European Enlightenment in subjective preference theory. In this approach, the coincidence of suitable technological innovation and socio-economic conditions in the UK in the eighteenth century produced a new organism in the form of industrial society. It was this birth that Adam Smith was struggling to understand and, even though his view was obscured by out-dated theories of artisan economy, he deserves much credit for his careful observation of the new experiences happening around him. But what Smith observed was only the beginning of the process of industrialisation and he failed to see that it was not an increased division of labour in itself that was important, as this increased division of labour was only the expression of the more fundamental process of mechanisation, the use of machinery on a larger and larger scale to increase output enormously.

Though Smith was able to observe that the new types of work being introduced were repetitive and monotonous and gave no scope for the exercise of initiative by the people performing them, it appeared 'utopian' to change the tasks and lose the tremendous gains in output. Only when Ricardo later demonstrated that these labouring people also faced inevitable pressures from market forces which pushed down their rewards towards a bare physical subsistence did utopian, rabble-rousing, 'socialism' acquire the dignity of becoming 'scientific' and respectable. The question of criticising the nature of the tasks performed by the labouring classes could then be ignored and replaced by criticism of the low consumption levels of the poor. This type of view which accepts as an ugly neccessity that many people will have to work in factories as unthinking adjuncts to machines, but that some social choice exists over their quality of life outside the workplace is typified in the work of John Stuart Mill writing in the UK in the mid-nineteenth century.

Mill felt able in those more prosperous economic circumstances to criticise the free market economy to a greater extent than Ricardo, whose support of capitalists against landlords in the conditions of 1815 led him to advocate loosening the controls over the movement of goods and people. Controls, he judged to be only in landlords' interests. Mill distinguished between the analysis of production and that of distribution. 'The laws and conditions of the production of wealth partake of the character of physical truths. There is nothing optional or arbitrary in them', whereas 'It is not so with the Distribution of Wealth. That is a matter of human institution solely'. Thus although the most exhausting and repulsive of work might be paid the worst of all, this was not because the method of production was at fault, but because of social conventions and the political powerlessness of the poorest. Therefore he concluded the government could, and should, go beyond policing contracts and do more directly and indirectly to improve the quality of life of the poor. Mill was also careful to point out that this criticism of the system of private property was aimed at its preservation, not its replacement by a communist system. He also was very firm on the point that the only legitimate agent of these reforms was a sovereign Parliament, and certainly not trade unions, as his denunciation of the 1851 strike in the engineering industry showed.

Alfred Marshall whose textbook, *Principles of Economics*, succeeded Mill's *1852* as the standard introduction to the subject in 1890, was even stronger in his defence of private property and attacks on trade unions, but the logic of his inheritance from Mill still pushed him towards a critical stand on distributional issues. He derived the conclusion that aggregate satisfaction in society would be increased by a reduction in inequality, as he could see no reason to assume that people were unequal in their general capacity for satisfaction. Therefore taking money from the rich and giving it to the poor would increase the happiness of the poor more than it would decrease the happiness of the rich. Marshall actually rejected the theory of marginal revenue productivity advocated in subjective preference theory as describing a natural law of distribution. Instead, he argued for a theory of bargaining power, in which labour was naturally weak because any particular day's labour is incapable of being stored, thus making distribution a political rather than an economic question. Marshall's ambiguity in the analysis of distribution and his dominance over economics in the UK was such that it is difficult to find any mainstream economists in the UK developing the logical case for distributional equality as a specific issue in the twentieth century until A. B. Atkinson in the 1970s. Equality became a political issue fought on ethical grounds in which the only economists who took part tended to be subjective preference supporters demonstrating the efficiency and equity properties of the inequality produced by free markets. A cynical cost-of-production view on th gap in investigation might be that poverty has been so far from the experience of professional economists that it is not surprising the paradigm developed in that direction. A more charitable observer might claim that the issue of poverty is subsumed under the strong concern with unemployment in much cost-of-production theory and policy advice, citing Keynes as an obvious example.

In fact, in the twentieth century, the general interest in distribution in cost-of-production theory shifted away from unnecessary poverty towards the unearned affluence which appeared to be its reverse side in immensely productive industrial society. In 1899 Thorstein Veblen's book *The Theory of the Leisure Class* was published in the USA. In that book Veblen attacked the lifestyles of the affluent, ridiculing their behaviour as 'conspicuous consumption' with an emphasis on display. Thus, Veblen argued, the wives of rich men were merely part of a tribal rite, displaying in their manners, clothes and jewels the property of their husbands. This biting picture of vulgar ostentation vividly contrasts with the sympathetic image of the rich as rational abstainers from immediate consumption who receive interest as justifiable reward in subjective preference theory. This deep disagreement helps explain Veblen's total lack of recognition in some texts and important place in others. Veblen's argument is that the consumption patterns of the affluent are socially determined, just as physical subsistence needs determine the consumption patterns of the poor. Veblen even suggested that in some extreme cases a rise in price would increase the quantity demanded because consumers would associate a good being more expensive with its being more prestigious. This flatly contradicts the subjective preference theory prediction about demand relationships.

By the 1960s, affluence appeared to have bitten deep into United States society and the consumption levels of the mass of the population were by any historical standards extraordinarily high. It now became possible to talk about a whole society as affluent and Veblen's work was revived by J. K. Galbraith in his book *The Affluent Society* (1970), and Paul Baran and Paul Sweezy in *Monopoly Capital* (1968). These writers up-dated Veblen's theory of the social determination of consumption patterns from the tribal rite, affirming status to subliminal advertising, manipulating wants. In other words, technological determinism now reached out beyond the workplace and penetrated all areas of life, completing a circle of production, distribution and consumption for the mass of the population. But it is one thing to throw doubt on the subjective preference assumptions that consumption is the free activity of independent individuals satisfying inherent tastes, and quite another to judge any pattern of consumption as undesirable.

There are two directions which can lead to negative judgements of present consumption patterns in the USA and other western societies from a cost-of-production standpoint. The first observes that affluence is still only local on a world scale and traces out the relationships between rich and poor societies, emphasising the deep interconnections and unequal power positions. Theories of international trade called dependency and unequal exchange derive from this reasoning and we shall return to these later. For the purposes of this section it is sufficient to note that this argument derives directly from Mill's objections to poverty and Veblen's objections to affluence combined with Marshall's assertion that redistribution from rich to poor will produce greater total happiness. Tackling poverty on a world scale is not fundamentally different to tackling poverty on a national scale and only requires the recognition by the rich that substantially reduced consumption does not mean anything like a proportional reduction in the quality of life.

The second line of criticism does not need to go beyond the boundaries of the affluent societies. Instead it goes back to Smith and his original doubts about the effect of industrialisation on human personality. Mindless, wasteful consumption is then the inevitable outcome of mindless, alienated employment. From this point of view, industrialisation can appear as an enormous mistake in which potentially active, curious, independent human beings were alienated from their true natures by monotonous work for which they were schooled into being passive, unthinking, automatons. Hints of this type of view appear in writings by William Morris (Briggs 1962) writing in late nineteenth century Britain and more recently have been strongly put forward in the works of Schumacher (1974), Marcuse (1964) and Illich (1973). For such writers there is very little quality in contemporary life and the needs of industrial technology have almost completely dehumanised society. But only 'almost', because somehow they themselves have managed to escape the trap to advocate various degrees of de-industrialisation. We shall return to this elite band in Chapter 7 when discussing the policies arising from cost-of-production theory. Even the most ardent technological determinist of this type would have to admit that some people in industrial society do *believe* they are making important decisions about production. More generally, all cost-of-production economists direct our attention to the context and content of production decisions to explain how the present inequitable situation arose and is reproduced.

6.3 The production decision: imperfect competition

Whilst Mill felt that decisions about distribution should be explicit social decisions, leaving production to be independently, technically ordained, he saw that, in practice, decisions about distribution in a society based on private property are intricately entwined with decisions about what, where and when to produce and the price at which the product is sold. This belief enables us to classify Mill, and all the other economists discussed in this chapter, as holding a cost-of-production theory of value. Mill and Marshall were both willing to admit that the analysis of consumption had a greater role to play in economics than that contained in Ricardo's writing. But, in the final determination, they maintained that consumption primarily acted through the quantity side and that it was production and distribution which together determined the value of a good. This value was equal to the total cost-of-production, which was the minimum price at which the present quantities of a good would continue to be produced over time, i.e. the natural price in Smith and Ricardo's language. The strength of this approach for Mill was that it gave a possible explanation of changes in level of economic activity due to apparent 'gluts' of goods in the United Kingdom economy at his time. As generally a producer had to pay money for inputs before sale, then this cost-of-production could easily be higher than the money price actually obtainable when the output was ready to be put onto the market. Under such circumstances the producer might decide not to sell all the output and instead build up stocks, resulting in temporary, but significantly, reduced production and employment.

By the end of the nineteenth century the increasing size of major industrial enterprises encouraged Marshall to make some reference to the implications of situations in which the cost of producing a unit of a good fell as an enterprise increased in productivity capacity.

In Fig. 6.1 we show such a situation in the analytical framework we used in Chapter 3. If the natural price is determined by the average unit cost-of-production, then a large enterprise is always able to force smaller enterprises out of the industry by pricing at its lower cost-of-production. In the extreme case of total monopoly, the enterprise becomes identical with the industry and is largely freed from the pressure of competition, including the threat of new entry. Marshall saw this situation as arising out of the natural technical conditions of production in particular industries, for instance, the extension of public utilities like water, gas, electricity and railways into new areas might be done with less inputs by already existing enterprises.

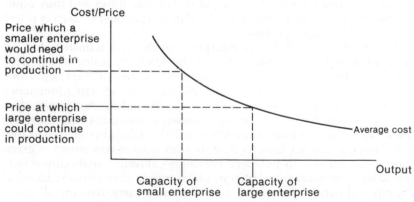

Fig. 6.1   Natural monopoly with falling average costs

The behaviour of an enterprise under conditions of natural monopoly cannot be predicted in the sense that we demonstrated for the entrepreneur facing perfectly competitive conditions in Chapter 3. There, the marginal entrepreneur had effectively no choice over price or level of output, but here, the enterprise decision-maker can choose one or the other, if the enterprise is a monopoly. The production decision-maker can choose to restrict output and thus obtain a higher price than the unit cost of production, or choose a high price and only sell that output which will be purchased at that price. Either way, the consumer seems to lose out and the producer gains compared with the perfectly competitive situation. It is possible to describe formally the conditions under which the surplus of revenue over total costs is maximised but for our purposes here it is sufficient to note that there is a strong temptation, to say the least, for production decision-makers to charge a price above the cost of production and appropriate a 'surplus' for their own use. In such a situation, Marshall argued, 'it might often be to the interest of the community directly or indirectly to intervene, because a largely increased production would add much more to consumers' surplus than to the aggregate expenses of production of the goods' (Marshall 1947: 503).

Whilst criticism based on natural monopoly in decreasing cost industries appears awkward for subjective preference theory, it does not present a fundamental challenge. At worst, it identifies a few problem industries which may be the exceptions that, in effect, prove the rule that most economic activity can be guided efficiently and equitably by the free market mechanism. A subjective preference fundamentalist like Hayek could then argue that to undermine the principle of individual liberty in order, for instance, to lower rail fares reveals a rather odd set of priorities. Also the responsibility for identifying industries with increasing returns falls on the critics and this has proved empirically difficult. For instance, Milton Friedman argues that if the stock exchange works efficiently then the book value of a company will always be equated with the value of its revenue flows and thus economists cannot identify cost-of-production independent of market prices from such accountancy data.

In the 1920s and 1930s, as enterprises in the new industries like oil and automobiles were established in the USA on scales which were enormous by all historical standards, new theories of imperfect competition were put forward which challenged the subjective preference model of perfect competition more generally and fundamentally than natural monopoly theory. The best known is associated with the name of Chamberlin, writing in the USA in 1933. Chamberlin argued that an enterprise did not have to treat its sales market conditions as given but could attempt to influence consumers through artificially differentiating its product from other products which were virtually identical in physical nature. Presenting a product as a particular 'brand' could result in customer loyalty giving the enterprise the ability to raise its price above its main competitors without losing all its customers as would happen under perfect competition. He went on to argue that every enterprise, including potential entrants, would be aware of the possibility of doing the same and differentiating its product. Therefore, the industry would be expanding in terms of number of enterprises, with each existing enterprise's demand relationship shifting, until every enterprise was just receiving its own cost-of-production and no surplus.

This situation is shown in Fig 6.2, again using the analytical framework of Chapter 3, and we can see that there is no need to assume decreasing costs or conscious manipulation to arrive at the conclusion that the economy is inefficient, i.e. not producing at minimum average cost, by the criterion that subjective preference theory would itself use. The strength of this criticism is that it does not require either enterprises to be large or the empirical measurement of increasing returns to scale. The mere existence of brand advertising places an enterprise under suspicion of being in a situation of so-called 'monopolistic competition'. This criticism placed subjective preference theory on the defensive, forcing the rather feeble responses that because the condition is so general it is likely to be weak for any particular enterprise or that, anyway, people actually get satisfaction from the advertising itself and to restrict advertising would deprive consumers of a choice which they value. Kaldor's response to this latter argument in 1935 still carries weight: 'This line of reasoning would only be permissible if consumers were actually confronted with the choice of having *either* a smaller range of commodities at lower prices *or* a larger range at higher prices' (Kaldor 1935: 403 – Kaldor's emphasis).

Undoubtedly, monopolistic competition was a more effective analytical tool to criticise the subjective preference theory of production

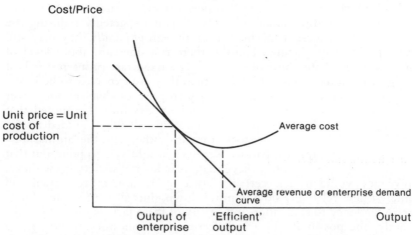

Fig. 6.2   Monopolistically competitive enterprise in equilibrium

than natural monopoly. Unfortunately, on its own, monopolistic competition did not lead very far in setting up a positive alternative theory of how a whole economy might work. Enterprises facing monopolistic competition respond in qualitatively the same way to changes in input prices, and are as keen to innovate and reduce costs and take advantage of favourable shifts in consumer tastes as enterprises in perfectly competitive situations. John Maynard Keynes, in our view, drew on the ideas about imperfect competition around him in the 1920s and 1930s on the nature of the production decision, gave them a new twist and produced a theory of the whole economy which did provide an alternative to the subjective preference general equilibrium model. Keynes's major book *The General Theory of Employment, Interest and Money*, first published in 1936, begins with a careful discussion of production from the standpoint of the production decision-maker.

Keynes's decision-maker lives in an industrial, monetised society based on private property. It is industrial, so one major part of the production decision is whether to purchase large units of machinery; it is monetised, so that the decision to buy inputs is separated from the ability to sell output; it is based on private property so that funds for purchasing inputs, beyond a very limited amount of own resources, have to be obtained through a market, where interest is charged as the price of borrowing other people's property. The decision-maker then decides how much to produce in the future subject to all the constraints that a monopolistically competitive type of enterprise might be expected to face, constraints normally excluded by assumption from the entrepreneur's decision in subjective preference theory.

Firstly, there is the estimation under uncertainty of future revenues; these cannot be simply calculated on the basis of, either, the current market price as under perfect competition, or, a self-chosen price as for a natural monopolist. Secondly there is the problem of future innovation which, when embodied in new machines, threatens to reduce unit cost of production substantially, thus unexpectedly reducing the *economic* life of present machines éven though *physically* they may still be capable of producing. Thirdly, there is a question about level of interest rates. Thus, borrowing funds at a fixed rate of interest is best done when interest rates are lower than they are expected to be in the future. Under such constraints it may surprise us that anybody ever decides to produce anything at all and Keynes himself claimed that decisions to produce became even more difficult when guided by the cold calculation of the joint-stock company rather than the 'animal spirits' of the early capitalist barons. Keynes's insight was to point out that there was good reason to believe that, as industrial society grew older, revenues would be less certain, future innovation more certain and interest rates relatively slow to move down, thus all reinforcing a long-term tendency to stagnation and, if any of these factors moved significantly, the possibility of a real decrease in economic activity, i.e. a depression. For Keynes, like Ricardo, the person who ultimately decided over production, whether called an independent capitalist or a joint-stock company managing director, feels besieged by circumstance and yet still makes the crucial decisions for society. But to show why Keynes thought these decisions were crucial for everybody requires us to move up to the level of the whole economy.

6.4 A cost-of-production theory of a whole economy: Keynes's political economy

John Maynard Keynes was an excellent self-publicist; he demands to be placed at a crossroads in economics, facing everyone with the choice of being Keynesian or anti-Keynesian. That we deny him that place in this book and locate him in a stream of thought running from Smith and Ricardo would probably have immensely annoyed him, as he regarded some of the mercantilists and Ricardo's contemporary critic, the Reverend Thomas Malthus, as his true antecedents. If, paraphrasing Shakespeare's Mark Anthony, we are about to bury Keynes not to praise him, then at least we can claim that, unlike Brutus, we did not stab him in the back. Others, like Leijonhufvud, have hailed his name but also totally removed the radical content of his ideas. The reader must choose whose claim is the strongest.

Despite coming from a background of privilege and ease himself, Keynes's concerns did embrace the unemployed, arguably through a sense of enlightened self-interest, but at least it was *enlightened* self-interest. Keynes, like other contemporaries such as Kahn and Myrdal, recognised the possibility that natural economic processes could be cumulative rather than compensatory. That is, once an economy started moving in a particular direction then that movement would be reinforced, not dampened, by the operation of markets. The major cause of this cumulative process for Keynes derives from assumptions about human psychology which are in direct contradiction to those of subjective preference theory but are close to those of contemporary strong technological determinists. Human nature for these writers is basically malleable and passive; to dramatise the contrast we could say that if subjective preference theory assumes individuals to be courteous heroes, then cost-of-production theory assumes we are all cunning victims. As consumers, savers and producers we calculate our interest short-sightedly and selfishly and are constantly surprised that our plans fail to materialise.

Firstly, consumption is passive in that, as incomes tend to increase, it fails to rise proportionately. The effect of this is to increase desired saving as a share of total income as productive capacity increases, which, as we shall see below, produces a dampening effect on long-term growth of the economy. Consumption is also malleable in that any drop in income produces an immediate response in a fall in consumption and threatens to turn a minor recession into a full economic

143

depression. The mechanism that describes this latter process Keynes gave the name the *multiplier*. If the first shock to the system is increased unemployment, perhaps due to simultaneous fires in a few hundred factories, then the newly unemployed will find themselves without the incomes they aimed to spend on current consumption. They will immediately passively cut back on consumption, which will reduce the effective demand (not the desired demand which will remain passively at the same level) for other products leaving producers with increasing stocks and depressed expectations about future demand. Producers will then lay off workers, meeting the reduced demand from their increased stocks. The laid-off workers will then find themselves with reduced incomes and reduce their consumption, thus continuing the process. The process will only stop when all producers are holding their desired proportion of stocks to substantially reduced sales.

But if this multiplier process has the appearance of responsible innocence, it is the vice of avarice that produces the damage we do as savers. For subjective preference theory, saving has the puritan virtue of abstaining from consumption, which merits the reward of interest. For Keynes, saving is merely the residual left after consumption has been met. Saving, then only becomes real economic activity with difficulty. Thus saving is first experienced as a withdrawal of potential demand in the form of money. If producers are conservative and only judge future demand on the basis of present demand then increases in saving will not be interpreted as pent-up demand in the future requiring tooling-up now, but as a loss of markets best met by laying off workers. It is only when savings appear as lower interest rates that they become visible to producers as an opportunity to increase productive capacity cheaply. But between the passive saver and the conservative producer stands financial markets dominated by speculation

Keynes's contempt for these markets is openly expressed in the *General Theory*, when he describes the Stock Exchange as a '*casino*' (Keynes 1936: 159). Those who deal on the financial markets, who we, following Keynes, shall call rentiers, gain through a high turnover of stocks on which they receive commission and high rates of return when they deal on their own account. Producers equipping factories have to take a view over several years, rentiers play the market on a day-to-day basis; the former are involved in enterprise, which Keynes called 'the activity of forecasting the prospective yield of assets over their whole life', and the latter are involved in 'speculation', which he called' the activity of forecasting the psychology of the market' (Keynes 1936: 158). Governed by rumours, rather than information, the rate of interest charged to any particular producer will rise if there are any doubts about the individual, the industry, the overall economy, or the future of the world. Whilst Keynes thought that the underlying tendency was for interest rates to fall as the mass of saving grew relative to output, leading to the painless 'euthanasia of the rentier', there are several points where his exasperation gives the impression that violence on rentiers at a more active age might be excusable.

Faced with inexplicable withdrawals of current demand by the unemployed and arbitrary rises in the cost of funds due to rentiers, the individual producer then has to take into account the possible actions of other competing producers. Little wonder then, that Keynes was content not to analyse that aspect in detail, mere competitors were the least of a producer's problems, especially if we are willing to assume relatively unabrasive monopolistically competitive conditions. The parallel with Ricardo should now be clear if, instead of landlords, we see rentiers as the villains of political economy, who gain at the expense of producers in general, with the cost being paid primarily in the form of unemployment. Producers exacerbate the problem by over-reacting to set-backs due to their own malleability and passivity, but the fact that they are in production in the first place is to their credit. In a world of acute pessimists, any producer must be a hopeless optimist by comparison.

We can also see why Keynes represented a fundamental challenge to subjective preference theorists. The heroes of subjective preference are the villains of Keynes's world. Despite Keynes's sincere protestations that he wished to preserve the system of private property through reform, his logic led him to the conclusion that free markets left to their own devices produced short-run depression and long-run stagnation. No longer was the cost-of-production criticism restricted to regulating a few natural monopolies, but now it aimed at the core of the economy, threatening a powerful minority interest, in two senses of that word, which subjective preference theory specifically justified. But the further development of this criticism proved difficult for two main reasons. Firstly, Keynes himself was confused by the radical implications of his economic logic, which went beyond the reformist liberal nature of his general political stance. He never resolved this himself, as the Second World War and his death soon after that War meant that debates on the *General Theory* had to take place largely without Keynes. Secondly, the language of markets deriving from subjective preference theory was so dominant that the *General Theory* had to be translated into that language. There were concessions to conventional economics in the *General Theory* itself as Keynes pointed out, but these were greatly increased by others, starting with John Hicks in 1937. Something may well have been lost in that translation to basically subjective preference language, a translation which forms the basis of the next section.

6.5 The General Theory as a special case of subjective preference theory: Keynesianism

The one area in which Keynes could unambiguously be said to have a general theory was in his explicit handling of the movements across long periods of time of an industrial, monetary economy based on private property. Here the responses by both Keynes's interpreters and detractors have usually been simply to ignore these parts of Keynes's work. It is the image that Keynes was only interested in the immediate future and with no views on the broad question of class interests in society, that we have tried to correct in the previous section. Our interpretation there does locate Keynes's thought firmly in the field of political economy and he emerges with some real insights in that field as a cost-of-production economist in the mould of Ricardo. But Keynes, like many famous men, is best known through those who claim to be his disciples. Therefore, we turn to the short-run macroeconomic market model into which Keynes's thought is conventionally compressed by those calling themselves Keynesians and show their failure to achieve a compromise with subjective preference theory, other than on the basis of complete surrender.

Part of the blame for this lies with Keynes himself. He did not spend much time on price determination in the *General Theory*. He was content to claim that the best measure of value for the economy as a whole was the number of people in employment, and for any particular good the total amount of labour embodied in a unit of output basically determined its price. This amount of labour could be calculated in money terms by multiplying each hour of labour by its own money wage. What determines those money wages is not rigorously examined, and Keynes only hints that relative wages might reflect relative contributions to production and nowhere does he suggest that the general level of money wages is an outcome of any identifiable economic law. This vagueness on price determination undoubtedly left Keynes' argument vulnerable to criticism from the subjective preference theory standpoint that he was just dealing with the special case of a fixed price economy and that better information flows given by freer market processes would rule out economic depressions.

In contrast, Keynes did give a good deal of space to discussing how the aggregate level of real activity in the economy changed. This relative emphasis in Keynes can be strikingly contrasted with the discussion on subjective preference theory in Chapters 3 and 4, where we saw that the prices of products were rigorously and carefully analysed as the outcome of the preferences of independent individuals, whereas the overall level of economic activity was basically the simple sum of all the individual decisions to consume or to produce. In Keynes's analysis the whole economy could not be understood as the outcome of a simple summation procedure. The level of economic activity was not simply determined by independent individual decision makers but the aggregate conditions surrounding individual decisions themselves feed back into the decisions of individuals, which only then give the final overall level of economic activity. Therefore the state of the whole economy becomes interesting in its own right as the beginning and end of analysis. It is for this reason that Keynes was vulnerable to being reduced to purely a 'macroeconomist', concerned only with some special problems at the level of the whole economy with little understanding of decision-making processes at the level of individual decision-makers, which were claimed to follow the general principles of subjective preference theory. To move from Keynes to the Keynesians requires a translation as we mentioned above, from the language of interest groups to the language of markets. This translation can be treated in three separate parts

The first translation is from the unemployed worker unable to meet a desired level of consumption because of a lack of effective demand to a general market for savings and investment linked by the rate of interest. Keynesians hold the view that the saving is a residual between consumption and current income, rising sharply with increases in incomes but not falling to zero with falling incomes. In this model there is no reason to expect the flow of savings to be very sensitive to changes in the rate of interest. Also the rate of interest that has to be paid for borrowed funds is only one of the factors which a production decision-maker has to take into account when deciding to invest in a piece of machinery, so here again responsiveness to changes in the rate of interest might be expected to be small. Therefore if an economic policy is designed to manipulate rates of interest it might not be effective in changing real decisions, but to say that is not to contradict subjective preference theory which disagrees with manipulating any prices, including rates of interest.

The subjective preference response on the supply of savings is to argue that we are stronger-minded individuals than the Keynesians suggest, and make our decisions about current consumption on the basis of a hard-headed, long term view of income flows, not immediate income alone. Therefore we are less likely to be surprised by income fluctuations than the Keynesian position suggests, maintaining consumption in the face of temporary falls in current income and thus reducing saving significantly, so as effectively to maintain current demand and hence general producers' confidence. Analytically this can be seen as a question of the size of a variable called the marginal propensity to consume out of current income (hereafter, MPC). This is defined as the proportion of any unit increase or decrease in current income which is consumed. Keynesians would argue that the MPC is relatively high compared to their subjective preference critics.

The effect of this disagreement can be seen through a simple numerical example. A sudden loss of income to an economy of £1000 will have the following differing impacts if we assume MPCs of 0.9 (Keynesian) and 0.4 (subjective preference). By definition the immediate effect will be to reduce consumption by £900 and £400 respectively. But this consumption immediately reduces incomes for the producers of those consumption goods in the economy who will by definition reduce expenditure by $0.9 \times £900$ or $0.4 \times £400$ on immediate consumption and, thus, reduce by £810 or £160 respectively incomes for those consumption good producers. In the next round those reduced incomes produce further reductions of $0.9 \times £810$ or $0.4 \times £160$ in immediate consumption. Summing up the decreased activity in the two examples, we have $£1000 + £900 + £810 + £729 = £3439$ for the Keynesian MPC and for subjective preference MPC we have $£1000 + £400 + £160 + £64 = £1624$. A dramatic difference which will be enhanced if we went through further rounds of this process. Thus by varying the assumed size of the MPC it is possible to dampen the theoretical impact of unexpected shocks to an economy. This applies whether those shocks involve initial decreases or increases in income. Empirical investigations of MPCs for actual economies are complicated by the necessary introduction of government and international transactions. Also the precise specification of current consumption is open to debate on what should be excluded as durable consumption and thus statistical investigations have tended to be inconclusive.

On the demand for funds for investment, many Keynesians seem analytically willing to accept that changes in the rate of interest are the most significant influence on producers' decisions, by assuming that the flow of revenues yielded by a planned level of output and the economic life of machinery are both known with certainty. Thus if the current market price of a machine is £1000, if its economic life is three years, and if the net revenue in each of the three years is £400, the maximum rate of interest which will be paid for borrowing that £1000 is a discount rate which equates the cost of the equipment with the expected net revenue. This is given mathematically as follows:

$$£1000 = \frac{400}{1+r} + \frac{400}{(1+r)^2} + \frac{400}{(1+r)^3}$$

where r is the discount rate expressed as a fraction.

The solution is a discount rate of about 10 per cent per annum, since

$$1000 \simeq \frac{400}{1.1} + \frac{400}{(1.1)^2} + \frac{400}{(1.1)^3}$$

If the current interest rate which has to be paid is higher than 10 per cent, then the machine will not be purchased. If it falls below 10 per cent, then it will be purchased by a rational producer. In the simplest Keynesian model there are no other specific factors influencing the investment decision, and the predictions of the Keynesians and subjective preference theory are at least non–contradictory qualitatively. As the empirical identification of aggregate investment relationships is also complicated by uncertainties about which interest rates influenced which purchases, disagreement could hardly be conclusively tested empirically anyway.

But, even if the reaction to falls in the rate of interest is to increase the amount of investment, there is still a question about under what conditions the rate of interest might be sticky and not fall easily, thus not encouraging investment. The rate of interest is, for Keynesians, a monetary phenomenon, not necessarily reflecting the real condition of the economy. This is because money is not just a medium of exchange but also a store of value. To understand the implications of this it is necessary to understand the relationship between the actual rate of interest and the market price of a financial asset. In buying a financial asset, say a government bond, paying fixed interest, the buyer becomes entitled to a regular fixed cash payment. In Keynesian language this interest is the compensation paid for hazarding purchasing power, i.e. foregoing liquidity. Thus interest is not the reward for saving as such, but the reward for not holding those savings as money. Each person has to decide the forms in which savings are to be held, i.e. what is to be the allocation between different stores of value. Some amount of total savings could be held in the form of money, as money facilitates immediate command over consumption at any future time with the certainty of that consumption having a specific monetary value. The rest of savings would be held in the form of financial assets, thereby sacrificing immediate and certain (in money terms) command over future consumption in return for an interest income.

The basic conditions of choice can be simply presented. A person buys a bond issued by the government or a company for £100 and repayable in the distant future and that bond carries an entitlement to be paid by the issuer a fixed rate of £10 per year, i.e. 10 per cent per annum at that purchase price. If, while this person holds the bond, there is a general expectation among investors that interest rates will rise, then investors will refrain from buying bonds and hold money until the reduced demand for bonds has depressed bond prices and effectively raised interest rates. Interest rates will settle at the 'safe' or expected level. But in the meantime the person who bought the bond for £100 will find that the market price of the bond will have dropped, since the price (p) of the financial asset will be equal to the annual income (v) divided by the interest rate (i). Thus if, in our example, the interest rate stabilises at 15 per cent per annum, the bond which was bought for £100 will now be worth only £66.70 on the market, since in math-

ematical terms: $p = \frac{v}{i}$ or $p = \frac{£10}{0.15} = £66.70$ Thus the investor will have

made a 'capital' loss of £33.3 on the investment for which any interest income accruing in the meantime will provide inadequate compensation. Thus, even if the government increases the money supply as a policy measure, interest rates may not fall.

This situation is called the liquidity trap and as we remarked in Chapter 4 has never been found empirically. Unfortunately for Keynesians it has also proved theoretically vulnerable. Assume that many people are holding money waiting for interest rates to rise so that they can buy bonds at a cheaper price (remember that as interest rates on new bonds rise then any existing bond which pays a fixed amount a year will fall in price if it is to be comparable with new bonds in overall return). But all this money demanded as a store of value means people not consuming, which means producers not selling, and a pressure on prices to fall in order to dispose of unplanned stocks. If prices generally fall then the money held for speculation as a store of value will become more valuable in purchasing power. Thus, if people are really interested in their ability to command real resources, the current demand for consumption goods will start to rise and encourage production as the money balances become more valuable in purchasing power, even if interest rates do not fall. This 'real balance' or 'Pigou effect' has proved a very telling blow to the Keynesian theory of interest among economists because of its strong rationalistic basis.

As an aside, it is tempting to argue from this observation that if you really want to squash modern economists you should say they are illogical, not that they have their facts wrong. So, looking at the demand side of the money market analytically and assuming a fixed supply of money, it would appear that after a depressing shock to the economy either interest rates would fall and encourage investment or general prices would fall and encourage increased current demand for consumption goods; only with totally fixed interest rates and prices would neither occur.

The third part of the translation of Keynes into the language of markets involves seeing producer and worker relations as a market with buying and selling of labour. Keynesians are willing to assume that we are talking about a short-run situation, that is a time-period in which the stock of productive machines in the economy is fairly fixed because, on average, there is not sufficient time to design, build and bring into production new machines. A period of a calendar year would certainly be considered the short-run by this definition. This fixed supply of machines is put to work with wage labour and assumed to allow some flexibility in degree of labour use, depending on rises or falls in the wage rate. If wages are relatively low in broad terms of the amount of output distributed to labour for a unit time period of work, then we might expect more time units of labour to be employed because the machines could be worked more intensively, i.e. with more labour time, and still make a surplus to pay the interest charges. So only if the technology were completely inflexible, i.e. only a fixed amount of labour time could be employed with each machine, might we not expect an increase in labour time demanded (and hence a probable fall in unemployment) with a fall in the amount of goods distributed to a labourer for an hour's work, i.e. a fall in the real wage rate.

This only leaves the supply side of the labour market in question as the cause of prolonged unemployment. But with the unemployed outside the gates of factories willing to accept lower real wages in order to get work, then in whose interests is it to keep them there? Not the employers who could reduce their costs and not the financiers who would find less pressure on their dividends and interest payments. The only people who unambiguously benefit are the employed, who are getting the higher wages, and the only way they can enforce and maintain this position is through Trade Unions and the threat of collectively disrupting production. A disruption that would increase costs for the employer more than hiring cheaper labour would decrease costs. It has been argued, in an attempt to keep some shreds of Keynesian disequilibrium theory intact, that trade unions have to negotiate for money, not real wages and employers simply add on a margin to the wage bill for interest payment and themselves, i.e. 'prime cost plus' theory of price formation. Therefore, if money wages fall then prices fall and the economy ends up in exactly the same real position, including level of unemployment, only with lower money wages and money prices. But all we need to do to counter this is to recall the real balance effect and its conclusion, that as money prices fall then money balances become more valuable, thus encouraging increased current consumption expenditure.

Thus, in the final rigorous Keynesian analysis, it is the unemployed themselves who are mainly to blame for their condition. Firstly, if they had been more rational and accurately forecasted their flows of income then they would have not had suddenly to cut back consumption when faced with a spell of unemployment, but instead would have drawn down savings. Secondly, they should be more determined in seeking and accepting work at wages lower than those currently paid. The government is also at fault if it has by chance allowed the money supply to contract violently and thus dampen down the real balance effect. Employers are at fault if they passively allow trade unions to determine real wages. The final irony of the Keynes versus the Keynesian arguments is that the role of bankers, insurance companies and financiers becomes the most positive of any group in the hands of the new selfstyled Keynesians, like Leijonhufvud writing in 1968. Financial institutions connect the present with the future through transactions involving purchases now in exchange for repayments in the future. They thus help desired demand to become revealed and, in general, the smooth running of the monetary system means that the real balance effect can operate to maximum effect. The Keynesians have thus turned Keynes on his head and left themselves no grounds on which to be rigorously distinguished from the subjective preference school of thought. As effective academic economics, the conventional translations of Keynes's thought were dead by 1970, at about the same time they died as effective politics as we shall see in the next chapter. This simultaneous demise in the realm of politics and the realm of ideas should however not encourage the simple view that ideas and politics are always inseparably linked together and have no autonomy.

6.6 The cost-of-production revival: back to the roots

Subjective preference theory after defeat in the capital controversy was taken back to its theoretical foundations and found new strength in the 1960s, similarly cost-of-production theory gained from the surrender of Keynesianism and rediscovered a new vigour in the 1970s. The revived cost-of-production approach to the theory of value rested on the assumption of an industrial technology which combines physical inputs in a rather inflexible way. Valuation is a social and well-defined process because industrial technology requires large numbers of people to be brought together virtually totally independently of their own wills and desires. Thus the theory starts at the broad societal level and plays down the effects of demand. The broad requirement is then imposed that the economy be able physically to reproduce itself indefinitely over time. It is the search for the pricing conditions that satisfy that requirement which is the first goal of cost-of-production theory in its neo-Ricardian mould.

The theoretical restatement of the cost-of-production school's position which precisely followed these criteria appeared in 1960 with the publication of Piero Sraffa's *Production of Commodities by Means of Commodities*. Sraffa freely acknowledged his inheritance from Ricardo and thus reasserted the Ricardian roots of the cost-of-production approach. This encouraged Sraffa's radical sympathisers to accept the heretical label of neo-Ricardian as they joined the growing movement in the 1970s in defiance of the noe-classical orthodoxy. The sub-title of Sraffa's book was 'Prelude to a Critique of Economic Theory', and in his preface Sraffa expressed the hope that someone would base a critique of neo-classicism or, in our language, subjective preference theory, on this foundation. Thus, in looking back rigorously to Ricardo and antagonistically at contemporaries in the subjective preference school, Sraffa's book gives an excellent basis from which to survey modern cost-of-production theory. Sraffa's book was concerned with one aspect of the same problem over which Ricardo had puzzled, the relationship between prices and labour values. Sraffa looked at this general problem from the perspective of discovering an invariable standard of value reflecting only the basic technological characteristics of a society.

In the formal language of economics, the problem can be seen as showing logically the existence of a set of prices; prices which are consistent with the physical reproduction of the economy, and subject to laws of value showing the way that they change when subject to specific external shocks. Ricardo had been worried about the divergence of relative labour time inputs from the relative final prices of outputs in a society with profits, but had left the matter finally unresolved. This was the problem that Sraffa solved, stimulated no doubt by editing the *Works and Correspondence of Ricardo* into some fifteen volumes. This latter experience might also explain why his own major work is so short and took about forty years from conception to publication, but even then it was both stimulating and a few years ahead of its time!

Sraffa begins by examining an economy which is simply ticking over. That is, he starts by examining an economy in which the outputs are exactly equal to the inputs, including the bare subsistence needs of the labour employed. There is no surplus i.e. a fall in output would produce a fall in the labour force and vice versa. The example he gave is a two-good economy, with the following necessary technical organisation:

280 quarters of wheat + 12 tons of iron produce 400 quarters of wheat;

120 quarters of wheat + 8 tons of iron produce 20 tons of iron.

Thus a total input of 400 quarters of wheat and 20 tons of iron at the beginning of a period is used to produce the same amounts of wheat and iron as final products at the end of a time period. Sraffa assumed that the subsistence needs of the labourers were included in the inputs so that the system simply ticks over year after year, with no growth. It is clear that, looking at the inter-industry transfers, in the iron industry there are twelve tons of iron available (twenty minus eight) to exchange for the 120 quarters of wheat needed to keep the production of iron going. Thus the price of one ton of iron must be ten times the price of a quarter of wheat. This price is consistent with the need of wheat producers to exchange their net production of 120 quarters of wheat for the twelve tons of iron needed to produce the next year's amount.

This is the only relative price structure consistent with the reproduction of the economy. In mathematical terms this can be obtained by solving the simultaneous equations:

$$280 \, p_w + 12 \, p_i = 400 \, p_w \text{ (that is the total value of wheat in the economy)}$$

$$120 \, p_w + 8 \, p_i = 20 \, p_i \text{ (that is the total value of iron in the economy)}$$

where p_w is the price of wheat per quarter; and p_i is the price of iron per ton.

As we are discussing only relative prices, one physical unit of either of these goods can be used as a base price, numeraire, or unit of account. If we express the price of iron in terms of wheat by using one quarter of wheat as the unit of account, then the equations become:

$$280 + 12 \, p_i = 400$$
$$120 + 8 \, p_i = 20 \, p_i$$

Or, in either case, $p_i = 10$ quarters of wheat.

So we have just one set of prices which is consistent with the reproduction of the economy. This solution involves no explicit discussion of demand, as the set of prices is only a product of physical relation-ships, including the subsistence needs of human beings to reproduce their labour indefinitely.

But things are not so simple once we move from this simple ticking-over economy to the situation in which a surplus above subsistence is produced. Sraffa shows this by changing the above example so that the amount of wheat produced rises from 400 quarters to 575 quarters. There is now a surplus of 175 quarters per time period which can be distributed in any manner we choose without apparently changing the ability of the economy to be reproduced. In this state of improved tech-nology, one possible mode of distribution is simply to allocate the sur-plus in proportion to the basic value of the output, that is through an equalised rate of profit, which is formally the equal fractional addition to value which just exhausts the surplus. The production equations in price terms will now be:

$$(280 + 12\ p_i)\ (1 + r) = 575$$
$$(120 + 8\ p_i)\ (1 + r) = 20p_i$$

where r is that rate of profit or fractional increase, and a quarter of wheat is once again taken as the numeraire.

Each of the total input values is now multiplied by $1 + r$, r being the rate of profit, and the value of inputs is not just being replaced but also carrying or 'earning' a constant rate of profit. There are now two things or variables to be discovered (p_i and r) in the two equations; this is generally soluble and can be calculated as $p_i = 15$ and $r = \frac{1}{4}$ or 25 per cent in this example. Thus once again there is a unique relative price for iron in terms of wheat consistent with the reproduction of the econ-omy.

But supposing the surplus is to be shared between profit and enhanced wages, i.e. the assumption that wages are equal to subsistence is dropped. If we assume that labour shares in the surplus produced, then we have a further variable, namely the wage rate, so that there are three variables in two equations. The system of prices is insoluble, unless the distribution between wages and profits is first specified. If the whole of the surplus goes to labour then relative prices will almost certainly differ from those established when only part of the surplus goes to labour. When the whole of the net product goes to labour, we, in effect, revert to a subsistence economy – in the sense that the rate of profit is zero – and the equilibrium prices of the different products will be proportionate to the different quantities or times of labour which have been directly and indirectly employed to produce units of them. But when less than the whole of the net product goes to labour then the prices will not, in general, be proportional to the labour times per unit of output. Thus the prices will change according to changes in distribution between labour and capital. This is what the example on Ricardo at the end of Chapter 5 demonstrated.

Sraffa succeeded in finding a 'solution' to this problem of the invariable standard of value. The solution consisted in showing that a thing called the standard commodity always existed and, in principle, could be calculated by taking bits and pieces of many commodities in the economy. The relative sizes of the bits and pieces could always be calculated in any specific case so that this composite commodity would provide an invariable standard of value; invariable, that is, to changes in overall distribution between wages and profits. Thus, the theoretical problem that a set of prices purely dependent on the physical characteristics of technology would always exist in a non-subsistence economy was solved without any explicit reference to demand. But even more significant was the proposition that, more generally, equilibrium prices of production, to which markets would tend, could always be found once the physical input-output coefficients *and* the distribution were known. Thus rigorous grounds were laid by Sraffa for both a renewed attack on subjective preference theory and new policy initiatives. The nature of the formal attack on subjective preference theory was to rework the models of subjective preference theory in terms of economies with inflexible technologies. Economists' use of linear mathematics, including linear programming and input-output analysis as techniques of analysing individual production decisions and whole economies respectively, increased rapidly. These were appropriate methods for representing economies in which the ability to substitute inputs for each other was zero, known formally as a fixed coefficient economy. Most of subjective preference theory survived this critical examination in broad qualitative terms, although increasingly the qualification was added to their theorems that the effect of this or that price change was non-negative or non-positive rather than more boldly positive or negative respectively. Sensitive price responsiveness was therefore challenged, which somewhat undermined the subjective preference case. A more telling criticism has already been mentioned, the capital controversy, which was totally conducted in terms of such linear methods and did result in a subjective preference defeat. But, in general, the main impact of the criticism that Sraffa inspired was not to replace subjective preference theory with a new paradigm, but to rally believers in free markets around the subjective preference flag.

On the more positive side, the development of Sraffa's ideas spawned a whole new economic literature on distribution, growth and international trade. Distribution has been a major issue in cost-of-production theory, certainly since Mill's division of economic analysis into socially determined distribution and technically determined production. Sraffa's conclusions echo that view of the world, saying that, whilst we can theoretically exclude distribution from price determination by using the standard commodity, distribution is in practice crucial to the determination of prices. This raises the question of how distribution is determined itself and whether there are any criteria that can be used to evaluate one pattern of distribution as superior to another. The determination of distribution we will leave to the next section when we will discuss the behaviour of the large corporations as the typical institutions determining distribution in late industrial society. In this section we will discuss the evaluation of distributions as it can be discussed using a basic, aggregate Sraffa approach.

Any arguments about the justice of a particular pattern of distribution in cost-of-production theory tends to start from the weak egalitarian principle that the essentials necessary to an active physical existence are a basic right for every human being. A society, where such basic needs are not met and many of the population are not fed, sheltered and suffer ill-health so as to be identifiably absolutely physically deprived, is unambiguously underdeveloped from a cost-of-production point of view. The literature on underdevelopment in the mid-1970s has been dominated by cost-of-production theory, and strongly influenced by the concept of 'basic needs'. Research projects attempted in the mid-1970s to measure deficiencies and design distribution programmes to make up these deficiencies. Such rationing programmes would unambiguously improve the distribution pattern by cost-of-production criteria even though they aim to divert considerable resources away from the affluent without their consent. But this strong criterion of eliminating poverty is lost once we examine industrial society, where the technology is immensely physically productive, and have to see distribution questions in terms of a struggle over surplus. Egalitarianism in terms of an equal right to an active physical life is a principle which is of limited use in deciding who is to be the next proud owner of a video-tape player.

Any national distribution pattern in industrial society cannot be rigorously criticised in cost-of-production theory, although it will certainly be attacked. At its most unified, many economists would accept that the simple principle of fundamental human equality can be used in industrial society to draw attention to the need for state aid to deprived minorities like the aged and handicapped. Fewer would assert that the theory provides no basis for justifying profit, as defined by Sraffa, as a necessary mode of distribution, and therefore all the product should be distributed according to labour time contributed. But even this distributional 'socialism' would be criticised by the tiny group of rigorous, if more utopian, socialist economists claiming that the Sraffa model shows no necessity for wages either, beyond a few basic needs. In this last case, nobody has a natural right to any reward and so distribution can be totally separated from activity in production. Thus, a general conclusion pointing towards the desirability of greater equality in incomes and consumption can be derived from a Sraffa-type model agreeing with the similar equity conclusion of the earlier cost-of-production writers from Mill onwards. This conclusion allows for a variety of positions with respect to policy on inequality from mild welfare measures, for which some case could be found in subjective preference theory, to total income equality for all members of society. This overlap is much reduced in discussions of the relationships between distribution and the process of economic growth, and distribution and the process of increasing international trade. For both these processes, subjective preference theory predicted that inequality (almost inevitably) would be automatically and naturally reduced, thus diminishing any need for conscious intervention on distributional grounds. Cost-of-production theory produces a strong case against this.

Economic growth has been a continuing important concern for cost-of-production theory from Ricardo's time. Industrial society is seen as having a large growth potential because knowledge of possible technological change is institutionalised and cumulative in industrial society. This advance in technological know-how always allows higher production per head of population although its actual expression may be in the forms of improved machinery, improved labour skills or both. The implementation of this knowledge in production requires the use of part of the general surplus, i.e. savings, to support some part of the labour force in addition to that part required to reproduce the economy and keep it ticking over. Now we have put technological determinism in this dynamic form, we can ask what is the role of distribution in this analysis. We shall assume that distribution in the society involves an equal rate of profit and a standard wage as the modes of distribution of surplus. Saving out of profits is proportionately higher than that out of wages, possibly because profit receivers are generally richer as individuals than wage receivers.

As the population grows, then the economy may suffer from increasing inequality. Thus, if the rate of general economic growth is lower than the rate of population growth then this imbalance threatens to bring about a form of Ricardian stagnation as a final economic state, and increasing unemployment in the immediate situation. This seems bound to occur if the rate of population growth is assumed to be natural and not checked by unemployment, and the technology so inflexible that each machine employs a fixed amount of labour time whatever the wage rate. The economy would then apparently only achieve continuing high employment by accident and would otherwise have increasing inequality in the form of the unpaid unemployed. However, Kaldor (1960), amongst others has pointed out that some compensating changes in distribution might occur automatically. As unemployment grew and wages therefore showed no tendency to increase, then any economic growth, due to technological change making labour more productive, would tend to redistribute income towards profit receivers who save relatively highly and thus provide increased funds for investment, i.e. machines, to put the unemployed to work. But it is important to see that in this growth model it is the distribution mechanism which puts people to work, not increased conscious abstaining from consumption by more virtuous individuals, and certainly not the acceptance of wage decreases by workers. Also this mechanism seems rather clumsy, and has no claim to any greater justice, compared with the orderly implementation of technological innovation (the basic motor of growth) by a benign central authority.

International trade theory in the twentieth century has been dominated by the proposition, associated with the names of Heckscher (1919) and Ohlin (1933), that, even if inputs were relatively immobile, there would still tend to be an equalisation of their rewards providing outputs were freely traded on world markets. This proposition was doubly convenient to subjective preference theory because it fundamentally supported free trade and yet argued that the threat to national identity posed by unrestricted immigration would not be necessary to achieve the equity benefits of such trade. However, put in a cost-of-production framework with the assumptions that (1) wage rates in two industries are unequal and two countries are totally specialised, one in each industry, and (2) the profit rate and prices of outputs are equal, then a model can be built of a Sraffa type which does not produce the Heckscher-Ohlin result of equal wage rates. For instance, a single set of output prices and a uniform profit rate can be calculated from a set of Sraffa equations in which a different wage rate is used for each of the two countries. A situation Arghiri Emmanuel (1972) would call 'unequal exchange'. In simple mathematical terms, it is possible to show this by slightly augmented simultaneous price equations from above (remember one country produces only wheat and the other only iron):

$$(280 + 12\ p_i)\ (1 + r) + \bar{w}_1 L_1 = 575$$
$$(120 + 8\ p_i)\ (1 + r) + \bar{w}_2\ L_2 = 20 p_i$$

where $\bar{w}_1$ and $\bar{w}_2$ are the fixed wage rates in the two countries and L_1 and L_2 are the two labour forces. These equations are, in principle, soluble for p_1 and r, given the wage rates and the size of the labour forces. Thus, providing the two labour forces can be kept separate, then the inequalities in the economic system can be reproduced indefinitely.

In this case, unequal distribution has not even the claim to being a clumsy mechanism for benefiting the poorest by increasing the total size of the economy as it did in the Kaldorian growth model. The inequality becomes especially questionable if the lower wage fails to meet the elementary criterion of basic needs which some of the proponents of the theory would argue is the case at present on a world scale. Also, dividing wage-earners into two groups leads to the political conclusion that higher-paid workers are as likely to oppose lower-paid workers as they are to oppose profit-receivers in attempts to maintain their living standards. The international distribution pattern is thus a vital, complex, political question for cost-of-production theory. Vital because many low wage-earners fail to achieve basic needs and future economic growth is more likely to benefit profit-receivers and high wage-earners than low wage-earners. Political because technology is essentially given and altering distribution is a political decision which does not feed back strongly into technological change and fundamental economic growth. Complex, because at least three different interest groups are now involved and the poorest wage earners are the least able politically to represent themselves.

Thus at the aggregate level on a world scale, Sraffa-type analysis has proved a powerful tool for criticising some general subjective preference theory conclusions about the working of the market system, showing conditions under which distribution follows no particular natural laws; growth causes saving not vice versa; and, international inequalities are reinforced. This challenge in itself is important today, but we can see that its assumptions follow directly from those of J. S. Mill about the separation of technology and distribution, who in turn built on Ricardo's essential technological determinism, which is so central to the cost-of-production theory of value. The other important aspect of cost-of-production theory is the location of significant economic decisions in the sphere of production. In the next section we move on to look at a model of such decisions in the production units of advanced industrial society, a model which is highly consistent with Sraffa's analysis at the aggregate level of the whole economy.

6.7 Who runs the large corporation and to what ends?

In the twentieth century the giant corporation has become the most dramatic feature on the production landscape, especially in the USA. It would be argued by a supporter of cost-of-production theory that subjective preference theory never came to terms with that reality, instead becoming trapped in the fiction of the lone entrepreneur, who simply acts as the central link in a number of essentially individual contracts. One of the crucial distinctive characteristics of the corporation for cost-of-production theory is that it is the formal property of large numbers of shareholders and employs full-time professional executives organised in a management hierachy. These executives carry out specialist functions in divisions like engineering, marketing (advertising is also a feature of the corporation) and research and development. Also the large labour force is organised into one or more trade unions, which will often cross the corporation's boundaries and negotiate on an inter-corporation basis. For this reason and others, the corporation management will have links with rivals, major suppliers, largest customers and government departments, which are not anonymous market relationships.

The question of who runs the corporation and with what ends in view is thus very complicated. All the important characteristics may be agreed upon by most cost-of-production writers but there can still be much disagreement about who actually wields power. The very concept of power is a problem in itself. Power cannot be directly observed and measured. Cost-of-production theory then has a problem by the standards of its own methodology that one of its crucial concepts is as abstract, metaphysical and tautological as utility in subjective preference theory. This dilemma is in practice resolved by asserting that most people do *not* have power, because their interests seem to be harmed in one way or another by particular decisions, and therefore that real power must lie with the group whose real interests are best defended. Power exists in every human situation according to this view, and if no one will admit to it then someone is conspiratorially concealing it. One research task for the cost-of-production school is to locate these concealed seats of power in advanced industrial society, and unveil them. Discussions of the large corporation can be seen in this light, the decisions made inside these institutions appear to reach out into all our lives and this is prima facie evidence of power, the problem is to find who wields it.

Analytically, the model of natural monopoly in section 6.3 can be extended to give one possible indication of power. Power is the ability to use the surplus (or in subjective preference language, a rent) over the prime cost of production. This surplus is a resource available within a monopoly which can be used for any purpose without putting the corporation at economic risk. Within the corporation, three groups are identified who might claim this resource: shareholders, salaried managers and wage labourers. Of these three groups it is the managers who are the favourite cost-of-production target as the ultimate shy, and sly, holders of power. Shareholders as a group have formal ownership rights but their dispersed numbers and lack of information are against them controlling the surplus. Wage labourers have the power and the organisation to withdraw their labour collectively but their economic vulnerability to long-term loss of income and the relative mobility of modern industry limit their ability to exercise control over the use of surplus.

The weakest version of the managerial control theory implies by this elimination that the surplus is used for the managers' own collective and individual aggrandisement. Large offices, plush carpets, large expense accounts, and executive dining rooms and cars are evidence of corporate conspicuous consumption in the interest of managers as a group. More significant for the actual level of economic activity than this simple redistribution of consumption opportunities from customers to managers is the discretion that control over surplus gives managers in terms of the overall strategy of the corporation. The strategic goal that has been advanced most frequently as the alternative to profit maximisation by economists like W. J. Baumol, R. Morris and J. H. Williamson is that managers aim to increase the sales of the corporation as fast as possible, a goal pursued subject to meeting a constraint in terms of some minimum dividends paid to shareholders to prevent them selling their shares to a take-over raider. This is curious because as we saw in section 6.3 a major criticism of monopoly is that it has a general tendency to *restrict* sales with the aim of getting a higher price. Thus the 'modern' theory of the firm, which puts forward sales maximisation as a managerial goal, seems to erode rather than support the older criticism of large corporations.

The view that this managerial power is functional to the success of industrial society was at its strongest in the first half of the twentieth century but still finds some supporters today. At that time bureaucracy was a word with slightly less pejorative undertones than it came to have in the latter half of the century. Analytically Max Weber had arrived at the conclusion that bureaucracy was an effective form of authority, in that its principles of organisation allowed the performance of very complex tasks, i.e. just those tasks which are at the core of industrial society performed by the large corporations. Certainly one way of approaching Keynes's work is to see economic depression as partly the outcome of too much influence by owners over managers, albeit indirectly exercised through the stock market rather than directly through the Annual General Meeting of shareholders.

In the 1930s, the rapid industrialisation of the USSR under Stalinism and economic 'successes' in Italy under Fascism and Germany under Nazism encouraged a large literature on managerial power at the national and international levels. This literature conceptually linked these events as different manifestations of the same essential, inevitable process, the growth of bureaucratic/managerial control. For those economies which limped through the 1930s like those of the USA and the UK, the literature was often sympathetic to this process, in the broad sense that the process was envisaged as desirable relative to the other 'realistic' alternatives. This qualified support reached its peak in the book *Managerial Revolution* by James Burnham published in 1940. But the fall of the regimes in Italy and Germany in the 1940s and the revelations of the toll of Stalinism in the 1950s left this sympathetic position discredited and forced the more critical approach to managerial power which is dominant today. The essence of such a criticism can be found in Veblen's book *Theory of Business Enterprise* which was first published in 1904. In that book, Veblen can be interpreted as taking Mill's distinction between physical laws of production and social laws of distribution and representing it as a distinction between the roles of engineers and managers. Veblen argued that goods produced to the specifications of engineers would be durable and simply functional, qualities which were lost when production is controlled by managers.

In 1966, Paul Baran and Paul Sweezy gave full acknowledgement to Veblen for all his insights in their book *Monopoly Capital*. Their credentials in cost-of-production theory were already well established at that time. Sweezy had already participated in the imperfect competition debates of the 1930s when he proposed a model of oligopoly in which large corporations treated their demand relationships as very sensitive to the retaliatory actions of a few major rivals leading to a great reluctance to change prices. Baran had written a book on development, *The Political Economy of Growth* (1968), which in the 1960s and early 1970s was almost the standard text on the cumulative nature of underdevelopment and the perpetuation of poverty. In *Monopoly Capital*, they start from a model of the whole economy which has strong analytical connections with Sraffa's but with the specific additional distributional assumption that control of a vast surplus is vested in the hands of a small group of chief executives of major corporations. To identify (and indeed attempt to measure) the surplus Baran and Sweezy start by trying to identify what constitutes non-valuable activity. A major difficulty immediately arises because they see all products as being a complex mixture of functional necessity and unnecessary waste. Items such as defence expenditure can be commited to the category of waste virtually in their entirety, but most products reflect the interpenetration of use and waste; for example, an automobile's use as a means of getting safely from A to B comes packaged with non-optional selling features that have nothing to do with that function. Less ambiguously, but equally controversially, Baran and Sweezy regard whole categories of service activity as, in the broad sense, non-valuable, in that if only rights to private property were removed then complex legal and estate agency arrangements for protecting and transferring those rights would be redundant.

Thus, they arrive at the conclusion that the functional reproduction of the USA economy would require less than half the human and natural resources actually used. This large proportion helps justify concentration on the surplus rather than the 'subsistence' element of the economy as the dynamic force in the economy in their book. Sraffa turned on his head, perhaps, but nevertheless recognisably Sraffa in conceptualisation. Sraffa's concern is with the economic reproduction of society, Baran and Sweezy's is with general crisis and change. The method used shows the tendency of surplus to rise, the difficulty of absorbing this surplus through conventional channels, and hence the inevitability of crisis and the possibility of radical change. Surplus tends to rise because even the largest corporations are faced with an element of competition which encourages expansion of capacity and technological innovation as protective measures, i.e. a variant of technological determinism. The absorption problem comes with the difficulty of distributing the extra product to shareholders, workers and the government. The controlling managers have conventions about low dividend payments to shareholders, oppose higher wage payments to workers and overall exert influence to restrict government activity, as any of these groups could threaten their power, if encouraged by increased resources being available.

Instead of a general increase in welfare, selected privileged groups of workers receive a share of the surplus in advertising revenues which encourages consumption as well, and the government is 'allowed' to use part of the surplus in areas like the military, which do not compete with other avenues of surplus absorption. In so far as these channels and a few others fail to expand as fast as the potential surplus then the major economic appearance of the crisis will be unemployment. Being jobless in a society where advertising successfully encourages the view that the major meaning of life is consumption is an alienating, but not necessarily a radicalising, experience; as likely to encourage crime as the politics of change. Baran and Sweezy finally, almost completely, close the circle of reproduction themselves by showing racism and schooling as social mechanisms of control which socialise the vast mass of the population into a fearful complacency, in which the only alternative world is one which is worse.

It would appear then that the only aspect of this process which truly threatens continuing reproduction is where the search for surplus absorption outlets reaches out beyond the boundaries of the USA. Baran and Sweezy see this as inevitable, especially with a growing military establishment seeking to justify its existence. Events in Cuba and Vietnam in the 1960s then take on an extra significance as struggles which, if enlarged, could threaten the reproduction of the USA economy by removing three possible channels of surplus absorption; investment by the large corporations, aggressive overseas marketing by these corporations, and raising doubts about the effectiveness of further increases in military expenditure. For all its apparent independence Baran and Sweezy see the USA economy as vulnerable to changes outside its borders, although internally they see no substantial force for change as their subtle technological determinism forms a closed circle helped by the conspiratorial tactics of the controlling executives.

In his book *The New Industrial State* first published in 1967 J. K. Galbraith arrives at a slightly more optimistic conclusion from an analysis which in many ways resembles Baran and Sweezy's criticism of USA society. Galbraith widens the manipulative controlling group considerably to include most people who would call themselves managers or executives plus trade union officials and government employees who work in agencies closely involved with the large corporations. This group, the technostructure, has power because it performs the vital role in modern production of ensuring the smooth flow of resources through complex processes. It has also used that power to reduce the influence of market forces effectively to zero. The market economy is then a myth which exists in economics text books according to Galbraith. The choice is not between a market system and a command system of allocating resources but instead is about who shall do the commanding.

The problem with the technostructure is not that it is violent and wasteful, although it can be both, but that it is shortsighted and unenlightened. On issues like seeing the functions of advertising and military expenditure as rational activities for reproducing a fundamentally dysfunctional, irrational social system, Galbraith has much in common with Baran and Sweezy and the wider New Left movement of the late 1960s and 1970s. But he escapes their circle of despair by seeing the cure in the advance of the disease itself. Galbraith's evolutionary perspective on social change sees the removal of scarcity as a continuing process. The technostructure is the current constraint, and many more people are being educated at least sufficiently to remove that scarcity. This process produces people who are educated *and therefore relatively immune to advertising* but do not find employment in the technostructure themselves as scarcity diminishes *and therefore without the interest in self-perpetuation of those actually in the technostructure.* These people represent an internal constituency for change even in the most affluent society.

Post-Keynesian cost-of-production theory is thus a theory which is highly critical of the existing social order in affluent industrial society. It finds the possibility of a better society in a more equal distribution of current surplus production on a world scale *where previous cost-of-production economists emphasised redistribution at the national level* and sees the cost of that redistribution as small because most of the affluent are deluded into trying to buy happiness, which can only be obtained through non-economic activity. The enemies of this change are certainly those at the top of large corporations for whom the surplus is power, but may include many other relatively rich people. The friends of change are certainly enlightened intellectuals but the extent of support from other groups is uncertain. The struggle for change is joined primarily in the set of institutions we call the modern State and it is to the cost-of-production theory of the State and its policies that we now turn.

Further reading

The classic analytical text for modern cost-of-production theory is undoubtedly Piero Sraffa (1975) *Production of Commodities by Means of Commodities.* The most comprehensive introductory economics principles book in this vein is Joan Robinson and John Eatwell (1973) *An Introduction to Modern Economics.* Unfortunately, despite the shortness of Sraffa's book, their forms of presentation may make them relatively inaccessible to the student starting economics. In contrast, the writings of J. K. Galbraith (especially 1974) on the USA and Peter Donaldson (1973) on the UK are firmly in the cost-of-production mould, very readable, but lack a rigorous bite, which may seduce without giving the unsuspecting student the analytical tools to criticise effectively.

It is unlikely that students will get very much out of reading J. S. Mill's or Alfred Marshall's economic principles books in the original. Certainly interesting summaries of their ideas, and indeed other economists, from a broad cost-of-production viewpoint can be found in Guy Routh (1975) *The Origin of Economic Ideas* and Joan Robinson

(1962) *Economic Philosophy*, though they, like many others in our view, overstate the synthesising aspects of Marshall's work and understate his fundamental disagreement with contemporary subjective preference theorists like Jevons.

The imperfect competition models of the firm are summarised in all microeconomics introductory books but none that we know integrate them with a consistent macroeconomic theory. That is, perhaps, with the exception of J. M. Keynes (1936) *The General Theory of Employment, Interest and Money*, where the early chapters merit a careful reading on the nature of the production decision. Some of the most interesting writing on the firm in the cost-of-production spirit is found outside conventional economics texts in the works of Anthony Sampson (1975, 1977 and others) who has produced a string of investigative books describing the activities of large corporations in a number of industries.

Lastly, for those who want an equivalent to both the wide-ranging speculations and the Nobel Prize of Friedman, we can recommend Simon Kuznets (1965) *Economic Growth and Structure* as an unashamedly technocratic, but very readable, cost-of-production book written at the highest point of academic confidence in this approach.

Summary 6.1

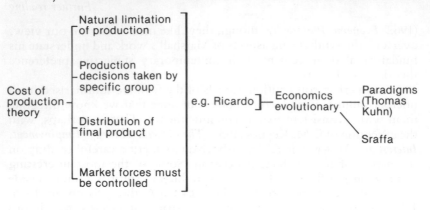

Summary 6.2

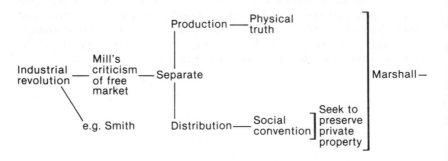

Summary 6.3

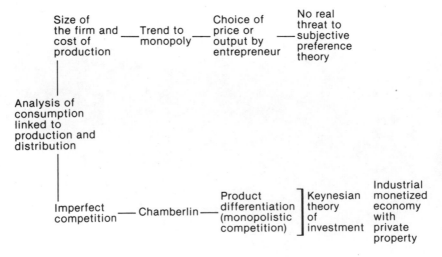

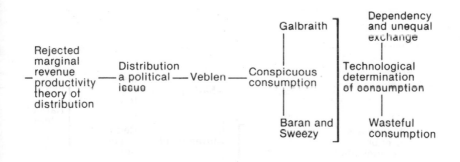

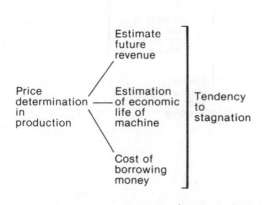

Summary 6.4

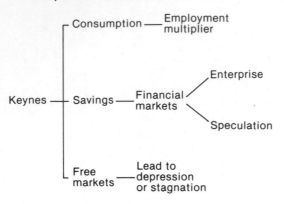

Summary 6.5

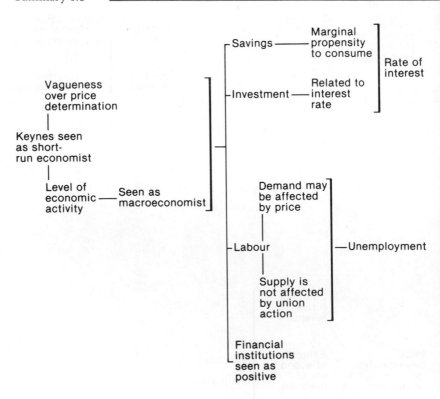

Money as store of value —— Reward for not holding money —— Liquidity trap —— Pigou effect

Unemployed should maintain consumption —— And accept work at lower wages

Maintain real balance effect

Trade unions should not determine real wages

Summary 6.6

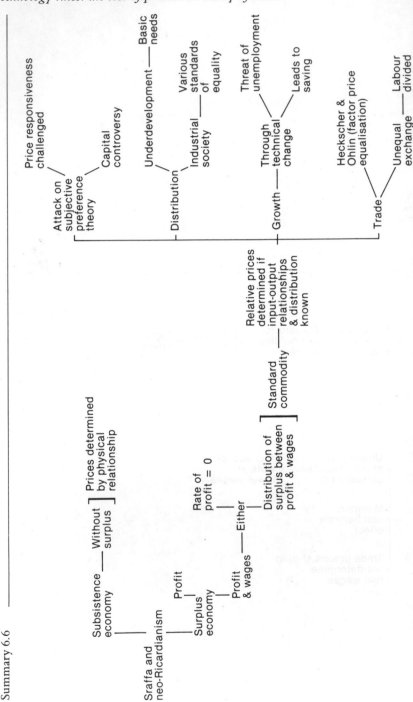

Summary 6.7

Large corporations — Source of power — Identification of power — Natural monopoly — Use of surplus by

Tautological

Share holders — Managers — Veblen — Managerial control — Bureaucracy

Maximisation of sales

Conspicuous consumption

Labour

Baran & Sweezy — Surplus controlled by executives of large corporations — Value determined by use

Surplus increases — Unemployment — Crime

Foreign investment

Galbraith — Technostructure — Social change towards removal of scarcity

Chapter 7

Social engineering:
the politics of cost-of-production theory

7.1 Social democrats and democratic socialists

Governments today claim to represent the interests of the great majority of the population subject to their sovereignty. That in itself is not new; what is new in many societies is the stress that is put on positive actions to improving welfare rather than protecting existing rights. Criticism of government activity is as likely to be that it suffocates its citizens through excessive care, as that it batters them with excessive violence. Thus governments claim to express our collective kindness to each other as well as repressing our more anti-social tendencies. In economics, cost-of-production theory can be used generally to justify the existence of such wide-reaching government intervention on two grounds. Firstly, that the increasing technological interdependence of industrial society increases our collective vulnerability to disruption if disputes over relative shares are allowed to fester. Secondly, that the increasing potential absolute surplus above any definition of basic needs leads to new distribution problems over the aggregate use of resources which can only have a social solution.

A feature of contemporary societies is à set of resource allocating instructions formally controlled in the last analysis by a sovereign legislature, which is apparently not required to accept market forces. Collectively, these institutions at the national level can be said to define the State. Together, they have a wide and deep influence on many aspects of our lives and therefore are subject to continuing criticism by those proclaiming individual liberty and the rule of market forces. But these institutions also have strong advocates among politicians and, under the general title of social democrats, these politicians have formed administrations in most western European countries many times in the past thirty years. It could also be argued more generally that the substantial influence of those who believe in resource allocation by the State can be found in every country, whether it be labelled capitalist, communist, socialist, or developing. For the purposes of this section, however, we will concentrate on the particular example of the Western European and North American social democrats to show the basic structure of the political programme, which is most closely associated with the cost-of-production theory of value.

Central to such social democratic political programmes is the belief that poverty in the form of physical or social deprivation is neither necessary nor excusable in industrial society. All citizens have the right to some basic material subsistence and it is the primary role of State institutions to redistribute resources towards the deprived. Where deprivation has an easily identifiable characteristic then resources can be specifically and purposefully directed through institutions aimed at particular targets, for instance, the handicapped, sick and old. Beyond these groups, social democrats will argue that there is a need to assist through State intervention the unemployed and the low paid as the free market system is as likely to exacerbate as to improve their economic position. From this perspective, the structure of taxation becomes a positive policy instrument, in that it can be evaluated in a redistributive role. Thus a taxation system is called 'progressive' if it redistributes income from relatively rich to relatively poor, and 'regressive' if income is redistributed towards the relatively rich. But whilst social democrats may agree on a general objective of a more egalitarian society the extent to which they are willing to intervene practically to bring this about still leaves much room for disagreement.

The free market system is not only regarded by social democrats as unlikely to remove glaring poverty, it is also suspected of being an ideological veil disguising a reality in which resources are allocated with little regard to the general social interest. Thus, even though social democrats may see the desirable features of free markets in principle, they point to the large corporations and trade unions in contemporary societies as prima facie evidence that the ideal of a free market in which large numbers of buyers and sellers come together with none exercising significant individual influence, is no longer an accurate description. Therefore, decisions about who is to be employed, and at what wage are no longer, if ever they were, the outcome of anonymous market forces. Rather the decisions are the outcome of power struggles between organisations expressing the self-interests of a relatively privileged minority. Large groups of people are discriminated against in obtaining higher paid employment. Also, when the wages of those who are fortunate enough to be so employed are raised, then the resulting higher costs are passed on by management in terms of higher prices thus further disadvantaging those on lower incomes outside the large corporations and associated trade unions. Finally, consumers are persuaded to buy at these higher prices by advertising pressure. It is this type of argument that has led to the adoption of various forms of institutional arrangements aimed at removing discrimination, restricting rises in incomes and prices and protecting consumers as important parts of social democratic programmes. But, like the criticism of inequality, there is still much room for disagreement between social democrats on the desired level and form of actual intervention, which can obscure the agreement on general principle.

This package of reformist policies which aims to diminish poverty and discrimination in employment and regulate agreements between large corporations and large trade unions to the benefit of us all in our role as consumers, ensures the place of social democrats close to the centre of contemporary Western politics. For those people who aspire to political office, this policy package constitutes a well-tried formula which has been advocated by a host of pragmatic, well-meaning ministers in social democratic administrations during times of general prosperity and low social tension. But, when social democratic political parties are faced with fighting elections at times of generally acknowledged economic crisis, a programme which does not go beyond some vague, if caring, redistributional good intentions is unlikely to gain the serious attention, let alone the votes, of a majority of the population. In such a situation, the social democratic doubts about free market forces harden and tentatively ally social democrats, claiming to exercise the majority's conscience in favour of a poor minority, with more radical socialists, claiming to represent the majority of society against a wealthy, powerful, amoral minority.

In this coalition, all markets are opened to critical scrutiny and assessment as to the need for regulation in the general, social interest. No market is safe from intervention. If there are too few corporations producing the good then there are doubts about monopoly power; too many and there are questions about the need for rationalisation. If the good is produced for mass consumption then the general consumers' interests may require protecting; production for the few raises doubts about whether society as a whole can afford to use resources for the production of such luxuries. One alternative to the free market allocation of a resource, whether the market is believed to suffer from excesses of either monopoly power or chaotic anarchy, is an institutional arrangement bringing all interested groups together for open discussion. A specific type of planning called 'indicative planning' requiring major organisations to agree broad targets for output and investment may be the outcome of such discussions on the national level. Such arrangements do not challenge the right to private property directly, but even this mild form of State intervention can raise questions about the desirability and necessity of private property in major production units.

Social democrats have no hesitation in raising such questions. They combine belief in a freely elected legislature as the legitimate voice of society with confidence in the technical ability of the State consciously to manage the economy. Generally, markets are suspected to be inequitable and inefficient in allocating resources and thus should be, and can be, replaced though taking direct State control over major industries. The precise industrial policy actually adopted by a particular political party at a given time will depend on the balance between social democrats and democratic socialists in its ranks. Continuing debates over 'nationalisation' in the UK Labour Party are an obvious example of failure to resolve this question. In recent times such debates have been complicated further by the increasing economic prominence of the very large corporation operating in several countries. This has raised the broad issue of whether control by nationals of a society over the economic decisions concerning that society is desirable in itself. In such circumstances, 'nationalisation' may mean the extension of control by nationals with or without State ownership. Even if the general principle of formal State control is agreed there are still pressures to move that control downwards from national legislatures to regions or upwards to supranational legislatures. Any of these legislatures may claim the right to control an economic activity in the name of its constituency. So, again it is probably easier to agree in principle that private property rights should be superseded than to agree how precisely that should be achieved.

Thus, particular markets may seem to require regulation and, in the last instance, it even may seem necessary to take an industry under State control. This proposition might be acceptable to some less dogmatic subjective preference theory supporters as acting in the national interest, even if they would want to add the word 'temporarily' to the previous sentence. However, social democrats and democratic socialists can unite against such bad weather allies in the belief that there are always major problems at the level of the national economy, even if all markets operated as freely as subjective preference theory assumes. It is this belief in deep macroeconomic problems that is central to unifying social democrats and democratic socialists into a coherent political force in western economies and has ensured the posthumous fame of Keynes as the person who gave a logical basis to that belief. It is in this role that politicians and their economic advisers cease to be maintenance workers tinkering with parts of the market organism but become social engineers in control of the whole economic mechanism. The resulting economic strategy claims to face explicitly two fundamental problems. Firstly, that rapidly changing industrial production techniques are socially disruptive when adopted in a piecemeal fashion. Secondly, that total demand for the output of an economy is not a simple sum of individual desires but the aggregate outcome of complex interrelationships.

At the national level the strategy demands a number of indirect measures, usually presented in an annual government budget, involving many different types of taxation, adjustment of the levels of these taxes, and general subsidies to encourage consumption and investment in different forms in various places; these measures collectively make up the 'fiscal' policy of the State. Similarly, various forms of State expenditure become part of both general technology encouragement and demand management, not just the provision of minimum necessary services to particular needy individuals. At the international level, development is seen mainly as a process of planned technological change. A central concern is what kind of technology is used and under what conditions technology is transferred from technologically sophisticated economies. Also, as the end of development is the elimination of poverty, development can be aided by directing more of existing resources into the hands of the deprived, through improving the demand conditions for their present economic activities and thus increasing revenues from the goods they currently produce.

This political stance on economic policy is found explicitly in every society of Western Europe and North America and variations exist in all countries as parts of various reformist movements. The belief in State institutions as a possible alternative to markets in allocating resources is attractive because such institutions appear to offer certainty, universality and flexibility. The modern State can always intervene, since by definition it holds sovereignty over a given area, and it can choose to intervene in a whole variety of ways. Also, especially since Keynes, there exists a common belief that the State has a specific crucial role in managing the whole economy efficiently (in addition to regulating income distribution in the economy in the name of equity). But it is the very breadth of this appeal which forms a grave weakness. As it is difficult to get agreement other than on broad principles, it is tempting either not to act effectively at all, or to bulldoze through specific legislation on the grounds that the principle has been accepted at a general election. The first alternative means that social democrats fail to act as efficient agents of social change, the second that democratic socialists fail to institute such change democratically. We shall return to this criticism later after demonstrating more explicitly the links between the basic assumptions of cost-of-production theory and a social democratic political programme.

7.2 Social democratic politics and cost-of-production economics

Basic cost-of-production theory assumes that techniques of production have evolved at an increasing pace since an industrial revolution about two hundred years ago. At any one point in time these techniques can be represented as a general state of technology with complex combinations of inputs and outputs linking industries. Also, every society has evolved historically a number of income distribution categories including, for instance, rent, wages, interest and profits, whose precise pattern is the outcome of struggles between groups of people who depend on these various forms of income. Given a technology and a distribution, Sraffa demonstrated that a set of relative prices of goods can be determined which will allow the economy to reproduce itself. If, unlike Sraffa, we are unwilling simply to assume the reproduction of the economy, then more pessimistic models can be constructed. We will illustrate such models by drawing on a number of writers who start from basic assumptions similar to those of general cost-of-production theory of value about technology and distribution.

For instance, Ricardo concluded that technological advance in agriculture was an ultimate constraint on economic progress. The technological inability indefinitely to raise the fertility of a relatively fixed supply of land by increased application of labour time would lead to reduced profit rates. Transmitted through the price system, these reduced profits would slow the rate of introduction of new techniques across the whole economy, contributing to stagnatory tendencies. But, whilst Ricardo saw this process as inevitable, he also recognised the negative, exacerbating influence of landowners whose desire to maintain their wealth was backed by the power of the State in the form of protective legislation, especially in the form of high agricultural prices. Thus Ricardo reversed Smith's optimistic identification of the interests of landlords with progress and concluded that their abuse of influence on the State in their own distributional interest should be politically reduced.

In a somewhat different but related vein, Marshall saw trade unions as enemies of progress and, whilst Keynes saw them as victims rather than villains, in general, it is unusual to find cost-of-production economists advocating trade unions as agents of progress. This general atmosphere of antipathy is explicable in cost-of-production terms by reference to the tension between technology and distribution as the central issue in understanding economic change. Thus, because trade unions have developed as defensive organisations for the employed, they have an interest to resist technical change, both because jobs are put at risk directly, and as an indirect means to secure a stronger position in the distributional power struggle. Also the general struggle over the level of wages is conducted by trade unions on the basis of potentially or actually disrupting production, which cost-of-production economics sees as an undesirable confusion between the laws of technically efficient production and the laws of socially equitable distribution. This disadvantage is compounded when the trade unions are divided by crafts, industries, nationalities, and other sectional antagonisms, leading to a wages structure which cannot be justified in cost-of-production theory. For instance, the case of international 'unequal exchange' was briefly mentioned in the previous chapter, where substantial wage differentials between workers in different societies for precisely similar work were shown to be indefinitely sustainable, with organised better paid workers having an interest in restricting movement of the lower paid, whilst the employers in both societies remain virtually neutral.

It was Keynes who analytically added the receivers of interest, or rentiers, to the list of groups who are enemies of progress, though earlier writers, like Hobson in the UK and Veblen in the USA, had described those who merely sat back and received dividends from shares as parasitical on society. From the point of view of the basic assumptions of cost-of-production theory about technology and distribution we can place Keynes's argument in the context of this section. Thus, a team of managers deciding whether to purchase a machine embodying a new technique of production must treat interest payments as a cost of, and hence a disincentive to, that investment. High interest rates, which benefit rentiers, are thus a discouragement to technical progress in the form of new machinery. This depressing effect is likely to continue as interest rates fall slowly, if at all, due to the institutional arrangements around shares, bonds and money markets being biased in favour of rentier interests in the general distributional struggle.

The sum total of cost-of-production criticism of landlords, trade unions and rentiers would seem to leave managers as the only remaining candidates for guiding progress. But even managers have come under fire in some versions of cost-of-production theory, as we saw in Chapter 6. Managers, especially of large corporations, are not above the struggle over distribution as they control the use of the surplus (or profits in cost-of-production analysis) after everyone else has been paid. Some writers, like Baran and Sweezy and Galbraith, argue that this surplus has become easier to extract over the past thirty years, and criticise managers for wasting that potential in their own collective interest. In a cost-of-production framework, this criticism can be analysed in its technology and distribution aspects. In order to increase profits, managers are certainly willing to innovate technologically, but such technical change is as likely to be in the packaging and marketing of the good as in the essential quality of the good itself in consumption. Similarly, more directly in the struggle over distribution, it is in managers' interests to raise corporations' prices whenever possible, giving an inflationary tendency to the economy; and, in addition, to increase the pace of work and the volume of sales regardless of the damage this may do to the health of people as workers and consumers.

Putting all these criticisms together it appears that no group of income receivers can be trusted to guide society unambiguously in the direction of technological progress and the general good. Technological progress is largely the result of virtually autonomous inventions which are only implemented when all the obstacles to innovation by self-interested groups have been overcome. Struggles over distribution distort and delay general progress and much human energy goes into simply defending interests against perceived threats by other interests, when instead that energy could go into giving everyone more. The subjective preference answer that market forces should be allowed to operate freely between individuals is rejected on the grounds that it is unrealistic, in that free markets have effectively ceased to exist. It is also illogical in that, for cost-of-production theory, market prices are determined merely as an outcome of distributional power struggles. In contrast, for subjective preference theory, market prices are determined by the tastes and talents of individuals, with production inputs simply receiving their marginal revenue products.

The radical socialist proposal that the distributional problem could be simplified by abolishing private property and thus, at least, eliminating the categories of rent and interest, cannot be criticised as illogical from a cost-of-production perspective. But, such a proposal would certainly be criticised as foolhardy by social democrats in terms of causing enormous social disruption as the distributional conflict escalates into a struggle for the survival of whole groups. It could also be regarded as irrelevant in that the struggles between and within managers and trade unions will continue. Finally, the proposal could be seen as unjustified in that there are no *rights* for anyone or any group to consume any more than some level of basic needs and thus there are no grounds for discrimination against any particular interest. It is along these lines that social democrats could resist a democratic socialist programme for attacking private ownership, rather than on the basis of the basic principle being illogical. In cost-of-production terms, such social democrats could claim to give political expression to a fundamental separation of technology and distribution in order to adjust distribution in the interests of the deprived and reduce the disruptive impact on production of distributional struggles. This is to be achieved through politically arbitrating in struggles over distribution on behalf of the wider social interest.

There is yet a third political position which can be derived logically from the cost-of-production theory of value. Instead of using the separation of distribution from technology to make distribution serve a dynamic, fast changing technology as both social democrats and democratic socialists argue, it can be argued that technology should be restricted to serve some desired distribution. In its most radical form this argument is expressed in the form that industrialisation was an enormous mistake which has robbed *Homo sapiens* and the rest of the natural world of the possibility of continuing reproduction. The cost of industrial production is then the reduction of essential human values and the creation, not of wealth, but of fierce destructive struggles over the distribution of what little scarce value remains. In the mid-1970s there was not only a spate of anti-growth writing among economists like Mishan (1967), but also the widely publicised writings of people like Schumacher (1974) and Illich (1973) encouraged a growing ecology movement as a vocal, if small, political force in the industrial economies of the West and strongly influenced the debate on development strategies for the less-industrialised economies of the so-called 'south'.

Terms like 'appropriate technology' and 'basic needs', which came into vogue in the 1970s, only make sense in this political conclusion from a cost-of-production theoretical analysis. Both terms suggest that the interrelationship between methods of production and distribution is in need of conscious manipulation and that the most recently developed technique may embody large and unavoidable socially undesirable distribution features. Certainly the influences of this kind of thinking is now widespread and the atmosphere today is intellectually, and hopefully literally, more healthy due to the revival of anti-technology attitudes. But the movement against industrialisation finds difficulty in going beyond earlier romantic criticisms and forming a popular political programme. Liberating slogans calling for a de-industrialised, politically decentralised, deschooled, de-drugged, denucleared society appear to suffer in translation into positive political action. The apparent sacrifice required by the materially affluent is great, and those who continue to be materially deprived are unlikely to be convinced that they should be grateful for their spiritually superior condition. As such ideas have roots in a variant of mainstream cost-of-production thinking, the ideas of the ecology movement seem logically, if problematically, to be likely to find expression in social democratic political programmes.

Cost-of-production theory thus appears to provide a common underpinning to a number of political positions, including social democracy, a variant of socialism and environmentalism. The direction of economic strategy which would be adopted by an administration of such a type is relatively clearly dictated by cost-of-production theory but the precise specification of detailed policies seems impossible. This impossibility is consistent with a paradigm theory of knowledge. That is, it is only possible to recognise an existing situation as unsatisfactory by listening to the voices of dissent, which forces acceptance of a practical problem which the existing political approach, i.e. the current paradigm, cannot solve. Reinterpreting the flows of information in the light of observable technology and distribution conditions will then produce a different set of assumptions, i.e. a new paradigm, consistent with a number of new policy options. The choice of one particular policy is then a pragmatic choice after open consultation of all the conflicting interests. Thus, the precise policy to meet changing circumstances cannot be pre-ordained. In the area of economic policy the changing circumstances of the past twenty years have seen the fall of such a package of policies, generally called Keynesianism. The irony is that this particular relatively flexible package itself draws on cost-of-production theory, not on the supposedly more dogmatic, inflexible opposing subjective preference and abstract labour theories, which have if anything gained strength in the deepening crisis.

7.3 The demise of Keynesianism

Keynes's legacy seemed to offer the possibility of reconciling political liberalism, and its acceptance of private property rights, with the resolution of the aggregate economic problems which cost-of-production theory highlights as endemic to industrialised, market economies. This legacy was developed into a set of rules for indirectly managing an economy and a set of criteria for evaluating economic performance. These Keynesian criteria were the number of registered unemployed, the movement of some official price index, growth of measured National Income and changes in foreign currency reserves. In the 1950s and into the 1960s Keynesianism had achieved the status of economic orthodoxy, seeming to offer simple rules for a government to use a few policy instruments to achieve a target condition of the economy, specified in terms of a low level of registered unemployment, a slow rate of increase in the overall price index, a steady growth in economic activity, and a structure of international trade which does not run down the foreign currency reserves of the economy.

In its simplest form there are only three policy instruments, that is the government budgetary deficit, the level of interest rates, and the general exchange rate between domestic and foreign currencies. If unemployment is high, then the Keynesian policy recommendation is relatively to increase government expenditure and reduce government income. This response is one which only the government can make, since any private individual faced with unemployment is forced to diminish expenditure in the face of reduced income. The effect of the government's action is to increase effective (i.e. money-backed) demand for all the goods and services in the economy and thus encourage managers to increase production. If the price index is rising (i.e. inflation) then the government is advised to reverse the policy and reduce effective demand by relatively increasing taxation and reducing expenditure. Thus unemployment and inflation are two sides of the same coin being the result of an imbalance between effective demand and a relatively fixed production capacity. One policy instrument can therefore be used to deal with either the problem of unemployment or the problem of inflation.

Growth of real National Income is primarily the result of changes in technological knowledge which increase physical productivity and are largely independent of economic factors. But, in so far as such gains in knowledge are embodied in new machinery, then the introduction of such machinery as investment is encouraged by low interest rates, as interest payments are an additional cost to the managers on top of the going price of the machinery. Thus, if the State can give leadership through central bank policy to keeping interest rates low, then it can have a positive effect on growth. Also, as the market for investment funds is closely related to the money market but rather separate from other markets in Keynes's theory, low interest rate policy is possible without great effect on other markets. This is very different from Friedman's subjective preference theoretical framework which emphasises the strong interdependence of all markets (see Ch. 4). Lastly an overall monetary foreign trade imbalance can be coped with by negotiation with other governments to make orderly changes to exchange rates between different national currencies which tend to balance the inflows and outflows of foreign currency reserves for all countries involved.

In its heyday of the late 1950s and early 1960s, this broad approach to economic management was hailed as the answer to avoiding any violent fluctuations in the four major target variables. Economists claimed to be able statistically to discover stable aggregate economic relationships and calculate the sensitivity of responses in target variables to changes in policy instruments. The branch of statistics which economists had developed for this purpose, called econometrics, and the availability of computers, convinced many politicians, as well as economists, that they could 'fine-tune' the performance of the economy through variations in annual government budgets. Econometric models of whole economies were constructed using computers which expressed Keynes's broad relationships as hundreds of mathematical equations, calibrated by actual observations from the recent past. The implied sensitivity to changes in policy instruments were then calculated, assuming that people's behaviour is relatively habitual, at least when viewed on a group basis. Avoiding economic fluctuations in a context of steady growth not only appeared possible with appropriate government budgetary policy but also was considered impossible without such government policy. For instance, only governments could totally ignore the constraint of balancing their budgets and negotiate exchange rates for all currencies. Government intervention was judged to be a necessary and sufficient condition for economic health.

Confidence in intervention had grown so far in the early 1960s in countries like the UK, that political commentators were announcing the 'end of ideology' and pronouncing on a future where differences between political parties, and indeed whole political systems, would be largely removed by convergence to the rationalistic, technocratic principles of Keynesian macroeconomic management. Debate would still occur on the desirable distribution of economic activity between regions and the general distribution of resources between groups of people, but this would be a political question separated from the technical question of engineering growing aggregate material affluence. By the late 1970s this position had totally collapsed in that, in economics, subjective preference theory had totally undermined the logic of Keynesian argument and, in politics, social democrats were regularly losing political office to conservatives in western Europe and north America. The general economic crisis of the 1970s found its ideological reflection in the subject of political economy as a crisis of Keynesian economics and political expression in the decline of social democratic politics.

The logical inconsistency of Keynesianism can be understood if we see that Keynesian theory (as opposed to Keynes's theory) essentially synthesised the subjective preference theory of the independent consumer and perfectly competitive producer with Keynes's cost-of-production views on relationships between economic aggregates. As we have seen in Chapters 3 and 4 the natural logical outcome of assuming strong individualism in consumption and production is a general equilibrium system and a political theory of a State with a very narrow, albeit very important, field of intervention in law and order and defence. The Keynesian aggregate relationships were built on this sand of dis-aggregated individualism and the rigid structure was doomed to sink into the millions of grains which are the logical environment of fluid, flexible, general equilibrium as soon as a storm appeared. The storm conditions were provided by the combination of fast (in terms of 1950s experience) increasing registered unemployment and a fast increasing price index which occurred in the UK in the late 1960s and on a world scale in the 1970s. Keynesian theory logically ruled out this combination on the grounds that unemployment was a result of deficient aggregate demand and rising prices were a result of excessive aggregate demand.

A first defence was that in practice the Keynesian view accepted a margin of trade-off between rising prices and unemployment due to capacity bottlenecks in some industries being reached before unemployment had been completely removed. This trade-off relationship had been statistically examined for the UK in the 1950s by an economist named Phillips and gained fame in its graphical form as the Phillips curve, see Figure 7.1. The basic reasoning was simple and plausible and the conclusion totally agreeable to Keynesian thinking. As relatively uniform labour was increasingly employed, then increasing pressures could be exerted in the struggle over distribution between wages and profits by those already employed. The tendency would then be for money wages to rise and employment not to fall, as with a relatively fixed technology labour would not be laid off, especially if demand was buoyant. In addition, as managers largely determine prices, they are also able to offset increasing wage costs by increasing prices, thus producing a rise in the general price index associated with the decrease in unemployment.

The policy conclusion from this reasoning was that the government could choose an acceptable combination of unemployment and rising prices. In Fig. 7.1 this is shown as a combination of $2\frac{1}{2}$ per cent unemployment and a $2\frac{1}{2}$ per cent annual money wage rise. Such a wage increase would be expected to push general prices up by approximately the same percentage. This combination is produced by using the single policy instrument of the budget deficit (i.e. the government spending more than received in tax revenue) to yield sufficient extra aggregate effective demand to maintain this situation. In the 1970s the Phillips relationship no longer seemed to hold in the UK, as unemployment and inflation both rose rapidly. The Keynesian position then came up for attack and subjective preference theory provided an immediate logical explanation of the change. This explanation, naturally for subjec-

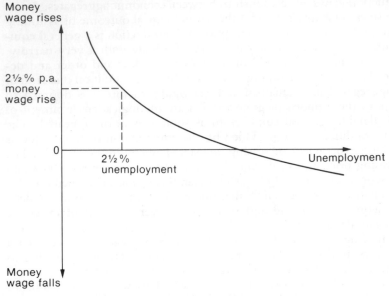

Fig. 7.1   A hypothetical Phillips curve

tive preference theory, drew on assumptions about rational individual behaviour which Keynesians were unable immediately to deny, as they largely accepted this model themselves.

Thus, suppose an individual requires a real reward higher than the current wage to perform a task, a wage that reflects a current general equilibrium situation. Now, if the individual's experience suggests that a money wage rise of $2\frac{1}{2}$ per cent will only just offset an expected rise in general prices of $2\frac{1}{2}$ per cent leaving real purchasing power unchanged, then the individual will want a money wage more than the current money wage plus $2\frac{1}{2}$ per cent to undertake the task. Only if that higher wage is offered will the rational individual consider undertaking that task. Thus *expected* price rises are built into the calculation of whether or not to sell labour. Once it is generally recognised that the government is building price rises into the economy then this becomes a factor in everyone's calculations, which can be seen as a shift in the Phillips curve in Fig. 7.2. All government efforts indefinitely to maintain a level of unemployment below the natural general equilibrium rate corresponding to zero inflation require continuing efforts by the government, in terms of increasing budget deficits in money terms, to outrun expectations of the mass of population about price rises in the next year. Creeping price rises inevitably become trotting inflation and then galloping hyperinflation and the Phillips curve disappears into the stratosphere. A stable Phillips curve seemed to rest on the assumption that people behave without any foresight or completely ignore experience.

184

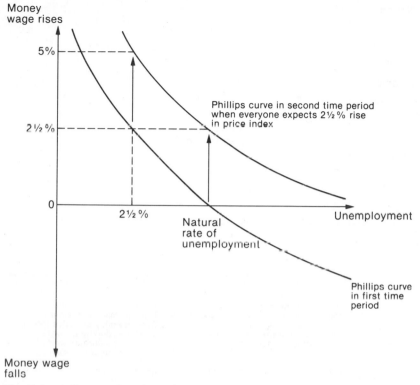

Fig. 7.2   A disappearing, hypothetical Phillips curve

This logical detonating of the overall Keynesian position was explosively completed by the practical failure to meet more and more complex political expectations. Intervention was not just to avoid deep depression but was expected to deliver resources immediately and precisely to specified groups of people in particular places through channels which left private property rights virtually untouched. Economists, encouraged by the information processing ability of computers, had tried to meet these expectations by designing multiple forms of taxes and subsidies and frequently altering the various rates of payment. But the time lags involved in gathering and processing information and then implementing policy proved to be long. Long lags make it theoretically possible for the problem of timing to be so acute that State intervention might actually exacerbate swings in economic activity rather than moderate them; a hypothetical example of this is shown in Fig. 7.3.

Thus social democrats in Western countries were increasingly faced in the 1970s with the problem of explaining their particular national economic crisis without effective support in economic theory. Some

Social engineering: the politics of cost-of-production theory

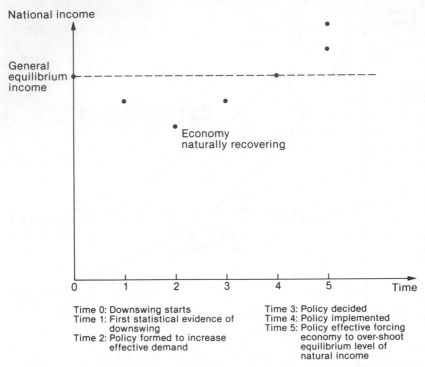

Fig. 7.3 Government policy exacerbating an economic cycle

combination of historically high unemployment, fast increasing prices, low economic growth and deteriorating foreign currency reserves was felt in all countries and in some cases, like the UK in the mid-1970s, all four occurred together. The only explanation which basic cost-of-production theory could offer was that struggles over distribution were disrupting all aspects of economic activity. The immediate policy response derived from this explanation was to increase government intervention in the arena of prices and incomes as an additional policy instrument to achieve stability in the price index, whilst using government expenditure to stimulate chosen areas of productive activity with apparent high growth and high employment potential. But action on prices and incomes proved difficult in the crisis conditions of the 1970s as it had been in earlier, less critical times and without trespassing on private property rights it proved virtually impossible to prevent rising unemployment. The crisis of confidence in social democracy goes beyond simple economic explanation but the demise of Keynesianism certainly has played its role.

The associated revival of more radical, fundamentalist cost-of-production ideas such as wider State control over industry, detailed intervention in wage bargaining and restrictions on international capital flows has eroded the shaky basis of the synthesis between liberal politics and reformist cost-of-production economics which dominated political economy through the 1950s and 1960s. This revival under the name of neo-Ricardianism had become the basis of an alternative economic strategy in the UK in 1980, alternative that is to both monetarism and Keynesian policies. By tackling obstacles to technological innovation directly through State directed investment, such a strategy aims to increase economic growth and employment. Also distributional struggles disrupting production at the national level are to be eased by close cooperation with trade unions, which are the major contemporary bargaining institutions. By offering a suitable mixture of private wages and general social benefits, called the social wage in this strategy, it is hoped also to remove inflation due to large sectional pay claims. And lastly, constraints produced by the international flows of goods, finance and people are also to be tackled directly by State intervention, especially selective controls on those imports which are believed to be priced under conditions of unequal exchange, monopoly power or State subsidies directly or indirectly. Thus the Keynesian target of economic growth under conditions of high employment, price stability and balance of payments equilibrium is still to be achieved but through more direct State intervention, not indirectly through budgetary instruments.

Internationally, Keynesianism had never achieved the policy dominance that it had nationally, even though Keynes's own last major policy activity had been in the area of international finance. The creation of the International Monetary Fund (IMF) after the Second World War as an institution for regulating changes in exchange rates between national currencies in a government-directed, orderly, non-disruptive manner certainly reflected Keynes's views on the need to eliminate destabilising speculation in all money markets. But by the 1970s the IMF had become the world representative and often enforcer of monetarist orthodoxy, intervening to restrict expansionist government policies as a price demanded for giving loans to meet foreign reserve fluctuations. However, one major consequence of increasing oil prices in the mid-1970s was that vast amounts of finance were suddenly injected into the international monetary system in the 1970s, well in excess of the relatively steady increase that had been the result of the US balance of payments deficit in the 1950s and 1960s. This *increase* in internationally mobile money, accompanying a world *decrease* in real production, encouraged Keynesian interpretations of the situation with a consequent pressure on IMF and other international economic institutions to act in a Keynesian fashion stimulating demand on a world scale. This view received greatest public attention with the publication of the Brandt Report in 1980. It is rather striking that, whilst it has been largely discredited at the national level, Keynesian economic ideas should seem to be moving into greater influence at the international level, even though these policy proposals have not been implemented. But perhaps not too surprising if the present crisis is seen to resemble an economic depression in the major characteristics that inspired Keynes's work in the 1930s.

7.4 Towards a critique of the cost-of-production theory of value as a democratic practice

Cost-of-production theory focuses our main attention on distribution and technology in industrial society. Industrial society is a complex, interdependent organism in which large organisations are technically necessary for production. The efficiency of the society is continuously threatened by struggles over distribution conducted on a massive scale between well-organised groups of people, struggles which are continually threatening to disrupt production. Also, market allocation of resources cannot be considered as equitable because such market prices are determined as part of the struggle over distribution and simply reflect inequality in the power of the combatants. Thus, on the grounds of productive efficiency in the sense of continuous employment for all of the population, and equity in the specific sense of reducing inequality, there is an apparent need for an independent exercise of power by some disinterested institution. Cost-of-production theory becomes obviously compatible with social democratic politics when the 'representative, modern State' is put forward as that institution.

There are two cost-of-production arguments in favour of such a State as the only overall rational agent in society, where rationality is defined by the criteria of compatible means and ends and sustainability of ends. The first argument is related to the struggle over distribution. Mass suffrage in any form ensures that representatives, or even delegates, from all major groups in society are elected to a forum where debates can be publicly reported and the reasons for decisions made clear. Thus if ignorance and prejudice are major causes of strikes and lock-outs, then strife will be diminished if not completely removed by some form of effective representation. The second argument is related to the requirements of technology, which in a large complex society means co-ordinated administration of resource allocation on a massive scale to carry out the diverse activities for which the market system is judged inadequate. The ideal form of the representative modern State is centred on a legislature of delegates roughly corresponding to the distributional interests in society presiding over a well-organised hierarchical network of implementing agencies. The legislature initiates and scrutinises the administrating agencies. The agencies execute the legislature's decisions through well specified chains of control, with sensitive feedback of information to continuously evaluate effectiveness.

Certainly in the last hundred years almost every society has been pressured to move in the direction of this ideal by self-proclaimed social democratic parties, even though this has been with considerable variations in desired forms of representation and ranges of activities undertaken by State organisations. But whilst cost-of-production social democrats claim to act in the great majority's interest, this claim is also put forward by subjective preference conservatives. Our argument in this book is that different ideals only find active political expression if they express different significant and real material interests in society. In the first instance, it appears that the specific interests that social democrats can most directly claim to represent are the chronically materially deprived. However, though the poor are always numerous and therefore form a large constituency for social democrats, there is the paradox that success in generally improving their position will result in the loss of support. Also, there is the special problem, that social democratic leaders rising from the deprived are then no longer deprived themselves and thus likely to be less enthusiastic about implementing radical redistribution against their new, improved real material interest. Thus, if cost-of-production theory only involved a concern for the poor then its political expression would be confined and restricted. But the argument in cost-of-production theory for greater equality in distribution is accompanied by a respect for technology, and it is this aspect which provides social democracy with much of its leadership and active support from outside the ranks of the immediately deprived.

For instance, all large organisations, especially those in manufacturing, have a logical structure dictated solely by the physical nature of the production process. The higher office-holders, who appear to control such organisations, are given a prominent and important place in cost-of-production theory because they operate at the crucial nodes where distribution struggles meet technological innovation. Invariably, in cost-of-production theory, control is judged to be far more important than ownership, but there is debate about whether the control is being generally exercised in a malign or benign fashion. For instance, control is malign when used to manipulate the mass of the people to purchase unnecessary luxuries, it is benign when used to persuade people that they do not need unnecessary luxuries. But this immediately raises the problem of who is to decide what is a necessity and what is an unnecessary luxury. The solution in cost-of-production theory is that benign people should be put in positions of authority in large organisations to make such decisions. Social democracy develops this idea one stage further by arguing that benign authority is more likely to be exercised by educated people acting as elected delegates and State officials than when they are acting as corporation managers and trade union leaders, even if the same individuals are involved.

The tension between trying to represent both the deprived and controllers in a society simultaneously can be partially resolved by setting up a large organisation with lines of control and information flowing from the mass membership to the leadership i.e. a social democratic political party. Consultation on policy is then largely undertaken through committees inviting authoritative specialists to give evidence, although adversely affected individuals and groups may have the right to appeal through formal procedures. The question of democratic control then depends on how far power can be devolved through the organisation and resist the tendency for control to concentrate at the top of the organisation where flows of information concentrate. In practice, however, expertise is likely to be highly valued and the mass membership of the party will tend to be treated as an electoral vote gathering machine, not a policy forming organisation.

Having achieved political office, the social democratic pattern of treating politics as a problem of organisation is likely to be repeated. Then, freedom can become the right to appeal, not the right to prior consultation. Criticism may well be tolerated but is likely to be buried in sub-committees, reporting regularly to committees, whose activities are periodically reviewed by working parties. Thus, if we understand cost-of-production economics theory and see its intimate relationship with a particular form of politics, then we can see how fascination with complex technology, distrust of the market, and genuine concern for the deprived gives rise to political forms which produce active, large-scale intervention to reduce inequality but on the terms of authoritative experts, not of the mass of the population. Cost-of-production theory seems thus to be, in the final analysis, a managerial ideology, capable of delivering to a deprived minority of us what a well-educated minority feels they need. At one extreme, it is muddled, benign and well-meaning if ineffective, at the other it is arrogant, manipulative and authoritarian if, in some narrow sense, efficient.

Further reading

J. M. Keynes (1936) *The General Theory of Employment, Interest and Money* is a crucial text for post-Second World War economics and thus worth persevering with despite its ambiguities. Virtually every book with 'macroeconomic' in the title will be basically Keynesian in its orientation. For a text written when Keynesianism was at its zenith in 1961 we can recommend Gardner Ackley (1969) *Macroeconomic Theory*. Since 1970 macroeconomic texts have shown a tendency to hedge their bets and not only criticise Keynesian thought on logical grounds (a muted criticism in Ackley's book) but also on practical grounds, perhaps leaving the student wondering why the analysis was undertaken in the first place! But strong support for Keynes's own contribution to economic understanding and policies can still be found in books by D. E. Moggridge (1976) *Keynes* and Michael Stewart (1972) *Keynes and After*.

Those who advocate deindustrialisation and no-growth economics have created something of a growth industry in publications themselves in the 1970s. Notable contributions came from the Club of Rome Reports, the second by Mesarovic and Pestel (1975) *Mankind at the Turning Point* being slightly more sophisticated than the first, and E. F. Schumacher (1974) *Small is Beautiful*. Expositions of social democracy have flowered with the development of an explicitly Social Democratic Party in the UK; David Owen and Shirley Williams have both produced books in 1981 which summarise recent political economic history from very much a cost-of-production standpoint. We explicitly use David Owen's book in Chapter 10 below.

Summary 7.1 _____

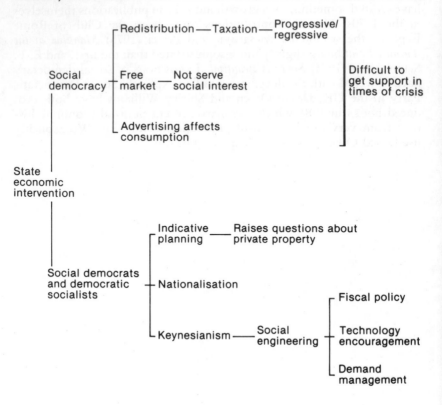

Summary 7.2 _____

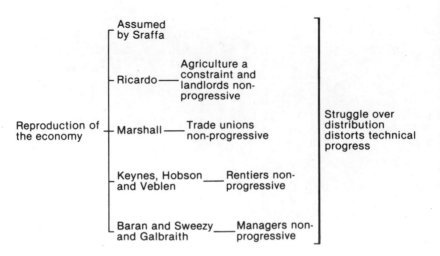

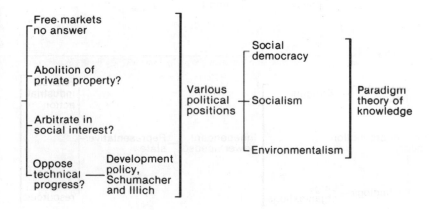

Summary 7.3

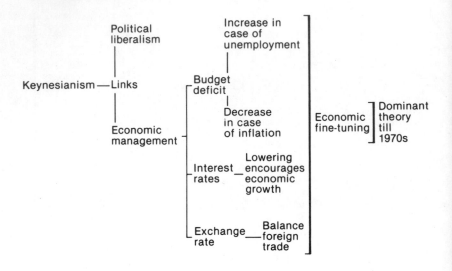

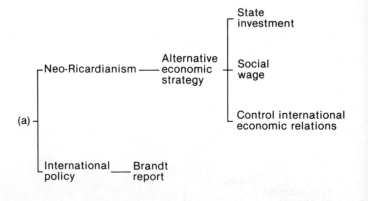

Summary 7.4

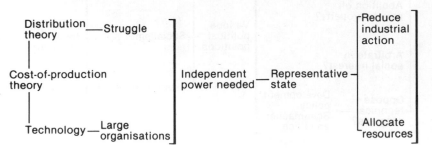

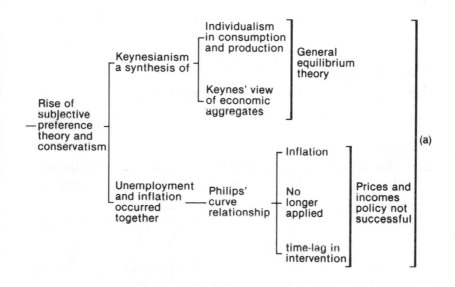

(a)

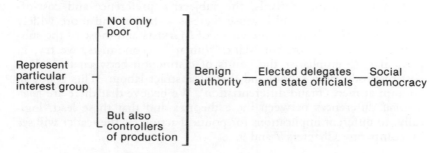

Chapter 8

Class struggle:
the abstract labour theory of value

8.1 The critique of capitalism as a mode of production: the origins of the abstract labour theory of value

Strife has raged about Karl Marx for decades and never has it been so embittered as at the present day. He has impressed his image on the time as no other man has done. To some he is a fiend, the arch-enemy of human civilisation, and the prince of chaos, while to others he is a far-seeing and beloved leader, guiding the human race towards a brighter future... He who opposes Marxism today does not do so because, for instance, he denies the validity of Marx's theory of the tendency of the rate of profit to fall. Similarly there are millions today who acknowledge Marx as their leader, but not because he solved the riddle of capitalist society. Perhaps one socialist in a thousand has ever read any of Marx's economic writings, and of a thousand anti-Marxists not even one (Nicolaievsky and Maenchen-Helfen 1976: ix).

The above quote, taken from what is in our view the best biography of Marx, was written in Germany at the time of rising Naziism, but has a freshness that could equally apply today.

The ideas of Marx and his long-time friend and collaborator Frederick Engels, and the school of thought based on their work, are, perhaps, the most widely discussed but least understood of all theories about society. It is the purpose of this chapter to present clearly the ideas contained within the abstract labour theory of value *not* by summarising the two thousand or so pages of Marx's main work, *Capital*, but by presenting our understanding of the theory in juxtaposition to that of its two major rivals, the subjective preference and cost-of-production theories. And because there is a sharper and more widely accepted contrast between the views of Marxists and those of the subjective preference – or, for Marx, 'vulgar' – economists, we try, in particular, to emphasise the points of distinction between the other, cost-of-production, school and that of abstract labour. This is not an attempt at mere 'brand differentiation'. We believe that there are *fundamental* differences between these theories and that these lead, logically, to different implications for political action, as the reader will see by comparing Chapters 7 and 9.

The abstract labour theory of value, as developed by Marx in the second half of the nineteenth century and by others since him, is essentially a critique of Capitalism as well as a critique of Political Economy, the latter explicit as the sub-title of *Capital*. In 1857 Marx had planned to contain these critiques in six books, one each on capital, landed property, wage labour, the state, foreign trade and the world market. But, nine years later, Marx decided on the production of only four books, one each on:

– the production process of capital – (Volume 1 of *Capital*)
– the circulation process of capital – (Volume 2)
– the process of capitalist production as a whole – (Volume 3) and finally,
– the history of political economy – (*Theories of Surplus Value*)

In this chapter, in attempting to explain the abstract labour theory of value, we follow a similar order to that followed by Marx in *Capital*, since, in general, this is a logical sequence. Thus our journey starts with capitalism as a distinctive mode of production, and then proceeds, through sections 8.2 to 8.4, to examine:

- the *dialectical* aspects of commodities, including labour power, and the nature of surplus value, exploitation. and of *class formation* within capitalism: (8.2);
- the *transformation* of values into prices and of surplus value into profit, rent and interest (8.3);
- the economic origins and *tendencies* to crises within capitalism (8.4).

Thus we broadly follow the order of exposition in *Capital* not because there have been no writers after Marx who have developed the abstract labour theory of value, but because it still seems to be the most logical sequence for expounding the theory. But the last section (8.5) of this chapter discusses some of the myths and controversies surrounding abstract labour theory. Section 8.5 is then followed, as in the other chapters, by notes on further reading.

The abstract labour theory of value, as a critique of capitalism and of political economy, was one of two strands of 'socialist' economics which developed in the nineteenth and early twentieth centuries. Since socialism is defined here to mean more than just the reform of capitalism, socialist economics can mean both the theoretical basis for understanding *and* opposing or even overthrowing capitalism, as well as the analysis of the problems of a society in transition to communism. It was only after the Russian Revolution in 1917 that the second area of socialist economics developed, whereas the rapid development of capitalism in the nineteenth century provided the basis not only for those theories which at worst sought to apologise for it or at best sought merely to modify it; but also for a fundamental critique of capitalism. Thus in tracing the development of this critique, we necessarily start at the beginning of the nineteenth century.

Marx, it has been said: 'obtained his philosophical training in his native Germany, his political education in France and Belgium and his understanding of economics in England' (Lichtheim 1978: 42). But it is in England, and in Ricardo, that the origins of the abstract labour theory of value can be found. As we emphasised in Chapter 5 it was Ricardo who picked up and persevered with the labour input theory, which Smith had tentatively toyed with. By contrast Ricardo, while persevering with the labour input theory, criticised and rejected the labour commanded theory which was later to be so enthusiastically espoused by subjective preference, or as Marx called them, 'vulgar', economists. And it was this perseverance with the labour input theory that led Marx to praise Ricardo as a 'scientific political economist'. At the same time, however, Marx criticised Ricardo for ignoring the historical origins of capitalism (see Marx 1970: 81). And since, according to Marx, Ricardo was one of the best classical economists, this criticism applied equally to others, and even to those who expressed anti-capitalist or 'socialist' sentiments. These socialist protests in the first half of the nineteenth century were mostly confined to Britain and France. The relative availability of land in America and the introduction of representative democracy following the American Revolution took the edge off the social protest there, although some agrarian populism emerged after the 1830s. But in Britain the development of capitalism in agriculture and the rapid growth of an urban proletariat created the conditions for the emergence of a socialist 'movement'. And yet, as Lichtheim has pointed out, a problem for the historian of socialism is that 'industrial capitalism was born in Britain, but the socialist protest against it found its most coherent intellectual expression in France, a country that was slow to absorb the impact of the new mode of production' (Lichtheim 1970: 41, 42).

However, the socialist theories which developed on either side of the Channel in the first half of the nineteenth century were later to be criticised by Marx and Marxist historians. These theories were extremely heterogeneous but few of the 'early socialists' attempted to analyse 'the contradictory interests of social classes which ensured that proposals for social change were always met with inertia and hostility' (Hardach, Karras and Fine 1978: 2). As Engels pointed out in *Anti-Dühring* these 'immature theories corresponded to the immature level of capitalist production and the immature development of classes' (Engels 1955: 365). Though equally immature, some were less acceptable to Marx and Engels who in their 1848 *Manifesto of the Community Party* analysed the socialist and communist literature of that time in three groups namely:

1. Reactionary.
2. Bourgeois.
3. Critical-utopian.

The reactionary 'socialists' were those, such as the feudal aristocracy and the petty bourgeoisie, who were perishing in the developing capitalism. Although the petty bourgeois group led by the Frenchman, Sismondi, analysed 'with great acuteness the contradictions in the conditions of modern production' (Marx and Engels 1975: 65), they wanted nevertheless to turn the clock back and restore a society of small producers. By contrast, the bourgeois socialists, with Proudhon being a prominent example, wanted to redress social grievances 'in order to secure the continued existence of bourgeois society' (Marx and Engels 1975: 69). They wished for a bourgeoisie without a proletariat. The third group, the critical-utopian socialists and communists, which included Saint-Simon, Fourier, Robert Owen and others, recognised the class antagonisms in the prevailing form of society, but at that time the proletariat were a class with no historical initiative nor independent political movement. Thus although the writings of the utopian group contain *'valuable materials for the enlightenment of the working class'* (Marx and Engels 1975: 73), this group opposed all political action on the part of the working class. Thus it was the bourgeois socialists (the Proudhonists), and not the utopians, who played an active role in the politics of their day and whose ideas seemed to many workers to make sense. It was the bourgeois socialists who believed it possible to modify the existing system, so as to produce a free and equal society. Marx did not believe this to be possible through reform and spent most of the latter part of his life producing a scientific analysis of capitalism that would be both a critique of the ideas of the bourgeois socialists and provide guidance for the action that would overthrow capitalism. As Marx and Engels put it 'The philosophers have only interpreted the world in various ways: the point is to *change* it' (Marx and Engels 1974: 123, – their emphasis). But to change it, it is necessary to study it not just in abstraction but through experience. This point was made graphically in the same German Ideology: 'Philosophy and the study of the actual world have the same relation to one another as masturbation and sexual love' (Marx and Engels 1974: 103).

This, then, was the political and historical context for the development of the abstract labour theory – the reason for Marx doing his painstaking research in the British Museum in London, after and while being politically active in working class movements in Europe. The fundamental criticism that Marx made of Ricardo also applied to the utopian and bourgeois socialists of the first half of the nineteenth century – namely their failure to place capitalism within its historical context. It was this failure to see commodity production as a social relationship within a historical context which was emphasised so strongly by Marx. Ricardo and the Proudhonists were guilty of being unable to distinguish between simple commodity production and generalised commodity production – between a system in which there is production for sale by independent producers or artisans and capitalism in which labour power itself is a commodity. Thus although, to their credit, they focussed on labour not just as the measure but also the source of value, they limited their attention to labour time in particular activities and not to labour within a particular *social* relationship. It is this abstract value-form of the product of labour in bourgeois production that 'stamps that production as a particular species of social production and thereby gives it its special historical character' (Marx 1970: 81). Thus Ricardo and the Proudhonists were unable to distinguish capitalism from other modes of production (see below), and the institutions and activities peculiar to capitalism were treated therefore as eternal and universal.

By contrast, Marx was very much influenced by the German philosopher, Hegel, and the latter's emphasis on the inevitability of change. For Hegel, the history of the world was a history of ideas, with each idea, as it is affirmed, bringing with it another idea which is its negation. The ideas do battle and out of this battle a new and higher idea arises, to be fought and conquered. This dialectical process of change is inevitable, but in the place of a battle of ideas, Marx substituted a battle of material or economic forces. Thus no class can rule without bringing into play an antagonistic class. And, in their writings, Marx and Engels argued that the foundation of a class, of social power (or of relative impotence) was the control (or lack of it) of economic resources. It was this that characterised a *mode of production*.

The study of economics is therefore part of a much wider analysis of the relationship between individuals and the social as well as the natural environment. Economic questions are not reducible to a system of exchange relationships (as in subjective preference theory), nor are they merely a question of individuals' relationships to nature (as in cost-of-production theory). Rather, we have to engage in a wider study of the fundamental basis of social relations, of the particular form that these relations assume in different societies, and of the way in which societies change over time or the internal dynamic of societies. Strictly speaking therefore, abstract labour theory as a school of *economic* thought does not exist.

The point of departure for Marxist theory, the fundamental basis of social relationships, is that there is a material environment which people have to come to terms with if they are to survive. Production, the process by which labour, technical knowledge and the natural environment are combined in order to satisfy human needs and wants, is therefore the key to understanding society. But, unlike cost-of-production theory, production is not seen as a mere technical relationship. The type of control that people exercise over nature through the application of particular technologies, or the level of development of the *forces of production*, will also imply a form of social organisation of production or *relations of production*, the type of control that individuals have over others.

Whereas the forces of production take the form of *technical* relationships, the relations of production take the form of *class* relationships, where class is defined with respect to the control or lack of control exercised over the use of the tools, techniques and natural resources, or *means of production*, in the production process. Thus there are always dominant and subordinate classes, with the power and interests of the dominant class being supported and justified by a legal, political and ideological system, or *superstructure*. Neither the forces nor the relations of production can be understood independently of each other, and taken together they constitute the *mode of production*.

The form assumed by the relationships contained within the concept of the mode of production will differ historically between societies and also over time. For instance, where there is generally a low level of productivity so that people have to spend most of their time producing basic commodities for subsistence, the society will be based upon agricultural production with very little division of labour. Further, the lack of a substantial surplus product will mean that most production is directly for consumption and not exchange. In such a society the basis of power is the control of land, and in the absence of established markets control of the economic surplus is achieved by the physical coercion of individual producers. Such was the basis of feudal society, the dominant form of social organisation of production in Europe during the fourteenth to sixteenth centuries where the opposing classes were the feudal aristocracy and the peasantry. Under modern capitalism however, where advanced technologies are utilised which require a more advanced division of labour with people specialising in the production of particular commodities or even parts of commodities, then production is for exchange, with a highly developed system of markets. As we shall see, in such a society the key to the control of the economic surplus is not direct physical coercion but control of the means of production. In this case the opposing classes are the bourgeoisie or capitalist class, and the dispossessed proletariat or working class. Table 8.1 summarises some characteristics of five possible modes of production; but it needs to be stressed that this summary is a highly schematic one and that the transition from one mode of production to another is likely to be neither abrupt nor clear-cut. In his *Wages, Price and Profit*, Marx pointed out that '... the present system simultaneously engenders the *material conditions* and the *social forms* necessary for an economical reconstruction of society' (Marx 1973: 78; his emphasis). Thus both the joint-stock company and the break-up of the nuclear family were, for Marx, examples of social changes which anticipated a later mode of production (see Marx 1970: 489, 490 and Marx 1972: 437, 438).

It is by closer examination of the antagonistic class interests inherent within society that we are able to understand the dynamic of society, the factors which motivate groups of people to behave in particular ways, and therefore the factors which promote social change. At the

Table 8.1 Main characteristics of five modes of production

Mode of production	Class of producers	Exploiting class/ elements of production owned by exploiting class	Purpose of production	Do producers organise production?	Which mode of production is likely to follow?
Slavery	Slaves	Slave owners/ producers	Use value	No	Commodity production
Feudalism	Serfs	Landlords/land	Use value	Yes on own land; No on lord's land	Commodity production/ capitalism
Simple commodity production	Artisans	No exploiting class	Exchange value	Yes	Capitalism
Capitalism	Proletariat	Capitalists/means of production	Exchange value	No	Socialism/ communism
Communism	Workers	No exploiting class	Use value	Yes, collectively	None (?)

Source: Based on Harrison 1978: 24/25.

most visible level, in modern capitalist society this dynamic takes the form of capitalists attempting to maximise profitability by minimising the costs of production, and workers attempting to maximise their earnings while minimising the amount of work they perform in exchange. But class interest plays a much more significant role in Marxist theory than merely providing a theory of distribution of the social product (as in the neo–Ricardian version of cost-of-production theory). It is through class struggle that the contradictions inherent in any mode of production work themselves out. Thus in order fully to understand the process of social change these contradictions have to be specified. We have to go *behind* the visible phenomena, the appearance of society, and identify the particular constraints that are placed upon the individual. We have to account for the invisible motivation that leads to the visible behaviour.

For example, why is it that in modern, western, capitalist societies, the wage bargain is of such importance, frequently leading to discontent, often to strikes or lock-outs, and occasionally to national states of emergency? The answer, according to Marxists, is that the social relations of society are not susceptible to conscious control. We are born into an existing social system and have to conform to certain patterns of behaviour if we are to survive. The means of production are controlled by a minority of the population. Initially we are either born into this elite or we are not. If we are not, we are forced to sell our capacity to work, although we may attempt to join this minority, perhaps by working hard and investing our savings in industry. But if we 'succeed', then even as capitalists our behaviour will be constrained. To stay in business we will be forced to compete with other capitalists by continually improving the product and cutting the costs of production. This necessarily brings us into conflict with the work force, who object to either being made redundant upon the introduction of a newer, more profitable, technique of production or to having their wages held down in the face of increased productivity. And as we shall see in the discussion of capitalist crisis, the competitive dynamic requires ever greater increases in efficiency just for the capitalist to maintain his position in the race for profits, leading to ever greater conflict between labour and capital, and ever greater competition between capitals. The picture we have here is not one of belligerent, money-grabbing capitalists on the one side and bloody-minded, politically-motivated workers on the other, each refusing to bend a little to take account of the interest of the other. Rather, it is a picture of people, who because of their relation to the means of production which defines their class interest, have no choice if they are to protect that interest but to enter into conflict sooner or later. It is not a question of the parties involved sitting down like 'rational' human beings and resolving their differences by compromise through the right institutional structure as cost-of-production theorists would have us believe. Each 'side' finds it 'rational' to behave in different ways and, furthermore, each will develop a view of the world based upon its own experience which will justify its relative position. That is, there will be opposing ideologies, although the dominant ideology in society will be that of the dominant class. However, if we accept that each will try to further its individual interest, why not let market forces arbitrate, as subjective preference theorists argue? The problem with this approach is that it only takes into account the social relations of *exchange* and therefore ignores the wider structure of social relations of *production, within which these exchanges take place*. They therefore take the social structure as given, and this abstraction from social change allows them to postulate a system in equilibrium.

But for Marxists the social structure is never static. The social (and therefore economic) life of a society can only be understood in terms of the relationship between the forces and the relations of production, and the contradictions or internal conflicting forces within this relationship. As soon as this contradiction is resolved in one way, it reappears in another form, giving rise to class conflict and always resulting in social change. As Marx and Engels wrote in the opening line of the *Manifesto of the Communist Party*, 'the history of all hitherto existing society is the history of class struggles' (Marx and Engels 1975: 32). Within capitalism the contradiction between social production and private appropriation is *expressed* in the theory of the tendency of the rate of profit to fall. The competitive battle between individual capitalists by which the strong take over the weak, involves a continuing process by which the labourer is replaced by the machine, leading to ever greater productivity and ever greater development of the forces of production. But, as we shall see, this development of the forces of production becomes increasingly incompatible with the private ownership and control of the means of production, the conflict coming to a head in periodic economic crises, such as the great crash of the 1930s and the recessions of the 1970s. Such crises provide both reactionary and revolutionary opportunities. Capital may be restructured at the expense of the working class and of weak capitalists, providing the basis for a new round of accumulation, or the working class may take over the means of production at the expense of capital, replacing capitalist relations of production with socialist relations of production. The result is not pre-determined.

The nature of the contradiction within a mode of production between the forces and relations of production is neatly summarised by Marx in the preface to his *Contribution to the Critique of Political Economy* first published in 1859. In that preface Marx stated that

The general conclusion at which I arrived and which, once reached, became the guiding principle of my studies can be summarised as follows: In the social production of their existence, men inevitably enter into definite, necessary relations, which are independent of their will, namely, relations of production appropriate to a given stage in the development of their material forces of production. The totality of these relations of production constitutes the economic structure of society, the real foundation on which there arises a legal and political superstructure and to which there correspond definite forms of social consciousness. The mode of production of material life conditions the general process of social political and intellectual life. It is not the consciousness of men that determines their existence, but their social existence that determines their consciousness. At a certain stage of development, the material productive forces of society come into conflict with the existing relations of production or – this merely expresses the same thing in legal terms – with the property relations within the framework of which they have operated hitherto. From forms of development of the productive forces these relations turn into their fetters. Then begins an era of social revolution (Marx 1977: 20, 21).

But this process of social change is not at all obvious. To discover it, we have, Marx argued, to penetrate behind the visible appearance of society, to identify the significant characteristics of the social structure. The visible or concrete appearance is explained in terms of an invisible or abstract reality. As Marx claimed in Volume III of *Capital*. 'All science would be superfluous if the outward appearance and the essence of things directly coincided' (Marx 1972: 817).

Often, Marxist methodology is described as going from the abstract to the concrete, but this is only true in the sense that the abstract categories are themselves implied by the concrete reality but in turn allow that reality to be understood. Thus both theoretical and empirical work inform each other and the conclusion of the analysis informs our behaviour. We need to dive down beneath the appearance of exchange and production techniques to uncover the nature of capitalist social relations, in terms of which the visible phenomena of exchange can be understood. In the methodology of the abstract labour theory, there is an integration of the spheres of consumption and production which is lacking in the other schools of economic thought. The subjective preference theorists give primacy to consumption whereas the cost of production theorists give primacy to production. However, in the abstract labour theory of value, each is seen as interdependent so that primacy cannot be afforded to one sphere alone.

This methodology of moving between the abstract and the concrete and of integrating the spheres of production and consumption is vividly illustrated by Marx's analysis of commodities, including labour power, with which he starts the first volume of *Capital*. It is to this that we now turn.

8.2 The dialectical aspects of commodities including labour, exploitation and surplus value

In societies in which there is an advanced division of labour, consumers must indicate their wants and needs to producers and products must be distributed from producers to consumers. Where such a society is also characterised by private ownership of the means of production we have *commodity production*, where the commodity has two aspects; it must satisfy a want or need and therefore have *use value* for the consumer and it is produced for exchange and therefore has *exchange value* for the producer. The use value and exchange value inherent within a commodity are brought into relation with each other by the *law of value*, the operation of which allocates the forces of production of society between alternative activities.

It is because the wealth of those societies in which the capitalist mode of production prevails presents itself as an immense accumulation of commodities that Marx begins his investigation into capitalism with the analysis of a commodity. And there are a number of important propositions about the commodity which need to be repeated here because of the countless misinterpretations of Marx that have been perpetrated as a result of ignoring these. It needs to be noted that

– a thing can have a use value, without being produced or having value. An example is the air we breathe:
– a thing can have a use value *and* be produced, yet still *not* be a commodity if it is not exchanged:
– thus, for a thing to be a commodity, it must not only have a use value but a use value produced for exchange:
– but for a thing to have value and be a commodity, it must be an object of utility. 'If the thing is useless, so is the labour contained in it: the labour does not count as labour, and therefore creates no value' (Marx 1970: 41).

Thus commodities are use values produced for exchange. Producers exchange their products, and there is therefore a social relation between producers born out of their dependence upon each other. Thus arises 'commodity fetishism' whereby relationships between people assume the fantastic form of a relation between things. This is analogous to the 'alienation' of the religious world in which 'the productions of the human brain appear as independent beings endowed with life and entering into relation both with one another and the human race' (Marx 1970: 72). Thus a form which people create comes, in the fullness of time, to dominate them.

But how does this domination occur? How does the law of value determine the rate of exchange of commodities or their exchange value, and therefore allocate productive resources? In what sense can two chairs, say, be said to *quantitatively* equal one table when they are *qualitatively* different, the use value of one being to sit on and the other to eat off? Marx argued that there must be one quality shared by both commodities for this comparison to be made; that is, they are both products of labour. The *value* in a commodity is therefore produced by labour and the *exchange value* of the commodity is its value compared to the value of another commodity.

The dialectical aspects of commodities

Thus the exchange value of a commodity may well fall as productivity rises, and Marx points out, as did Ricardo, that 'an increased quantity of material wealth [use values] may correspond to a simultaneous fall in the magnitude of its value' (Marx 1970: 46). Indeed, the extension of the social division of labour develops the contrast between use value and value, a contrast which is particularly evident in times of crisis (see section 8.5 below).

The value of a commodity can only be expressed through exchange, by means of which its value is equated to that of another commodity, and the labour of the producer to that of another producer. But of course in a developed system of commodity production, products are exchanged for money, and their exchange values *appear* as money prices. As a *measure of value*, the money commodity must possess value. In the case of a produced commodity like gold this value is related to the labour time required to produce gold like any other commodity. But where money takes the form of token or paper money issued by governments, its value is determined by the value of commodities for which it can be exchanged, and therefore the value of money is directly related to the quantity of money which is available, its speed of circulation and the aggregate value of goods exchanged. Thus money is the medium of circulation as well as a measure of value and it is from its function as a circulating medium that paper money arises. Money as the medium of circulation intervenes between the sale and purchase of commodities; but Marx anticipates the arguments of the latter-day monetarists in stressing that 'although the movement of the money is merely the expression of the circulation of commodities, yet the contrary appears to be the actual fact, and the circulation of commodities seems to be the result of the movement of the money' (Marx 1970: 116). And so money is the alienated form of the commodity, but it does not serve merely as a measure of value and medium of circulation. It also serves as a means of payment, which in the development of exchange and capital gives rise to credit, and when the production of commodities has sufficiently extended itself, money begins to serve as the means of payment beyond the sphere of the circulation of commodities. 'Rents, taxes and such-like payments are transformed from payments in kind into money payments' (Marx 1970: 140). Thus money serves as more than a medium of circulation. Here Marx goes beyond Milton (Friedman), which is perhaps not surprising, but his treatment of money as a means of payment is also different from Keynes's treatment of money as a store of value, as we shall see in our discussion of crisis in section 8.5. Here it is important to stress that money is the universal exchange value before which all commodities appear as mere use values or articles of consumption, and it is because of this monetarisation of exchange that the social relations between people inherent within any division of labour appear as a relation between things, each of which has a price. If value is *produced* by labour and yet only *appears* in the act of exchange as a rate of exchange or a price, then to understand what value *actually is* and how it is determined, we have to look closer at the operation of the law of value. Producers offer their products on the market at a price, which, given their previous experience, is likely to maximise their income. If, however, at this price, supply is greater than demand, then in order to sell the entire output the price will have to be lowered, or alternatively, if demand is greater than supply the producer will be able to increase the price and still sell out. Thus the level of market price is regulated by demand, by the wants and needs of the consumer. In turn the price mechanism serves to allocate productive resources to productive activity. If there is excess supply and the price falls then the producer in future will diversify into alternative products to increase sales revenue and therefore income. Alternatively, if there is excess demand other producers will be attracted to this market by the high profits being achieved. The level of *social* demand for the product therefore, determines the proportion of total labour time which *society* contrives to allocate to that particular line of production. Thus, for Marx as for Ricardo, 'supply and demand regulate nothing but the temporary *fluctuations* of market prices. They will explain... why the market price of a commodity rises above or sinks below its *value*, but they can never account for that *value* itself' (Marx 1973: 27, – his emphasis).

It is not then supply and demand that determines value but rather the labour time required for production. Those products that take longer to produce will have a higher value, this higher value will appear in a higher price of production, and if supply and demand paralyse each other, this price of production will be the same as the market price. Lazy or inefficient producers who take longer than the average to produce a particular commodity will have to be content with the lower average value of the product, which will reflect the average intensity of work, and the average efficiency of production. The latter will be affected by the tools and equipment utilised as well as by the degree of skill required, with skilled labour being weighted more heavily than unskilled.

The different proportions in which different sorts of labour are reduced to unskilled labour as their standard, are established by a social process that goes on behind the backs of the producers (Marx 1970: 44).

It is evident from this quotation that Marx is not saying that all labour is unskilled. The important point to note is that the value of a commodity is determined by the *socially necessary labour time* required for production. Value consists of *social* or *abstract* labour time, since it only appears through exchange and cannot be measured by a stop watch in a particular workplace. Value then is the social relationship that arises out of a division of labour. This concept of abstract labour is clearly quite distinct from that of Ricardo and cost of production theorists for whom labour time refers to the actual time required to perform a particular task given existing technical knowledge or what Marxists refer to as *concrete labour time*.

So far we have only looked at the use of direct or live labour time in production. But what relevance do the contribution of raw materials and the wearing out of tools and equipment have to the value of the final commodity? In as far as these inputs are produced by labour they will have their own value, and in as far as these inputs are consumed in the production of another commodity they will pass on that proportion of their value to the final commodity. Thus the socially necessary labour time includes both direct or living labour and that 'dead' labour which is embodied in the raw materials and machinery used up in production.

At this stage certain parallels can be drawn between the above discussion and subjective preference theory, or what Marx called 'vulgar economy': supply and demand, together with maximising motives, allocating productive resources to satisfy the wants of consumers, and the use of abstract categories to explain this allocation (utility and abstract labour time). These similarities exist, because at this stage of the argument we have concentrated on social relations of *exchange*. But whereas subjective preference theory remains at this level, abstract labour theory, in keeping with its underlying theory of history, has a different objective and goes further to consider the social relations of *production*. According to Marxist theory, the mode of production and therefore the class-based relations of production are the ultimate determinants of social relations in general and relations of exchange in particular, and by failing to consider this underlying structure of society and how it might change over time, subjective preference theory necessarily arrives at a universal, as opposed to a historically specific theory of exchange relations, and focuses on the tendencies towards equilibrium rather than emphasising the possibilities for change. Abstract labour theory then, is historically specific, where the characteristics of each historical epoch are defined by the nature of the social relations of production, which in turn will correspond to a particular level of development of the forces of production. And it is through the analysis of the relations of production that the particular form assumed by class relations can be specified and the possibilities for social change identified. Thus, whereas under capitalism the relations of exchange may be characterised by freedom (in agreement with subjective preference theory), the relations of production are characterised by coercion, leading to conflict.

To explore this further we need to understand the nature of capital for which the starting point is the circulation of commodities; since it is the end product of commodity circulation, namely money, which is the first form in which capital appears. The simplest form of commodity circulation is C-M-C, the exchange of one commodity for another using money as the medium of circulation. But from the sixteenth century onwards, with the development of money as capital, we get an inversion of this circuit into M-C-M. There are merchants who buy in order to sell, with the goal behind this circuit being exchange value. Now '*capital is money: capital is commodities*' (Marx 1970: 153). But merchants will not buy in order to sell unless at a profit; the circuit has to be M-C-M', where M' denotes a sum of money greater than that advanced. But they will not be able to sell at a profit, unless they have a monopoly of a particular trade. And with the development of capital in the hands of other merchants, they will find it difficult to hold on to such monopolies. Thus with the development of capital beyond the primitive or derivative forms of merchant and interest-bearing capital, we have to look for another source of surplus. 'Our friend, Moneybags, who as yet is only an embryo capitalist, must buy his commodities at their value, must sell them at their value, and yet at the end of the process must withdraw more value from circulation than he threw into it at starting' (Marx 1970: 166). He does this by finding, in the market, a commodity 'whose use value possesses the peculiar property of being a source of value' (Marx 1970: 167). This commodity is *labour power*.

Workers sell their capacity to work or their labour power for a definite length of time to capitalists. And like any other commodity, labour power has both an exchange value and a use value. It is this two–fold character of labour which was the best point of Marx's work, according to letters from Marx to Engels in 1867 and 1868. The exchange value of labour power is given by the labour time required to reproduce the workers' ability to work. Ricardo argued that population expansion would tend to drive the wage rate down to subsistence level, whereas Marx argued that, in general, it would be more than a simple physiologically determined subsistence level, that it would reflect the standard of living considered normal for the times, and that it would itself be the result of workers' struggles to share in the fruits of increased productivity. The use value of labour power is given by its combination with the means of production for a definite period of time, say eight hours, to produce other commodities and therefore other exchange values. The point about this *particular* commodity however, is that its use value, the amount of exchange value that it is able to produce (eight hours) is greater than its *own* exchange value, since it may only require the equivalent of, say, four hours of work to produce the goods that are bought with the wages earned. And if the labour embodied in the raw materials and machinery used in production is assumed to be passed on in the output, there will be a surplus produced, in this case the equivalent of four hours, which accounts for the difference between M and M'. This difference between the use value and exchange value of labour power is called *surplus value* and the means by which surplus value is extracted from the worker is called *exploitation*.

Here it is important to note that there is a clear distinction between the Ricardian concept of labour time and the concept of labour power in abstract labour theory. In the abstract labour theory, capital is seen as a social relationship in the exchange that takes place between the worker and the capitalist. Each has a use value that the other needs and thus each is dependent upon the other for its existence: the worker possesses labour power and the capitalist the means of production. Each class is defined in terms of the other. But it is a relationship that only exists because the means of production are controlled by a minority of the population. Herein lies the basis of coercion. A worker may choose *which* capitalist to work for, but in the end will still be working for *a* capitalist. The *exchange* relation between the two sides is characterised by freedom, so that the labourer is paid the full value of the labour power and exploitation is not the result of imperfections in commodity circulation, as cost-of-production theorists like Chamberlin and Joan Robinson have asserted (see Chamberlin: 1933 and Robinson: 1933). Instead exploitation is the result of the worker being free in a double sense: free to move from one capitalist to another, but also freed of the means of production. Once the labour power has been bought by the capitalist, the worker loses control over the use of that labour power and the fruits of that labour. And through the institution of private property, the legal foundation of capitalism, the surplus product takes the value form and becomes surplus value.

Thus capitalism is a system of generalised commodity production in which labour power itself is a commodity. It is the latter which distinguishes capitalism from a system of simple commodity production; and one thing is clear: 'Nature does not produce on the one side owners of money or commodities, and on the other men possessing nothing but their own labour power... It is clearly the result of a past historical development' (Marx 1970: 169). The free labour power is squeezed out of the system as modes of production are transformed and the descriptions of this process of 'prior' or primitive accumulation by Marx in *Capital* and later by Rosa Luxemburg in *Accumulation of Capital* make interesting reading (Marx 1970: VIII and Luxemburg 1963).

The recognition of labour power as a commodity means that the earlier presentation of the circuit of capital as M-C-M' has to be elaborated as M-C...P...C'-M' (see Marx 1970 (ii): 25). In this formulation the dots indicate that the process of circulation is interrupted by the process of production and C' and M' designate C and M increased by surplus value. They have increased because M, the money capital advanced, buys commodities: the means of production, and labour power. Thus the transformation of money capital into productive capital can be summarised as: M — C. Since the means of production, in the form of raw materials and machinery, is bought by one capitalist from another, these cannot be the source of surplus value for capitalists as a whole, although individual capitalists may gain at the expense of others through the occasional swindle. It is labour power which is the source of surplus value and it is the process of primitive accumulation which is the source of the coercion necessary for the surplus value to

211

be extracted. If the antagonistic yet interdependent relationship between workers and capitalists is the result of the minority control of the means of production and the institution of private property, then conflict between capitalists themselves is due to capital being divided into a number of competing units. Under capitalist relations of production, it is the maximisation and equalisation of profit which determine the prices of production. Capitalists will put their money, and therefore productive resources, where the rate of return on their investment is the highest, moving out of areas of low profitability into areas of high profitability, a process which creates a tendency for the rate of return to be equalised across sectors of the economy. As we shall see, such competition creates conflict, but for surplus value reflected in its money forms of profit, interest and rent, to be realised at all, there has to be an interdependence between capitalists. Here again we find a conflicting yet interdependent relationship. The root of this mutual dependence lies in the fact that workers receive less in wages than the value of the products they produce. Capitalists as a whole make their profits by extracting surplus value from the workers as a whole. It is this process of extracting and expropriating surplus *value* which is both the class characteristic and source of conflict within capitalism.

Through the war of competition, capitalists are forced to minimise their costs of production and maximise their rate of profit on pain of extinction. This process will have the effect of equalising the rate of profit across different branches of industry but, to receive anywhere near the average rate of profit, a capitalist will have to be as efficient as the competing capitalists. Thus each capitalist has continually to re-invest in new techniques of production in order to stay in the race. Those that are more efficient than the average will make more than average profits, but they will only remain in this fortunate position if they continually reinvest to maintain their lead. The relatively inefficient will be less profitable and therefore less able to reinvest in new techniques in order to catch up with the rest, and may well go bankrupt. Thus, although the forces of competition and supply and demand may equalise the rate of profit *across* branches of industry, *within* a particular industry there will be differential rates of profit according to differential levels of efficiency.

Thus each individual capitalist feels the forces of competition as external, coercive laws and is under constant pressure to increase the rate of surplus value, the ratio of surplus value to the value of labour power. The maximisation of the rate of surplus value can be achieved either by prolonging the length of the working day or by curtailing the necessary labour time by, for example, increasing the productivity of the labourer. The first of these Marx calls *absolute* surplus value, the second he calls *relative* surplus value (Marx 1970: 315). There are obvious limits to absolute surplus value, with capitalists themselves in the nineteenth century having to 'curb the passion of capital for a limitless draining of labour power, by forcibly limiting the working day by state regulations' (Marx 1970: 239). Thus the major avenue for increasing the rate of exploitation is through the production of relative surplus value. This process continuously 'revolutionises...the technical processes of labour and the composition of society' (Marx 1970: 510). This continual, revolutionary process separates town and country, on the one hand mental and manual labour, on the other: it tends to create a reserve army of unemployed which is itself recycled: and, on a country-by-country basis, it creates 'the weapons for conquering foreign markets [and for] ruining handicraft production in other countries' (Marx 1970: 451), so leading to the international expansion of capitalism.

But although the changing production techniques may be self-evident, the extraction of surplus value is not. Under the feudal mode of production whereby the serf was required to work for part of the working day on the lord's land, the extraction of surplus was plain for all to see. Under the capitalist mode, the wage payment to the labourer for, ostensibly, the whole of the working day hides the exploitation. 'The transaction is veiled by the commodity form of the product and the money form of the commodity' (Marx 1970. 568). And prices, the money form of the commodity, effectively fool not only the labourer but also the capitalist for, as we shall see in the next section, relative prices are unlikely to correspond to relative commodity values.

8.3 Values, prices and the transformation problem

The previous section stressed that capitalists are continuously under pressure to increase the rate of surplus value and to revolutionise the labour process. This is the source of both the progressiveness of capital in developing the forces of production and its 'callousness' in treating relations between people as relations between things. Thus the same competitive process which forces capitalists to revolutionise the labour process also hides from the capitalist the true nature of the capitalist mode. For individual capitalists do not receive the amount of surplus value which they manage to squeeze from their workers. Whereas surplus value, the source of profit, is *produced* according to the amount of live labour employed in production, it is *distributed* according to the total capital advanced for the production of the commodity. Thus although surplus value may be produced individually, it is distributed *socially*.

The value of a commodity, therefore, which reflects the amount of surplus value embodied within it, will differ from the money price of a commodity, which reflects the profit realised by its sale.

The value of a commodity (w) is given by the amount of labour time required for its production which in turn is made up of the exchange value of labour power (or what Marx calls *variable capital* – v), surplus value – s, and the value of the means of production used up in the production process (or constant capital – c). Marx refers to the value of labour power as variable capital, because, although it is capital, in the process of production it undergoes an alteration of value (see Marx 1970: 209). That is it is variable because the rate of exploitation or s/v, can vary. Thus the value of a commodity is equal to $w = c + v + s$. But this is likely to differ from the price of the commodity because whereas surplus value is produced by reference to v, it is distributed according to the total capital advanced. Thus the price of the commodity is given by $p = c + v + r(c + v)$, where c and v are in money terms and r is the rate of profit. This is the price of production of the commodity, and it is this which governs the market price.

To parody Marx's 'definition' of communism of 'From each according to his ability, to each according to his needs' (Marx 1972: 17), we can describe the process of creating and distribution of surplus value as 'From each capitalist according to his work force, to each according to his capital'. But this means that if, in general, capitalists make profits at all, then some capitalists will make more in profit than the surplus value which they produce. Thus prices will not be equal to values, unless r equals zero or the ratio of c to v (the 'capital intensity') is the same in all industries or sectors.

Now this is, of course, the conclusion that Ricardo had reached about half a century before Marx, as we saw in Chapter 5. Which is why some economists (such as Samuelson) have referred to Marx as a minor post-Ricardian. But whereas Ricardo was trying, through his use of labour time to determine relative prices, Marx's object was different. For Marx the concept of value was useful in stripping away the veil which money prices cast over the underlying social relationships. It is clear that Marx was well aware, long before writing *Capital*, of the deviation of prices from values, of what has since become known as the *transformation problem* – the transforming of values into prices.

But whereas, for Ricardo, this was a problem which was to be dismissed by arguing that price ratios would *approximate* to labour time ratios (see again Chapter 5), for Marx the deviation of prices from values had important consequences. Marx points out that 'The transformation of values into prices of production serves to obscure the basis for determining value itself' (Marx 1972: 168), and that the true nature and origin of profit is concealed not only from the capitalist, who has a vested interest in deceiving himself, but also from the labourer. But the labourer will realise, in discovering the true 'social' nature and origin of profit, that the whole capitalist system must be confronted and that workers should not limit themselves to unavoidable guerilla fights (see Marx 1973: 78).

But to say that Marx was well aware of the deviation of prices from values is not the same as saying that he correctly or completely transformed values into prices in Volume III of *Capital*. This 'failure' of Marx has been attacked by economists from other schools and the whole concept of value questioned. Ian Steedman, an English econ-omist, has, in a recent book, argued that '. . . the project of providing a materialist account of capitalist societies is dependent on Marx's value magnitude analysis only in the negative sense that continued adherence to the latter is a major fetter on the development of the former' (Steed-man 1977: 207). The basis for this argument is that the value system does not give a determinate price system and thus Steedman's argument is similar to that of Joan Robinson more than thirty years before and to those of others even further back – namely that statements about value are purely dogmatic statements (Robinson 1962: 38). Instead Steedman, Robinson and others in the cost-of-production school offer a Sraffian system of simultaneous equations so as to determine a set of relative prices from physical coefficients, where labour time is taken as a *technological datum* (in Marxist terms *concrete* labour) and capital is considered as a *physical input* (i.e. constant capital). From this formu-lation they arrive at the conclusion that analysis in value terms is superfluous. But this is hardly surprising since, for abstract labour the-orists, value is not so much the product of a *technical* relation between labour time and physical inputs, but more of a *social* relation of inter-dependence between consumers and producers, and workers and capi-talists.

In the analysis of simple commodity production (or Smith's 'rude state' of society) where the only interdependence is between consumer and producer (i.e. based upon the division of labour), market prices are directly proportional to labour values. For this limited case we agree with the neo-Ricardians that value analysis is superfluous. But as soon as we look at economic relationships in the historically specific form of capitalism, and therefore explicitly include a theory of history and social change, value analysis, as a representation of the invisible struc-tural relations of society, is crucial if we are to understand the visible appearance of society. Thus in the consideration of capitalist social relations, we see that the limited interdependence of producers and con-sumers of simple commodity production is complicated by the pe-culiarly interdependent, and antagonistic relationship, between capitalists as well as that between capitalists and workers. These relationships are expressed through commodity exchange and therefore ultimately through money prices, with the rate of profit being averaged and prices of production differing from values. Unfortunately, there is not space within this work to deal with the debate over the transformation prob-lem in greater detail, but for excellent introductions see Baumol 1974 and Fine and Harris 1979. For our own part, we go along with their analysis, which sees the problem, not so much as a *quantitative* one of converting numerical values into prices, but more as a *qualitative* one of moving from the relatively *abstract* category of value to the more *concrete* price of production, from the *social process* of value to the *accounting concept* of price of production. Marx's purpose was not to describe the price structure in *static equilibrium* but to explain the *dynamic process* by which it comes about, not to construct a theory of *relative prices* but a theory of *price formation*.

In a letter to Engels in 1867, Marx explained that his treatment of surplus value and of its conversion into profit had to *follow* the account of the process of the circulation of capital, and that therefore the deviation of prices from values could only be systematically dealt with in Vol. III. Also he argued: '. . . this method has the advantage of continually *setting traps* for these fellows which provoke them to untimely demonstrations of their asininity' (Marx quoted in Baumol 1974: 61; Marx's emphasis).

But regardless of this tongue-in-cheek jibe, Marx followed the method of starting with the somewhat abstract commodity and of ending with 'the *forms of appearance* which serve as the *starting point* in the vulgar conception: ground rent coming from the earth, profit (interest) from capital, wages from labour' (Marx quoted in Baumol 1974: 59; Marx's emphases). Thus it is not until Vol. III of *Capital* that Marx discusses the relationships between the industrial capitalist, and the owners of money or *finance capital*, and the owners of natural raw materials, or *landed capital*.

Surplus value is produced by labour power when combined with the means of production (machinery and raw materials) in a productive process under social relations of exploitation and the commodity is subsequently sold on the open market. But initially the inputs into the productive process have to be purchased, which requires money. Money therefore has a use value *as capital*, as a means to acquire profit. And, because we have a monetary economy, where money intervenes between sale and purchase, we have the possibility of those wishing to make purchases not having sufficient funds and those who have completed sales having surplus cash. Thus money capital becomes a commodity which can be bought and sold, and we have the conditions for *finance capital*; for the buying and selling of money in return for interest payments. But there is one important qualification. Commodity exchange is based on the exchange of equivalents. The use value of a commodity may be given up, but its exchange value is not. And it is for this reason that money is only lent or borrowed and not sold or bought. There would be little point in selling money since buyer and seller would merely exchange the same amount of money.

Since the use value of money capital is that it allows access to profits, its 'price' is limited by expected average profitability. Indeed interest payments, the price of money, are nothing more than a share of average profits and thus of surplus value paid by industrial capitalists to finance capitalists, with the rate of interest being determined solely by the supply and demand for money, with the demand being constrained by the average rate of profit. There is no exchange value for money capital as such and thus there is no 'natural' rate of interest around which the market rate might fluctuate. The rate of interest may well be negative in real terms, that is, in terms of purchasing power, but for a Marxist, any reference to this being in 'disequilibrium', as deviating from some hypothetically positive natural rate of interest is nonsense.

It is clear, then, that the finance capitalist's interest is a money share of surplus value. And since the development of the financial system has advantages for capital-in-general, industrial and finance capital are interdependent. One advantage of a comprehensive banking system is that it is able to bring together all the owners of idle money with all those who feel capable of converting this money into capital or self-expanding value. And further, a whole edifice of credit is built upon the relatively small cash base of banks, allowing the further expansion of productive investment. In addition to credit from financial institutions, firms may also extend credit by promising to pay each other at some point in the future when the inputs into production have been converted into commodities and sold. Thus the primary function of credit is to reduce the amount of capital held in the form of money, and finance capital takes on this specialist role of recycling surpluses and deficits. But the separation of the owner of money capital from the capitalist who organises production and disciplines the labour force leads to the emergence of joint stock companies, where each investor owns a small part of a large company. Effectively each share certificate is a title to a share of the profit received by the company, and these titles themselves become commodities being bought and sold through the stock market, with their price being determined by expectations about the prevailing rates of interest and company profits. A change in expectations therefore leads to a change in the price of capital, and for this reason, Marx referred to stocks and shares as *fictitious capital*, since their prices are to some extent determined independently of the value of capital, a position which Keynes was to restate some seventy years later. The emergence of the joint stock company opens the way for an enormous increase in the size of investments and thus an enormous increase in the scale of production. But there is also a negative side to the relationship. In Marx's own words, 'It reproduces a new financial aristocracy, a new variety of parasites in the shape of promoters, speculators and simply nominal directors; a whole system of swindling and cheating by means of corporation promotion, stock issuance and stock speculation. It is private production without the control of private property' (Marx 1972: 438). But there is a more important consequence. The ability of industrial capitalists to obtain credit means that they can rapidly enter those lines of production which are seen to be the most profitable, thereby speeding up the tendency for the rate of profit to be equalised throughout the economy. This increases the competitive pressure on all capitalists and thus the rate of re-equipment and reinvestment which, as we shall see in the next section, reinforces a tendency towards falling profitability and economic crises.

Apart from labour power, the other input into the productive process is the means of production, which includes raw materials and the products of the earth. But the earth too is privately owned. Particular individuals own particular parts of the globe and are able, in general, to demand a payment or *ground-rent* for the use of the natural properties of that land. Like money, land has a use value for industrial capitalists in that it can be used to put labour power to work and thereby receive profit, and they are willing to pay for this facility. But the determination of ground-rent is a little more complicated than the somewhat arbitrary way in which the rate of interest is determined. Again, like money–capital, the natural properties of the land do not possess exchange value in as far as no social labour has been expended in producing their particular socially useful qualities. But nevertheless some pieces of land, which may be especially fertile, endowed with minerals, or in a favourable location, are more productive than others in that their particular cost of production and therefore price of production of the particular commodity is relatively low and therefore profitability relatively high. That is, there is differential productivity and differential profitability. Thus for Marx as for Ricardo, there is *differential* rent, the difference in profitability between the least productive and the more productive pieces of land in the production of any particular commodity which is paid to the landed capitalist. But in his analysis of rent, Marx goes beyond Ricardo. The analysis of differential rent implies that no rent is paid for the use of the least productive piece of land, which in turn implies that this land is freely given over to the industrial capitalist, an assumption which is hardly compatible with land as private property, the very foundation of the theory of differential rent. If differential rent is the result of the price of production for a particular piece of land being less than the price of production for the industry in general, then for *absolute* ground-rent to be paid on *all* land regardless of the productivity of the land, the price of production must *always* be less than the market price of the commodity. But such a long-run deviation of price of production below market price suggests that there is some barrier which prevents industrial capitalists from entering the industry, thereby preventing an increase in the supply of the commodity, the lowering of the market price to the price of production and the redistribution of the surplus value produced within the industry to the average rate. Marx identifies such a barrier in the form of landed property. In Volume III of *Capital*, Marx argues that

'...if capital meets an alien force which it can but partially, or not at all, overcome, and which limits its investment in certain spheres, admitting it only under conditions which wholly or partly exclude the general equalisation of surplus value to an average profit, then it is evident that the excess of the value of commodities in such spheres of production over the price of production would give rise to a surplus profit which could be converted into rent and as such made independent with respect to profit. Such an alien force and barrier are presented by landed property, when confronting capital in its endeavour to invest in land; such a force is the landlord *vis-à-vis* the capitalist' (Marx 1972: 761, 762).

Landed capital, like finance capital therefore, provides a use value necessary for the production of a surplus value but is not the direct producer of that surplus value itself. It merely appropriates a share of the surplus value which results from the relationship of exploitation between industrial capital and labour. Thus, like finance capitalists, landlords are in an antagonistic relationship to industrial capitalists.

However, the nature of these antagonisms between the various fractions of capital (industrial, financial and landed) and between labour and capital in general, while they may be clear when laid bare by value analysis, may not be apparent to the actors themselves. The monetary veil presents reality in a different form. The visible reality is one where wages accrue to labour, profit to the industrial capitalist, interest to the finance capitalist and rent to the landlord. As we have seen in previous chapters, alternative explanations have been advanced to account for this appearance. Subjective preference theory, in keeping with its individualistic foundations, sees wages as the reward for the disutility associated with the time that is worked, profit as the payment for the organisational ability of the entrepreneur (who is also endowed with a fiery protestant ethic), interest both as the reward for postponing consumption and the product of the secret properties of the 'roundaboutness' or time of production, and rent as the result of the (temporary) monopoly control of markets. Cost-of-production theorists move closer to the Marxists in the sense that wages are necessarily decided by bargaining. But for the cost of production theorists the surplus is not a surplus value but a surplus *product*, determined more by nature and technique than by labour power working beyond the time necessary to reproduce itself. Interest is the *reward* for releasing liquidity and like rent accrues to those with monopoly power. Thus the technical product of society, which remains after the pickings of the monopolists, is distributed between the representatives of labour and capital through a bargaining process. And for the cost-of-production theorists wages are a payment for the labour *time* worked, not a payment for the labour *power* which is sold for a definite time.

Thus, Marx argues, bourgeois economists mystify the capitalist mode of production :

'In capital-profit, or still better capital-interest, land-rent, labour-wages, in this economic trinity represented as the connection between the component parts of value and wealth in general and its sources, we have the complete mystification of the capitalist mode of production, the conversion of social relations into things, the direct coalescence of the material production relations with their historical and social determination. It is an enchanted, perverted, topsy-turvy world...' (Marx 1972: 830).

It is only the categorisation of labour power as a *commodity*, which can lead to a theory of exploitation in *production*, the production of surplus *value* and the *transformation* of surplus value into profits, interest and rent. 'It is not abstinence that creates capital, but capital that requires abstinence' (Fine 1975: 31), and 'It is not because he is a leader of industry that a man is a capitalist: on the contrary, he is a leader of industry because he is a capitalist' (Marx 1970: 332).

As we shall see in the next chapter, the analytical distinction between surplus product and surplus value, between labour power and labour time, and in general between values and prices leads to important differences in the lessons that the analysis provides for political practice. And for the Marxist the guidance which the theory provides for political practice is the acid test of the theory. The theory must therefore unravel the dynamic of capitalism : an important part of that dynamic is the tendency for the rate of profit to fall. To this, we now turn our attention.

8.4 Capitalist crises – their origins and tendencies

We have seen in the previous sections how a system of production based upon private property and production for exchange generates certain antagonistic social interrelationships and a competitive dynamic to the economy. In this section we attempt to understand the operation of this dynamic and the way it affects and is affected by the social relation of society.

Competition, the process by which capitalists attempt to increase their particular rates of profit by reducing their costs of production to a level below the average for the industry, has contradictory effects for the general process of capitalist accumulation. In the long run, greater efficiency in production, defined in terms of more use values produced per unit of labour time, is achieved by the substitution in the labour process, of capital equipment for labour power. Thus the ratio of (physical) means of production to (actual) labour time employed, or the *technical composition of capital* will increase. *By itself* this process will increase the *value composition of capital*, which is equal to c/v, the ratio of the means of production and labour time expressed in terms of their respective exchange values and therefore in terms of socially necessary abstract labour time. 'To express this, I call the value composition of capital, in so far as it is determined by its technical composition and mirrors the changes of the latter, the organic composition of capital' (Marx 1970: 612).

Again, *by itself*, a generalised increase in the organic composition of capital will reduce the average rate of profit (in terms of both values *and* prices), since the rate of profit is given by: $r = s/c + v$. Dividing both the numerator and denominator by v, this beomes:

$$r = \frac{\dfrac{s}{v}}{\dfrac{c}{v} + \dfrac{v}{v}} = \frac{\text{the rate of exploitation}}{\text{the organic composition of capital} + 1}$$

It is clear from this that if the organic composition of capital rises, without the rate of exploitation rising, the rate of profit will fall. Thus attempts by individual capitalists to improve their *own* rate of profit create a tendency for the *average* rate of profit to fall. And it is quite likely that the more the rate of profit falls, the more bloodthirsty and ruthless will the competitive process become, thus speeding up the tendency for the rate of profit to fall. This law of the tendency of the rate of profit to fall is, for Marx, 'in every respect the most important law of modern political economy...[and] is from the historical stand-point the most important law' (Marx 1973(a): 748). But this is only a *tendency*, for there are other factors at work. We noted earlier in the discussion of the circuits of capital, how the sum of money realised at the end of the circuit was greater than the initial investment. The level of investment at the start of the second circuit therefore is greater than that for the first. Capital is expanding. With each round of investment capitalists will be attempting to increase productivity. There will be a relative substitution of constant capital for variable capital. However, capital equipment will only be substituted for labour power where the total labour time and cost of production required to produce the particular commodity ($c + v + s$) falls. Thus while, on the one hand, the technical composition of capital and therefore the organic composition of capital is rising, at the same time the total value of commodities is falling. Therefore even though the physical quantities of means of production relative to the labour power utilised may increase, the value of c relative to the value of v may not rise. In general, however, we argue that the value composition of capital (allowing for these feedback effects) is likely to increase, since the values of *both* c and v are likely to benefit from the general reduction in values. At this stage, however, it is important to note that there has been a considerable debate about the tendency of the rate of profit to fall and that this had a particularly international flavour about it with Japanese, European and American Marxists and non-Marxists all entering the fray. It is outside the scope of this book to outline the debate more than briefly but the central argument of those who deny the tendency is that capitalists will not introduce a new technique unless it *raises* the rate of profit (see Okishio 1961 and Steedman 1977:Ch. 9). The counter-argument by those who assert the tendency is that capitalist competition is such that individual capitalists are forced to introduce new methods of production if they give a competitive edge, that is, give a lower cost of production per unit of output. Thus what the individual capitalist thinks will give him the edge over capitalist enemies in the competitive war leads to a generalised fall in the rate of profit. In this process the capitalist is under compulsion. As Marx remarks, no capitalist 'ever voluntarily introduces a new method of production...so long as it reduces the rate of profit' (Marx 1972: 264). The new technique which reduces the cost of production can only be purchased at a 'cost' in terms of investment per unit of output. Thus the lower cost of production and *higher* initial profit *margin* leads to a *fall* in the profit *rate*. The increase in investment per unit of output is the cost incurred by capitalists to achieve the gain of a decrease in production costs per unit of output. The capitalist is caught (painfully) on the horns of a dilemma; 'his' (capitalists are rarely female, at least in the economics textbooks) rate of profit on total capital advanced *may* fall with the introduction of a new technique, but it will certainly fall if other capitalists beat him to it.

So far we have discussed this law in terms of a *tendency*; why not in terms of a certainty? The reason is simply that capitalists will always be striving to take steps which may, over short periods of time, push up the rate of profit. As Marx put it: '. . . the same influences which produce a tendency in the general rate of profit to fall, also call forth counter-effects, which hamper, retard and partly paralyse this fall. The latter do not do away with the law, but impair its effect. Otherwise, it would not be the fall of the general rate of profit but rather its relative slowness that would be incomprehensible' (Marx 1972: 239). What, then, are these counter-effects? So far, we have assumed a fixed rate of surplus value. But a fall in the rate of profit due to increase in the organic composition of capital may be offset by an increase in the rate of surplus value (or rate of exploitation, to use the more graphic term). If the value of a unit of labour power falls, with a given working day, the amount of surplus value produced and the rate of exploitation will be increased. For instance, if, in an eight hour working day, the first four hours are the equivalent of the exchange value of labour power (v), then the remaining four hours will constitute surplus (s). If the exchange value of labour power now falls so that it is equivalent to two hours, then s will rise to six hours and the rate of exploitation (s/v) will rise from 1 (i.e. 4/4) to 3 (i.e. 6/2). But herein lies another problem: in order to maintain a given rate of profit the rate of exploitation will have to become ever larger, for each increase in the *organic* composition of capital. This is shown in Table 8.2.

Table 8.2   The relationship between capital composition and rates of exploitation to give a fixed rate of profit

Organic composition of capital (c/v)		Rate of exploitation (s/v)		Rate of profit $\left(\dfrac{s/v}{c/v + 1}\right)$
c/v	% increase	s/v	% increase	
1	—	1	—	50
2	100	1.5	50.0	50
4	100	2.5	66.7	50
8	100	4.5	80.0	50
16	100	8.5	88.9	50

Marx's argument, then, is that an increase in the organic composition of capital will require an increase in the rate of exploitation to give a constant, let alone rising, rate of profit. Initially, the increased labour productivity that goes along with an increase in the organic composition of capital may be sufficient to offset the fall in the rate of profit, but at each stage an ever greater increase in the rate of exploitation is required to offset the same increase in the organic composition of capital. And it is Marx's thesis that sooner or later the increases required in the rate of exploitation will require ever greater investment in new techniques to increase efficiency which in turn will lead to ever greater increases in the organic composition of capital and only exacerbate the situation. But in addition to increases in the rate of exploitation there are further counter-tendencies at work. Capitalists will look at all elements of their cost of production to alleviate the underlying problem of a relative shortage of surplus value *vis-à-vis* the level of investment. In addition to attempting to increase the rate of exploitation by increasing the length of the working day, or by increasing the intensity of work, or by reducing the wage rate, a further offsetting tendency for capital within a particular nation may be provided by cheap imports. The import of cheap wage goods serves to increase the rate of exploitation by lowering the value of variable capital, while the import of cheap raw materials or machinery serves to lower the value of constant capital and the value composition of capital. But this importation of cheap food and machinery has obvious limits. If these imports are from other sections of capital, then this will be no solution for capital as a whole. And if these imports are from pre-capitalist modes they will evaporate as the pre-capitalist modes perish in the capitalist world. Thus the counter-acting tendencies to the falling rate of profit are only likely to provide a stay of execution for a limited time. Sooner or later the least efficient capitalists and consequently those with the lowest rate of profit will find it difficult to sell their products at a price which covers their price of production. The failure to realise expected revenue presents the prospect of defaulting on debts and even bankruptcy, leading them even further into debt as loans are contracted to ease them through their liquidity crisis. Thus credit will not resolve the crises, but merely extend them.

The increase in the demand for credit at a time of falling profitability will lead to an increase in the rate of interest, an increase in speculative activity on the stock exchange and probably to a fall in the value of fictitious capital. The increase in the rate of interest will of course be an added cost for capitalists who are already struggling. In this process, we can see the basis for Keynes's analysis of speculation hindering enterprise, but of course in this case any government action, as Keynes recommended, to limit speculative activity or to reduce the rate of interest will only have the effect of buying time. If the government does try to keep the interest rate down to limit bankruptcies and maintain the level of employment, the money supply is likely to rise and inflation is likely. But note that it is not the increase in money supply which is the fundamental *cause* of the rise in prices as the monetarists would have us believe; rather with falling profitability, further credit and therefore money is *required* to allow the realisation of surplus value at higher prices. But the rise in the price level may have a beneficial effect on the rate of exploitation if wages do not rise as fast, since this will effectively lower real wages and therefore the exchange value of labour power. If, on the other hand, workers are able to maintain their standard of living, then this will provide evidence for the cost–of–production view that it is trade union militancy leading to increased money wages which lies at the root of inflation. But 'Nothing is more absurd for this reason, than to explain the fall in the rate of profit by a rise in the rate of wages, although this may be the case by way of an exception' (Marx 1972: 240).

The government may follow even more interventionist policies by providing industrial aid and subsidies and even nationalising firms that are in trouble, as with Rolls–Royce and British Leyland. In so far as this is paid for by taxation, exacted from workers, a portion of wages is being used to maintain the rate of profit: in so far as the taxation is exacted from capitalists then it will be the more efficient firms that will be supporting their weaker competitors. In so far as intervention is paid for by printing money there may be an increase in the price level. Of course, any increase in the price level is likely to lead to an expansion of government expenditure in all its other spheres of activity (welfare services etc.) so that again the increase in the price level will appear to be caused by government expenditure, rather than through the government reacting to the crisis of profitability. The tendency for the rate of profit to fall, then, may appear in a number of guises, each of which has been elevated by either subjective preference theory or cost–of–production theory to *the* causal relation.

However, each of the above policy alternatives can at best delay the trend and at worst make the crisis deeper. Because the falling rate of profit is a tendency, the extension of credit must get ever deeper, the rise in prices ever higher and government intervention ever greater. But this means that when bankruptcies do occur, the effects will be more widespread. For Marx, this is a theory of capitalist *crisis*. 'The crises are...violent eruptions which for a time restore the disturbed equilibrium' (Marx 1972: 249). Crises are not movements from equilibria or detours from a path of social evolution, but they are an inherent part of the process of social development. A crisis is not a flaw in the mode of production but is fundamental to it. It is above all a time of social change, a time when capitalism must either restructure itself or be superseded by a superior mode of production, namely socialism. Capitalist crises have occurred in the 1870s/80s, the 1930s and the 1970s. Their particular form cannot be predicted without detailed historical analysis, but the hallmarks are there. Deep economic depressions cannot be overcome merely by offering investment incentives or by changing the climate of business confidence. Rather there has to be a restructuring of the economy. The less efficient firms have to go to the wall and their assets have to be devalued, allowing them to be bought up cheaply by their competitors. We get the *concentration* of capital into fewer and fewer hands. The production process itself has to be rationalised. Smaller and older inefficient plants are closed down so that we get the *centralisation* of capital into larger units based on the latest technology, and here the government might take an active part in industrial rationalisation as in the case of British Leyland where, at the time of writing, there are plans to close several plants and to lay off up to a quarter of the labour force. But this dog-eat-dog behaviour does not just go on within industries. Whole industries may be threatened. Because the point about capitalist crisis, as opposed to a cyclical slump, is that it affects the capitalist *world* economy. The signs began to appear in the mid-1960s, first of all in those countries with the least efficient industry like Britain and Italy, but later generalised to all the capitalist industrialised economies; inflation, unemployment, falling profitability and growth rates, industrial unrest. Thus, for instance, the shipbuilding industry in Britain is in competition with the Japanese, etc., and if the British industry collapses, as has largely been the case, then whole regions are threatened with economic decline. Indeed regions such as the Northeast of England which were economically devastated in the crisis of the 1930s still have not fully recovered. Of particular concern to Britain in the present crisis is the state of whole sections of manufacturing industry whose imminent collapse threatens to turn the industrial Midlands, indeed the whole of the northern part of the UK, into an economic wasteland. It is the severity of the crisis that has thrown orthodox economic theory into disarray. The Keynesian postmortem of the 1930s identified the virus as insufficient effective demand, and the carrier as parasitic speculators, with the patient suffering from a generic tendency for the marginal efficiency of capital to decline which lowered its resistance to infection. Still, as long as the economy was placed in the intensive care of the government which regulated both the effective demand and the rate of interest, there should be no reason why heart flutters should develop into seizures. But in the late 1960s and 1970s when the economy failed to respond to treatment, and indeed displayed hitherto unimagined symptoms of inflation *and* unemployment, or what came to be known as 'stagflation', economists retreated into *ad hoc* explanations; first it was due entirely to rising wages and then later to both rising wages and rising commodity, particularly oil, prices. But it is the failure of the prevailing orthodoxy of Keynesianism to provide plausible explanations and therefore viable policies, which has set the scene for a return to pre-Keynesian economic thought and a revival of the explanations offered for economic depression in the early 1930s in the form of monetarism. We are once again in a world of inherent stability, and if we are knocked off course by exogenous factors such as ignorant workers who believe that they can increase their welfare through their bargaining strength, or greedy Arabs who try to hold the industrialised world to ransom, then as long as the government removes obstacles to price flexibility and promotes competition, sooner or later we will be back in the land of prosperity. It is a vision that becomes real as long as you have the faith, but also provides a cover for massive deflation or repression or both. For Marxists the stakes are inevitably higher. It is the very continued existence of capitalism as a system which must be questioned. Capitalist crisis is at one and the same time the result of too much capital and too little capital; too much capital in relation to the production of surplus value and too little capital to produce sufficient surplus value.

As it is, massive deflation may resolve the crisis for a while as capital is devalued and the rate of profit jacked up, but the rising unemployment, the consequent dirth of effective demand, and the collapse of confidence in financial markets will make recovery a long haul. In the crisis of the 1930s full employment only came about with the onset of the Second World War. At one level therefore, the speed of recovery will be determined by the lifetime of the capital equipment still in use, with new investment creating a multiplier effect and leading to increased confidence and an expansion of economic activity. But in this discussion we have abstracted somewhat from social relations. We have not translated the crisis into human terms. Bankruptcy and financial collapse mean unemployment, people fighting for the right to work, trade unionism in defence of living standards, whole areas in economic decline, decline in social services, the decay of inner city areas, an increase in crime, riots etc. In short, an increase in the level of class struggle. And the outcome cannot be predicted. If the organised working class is relatively weak or is being side-tracked into a reformist cul-de-sac and therefore is unable to protect and further its interests, then it will suffer and capitalism may be allowed to restructure itself for another round of accumulation. Alternatively, resistance may be met by repression leading to defeat and the institution of a right wing or militaristic regime. But increasingly the continued development of the forces of production and therefore the continued development of social productivity is incompatible with and held back by production for profit. 'The real barrier of capitalist production is *capital itself...* The means – unconditional development of the productive forces of society – comes continually into conflict with the limited purpose, the self-expansion of the existing capital' (Marx 1972: 250). Whether and when this conflict will lead to the expropriators being expropriated by a working class – a class in itself – which has become a revolutionary class – a class for itself – is an open question, but one which is discussed further in chapter nine.

8.5 Monitoring myths about Marxism

The previous four sections of this chapter have attempted to set out the main elements of the abstract labour theory of value. In so doing, we hope that many common myths and misconceptions about the theory have been dispelled. But just in case some of the misconceptions still linger, this section briefly discusses and dispels some of the major misconceptions. As we pointed out in the first section, Marx and his theories are probably the most widely discussed but least understood of all theories about society. The purpose of this section is to attempt to remove some of the misunderstandings, rather than to discuss the more 'advanced' debates in and around Marxism. (For the latter, the reader is referred to 'Further reading' sections for this chapter and for Chapter 10). These then are some of the major misconceptions about Marxist theories and brief counters:

1. *There is no demand in Marx's theory – only production – there is; it is an integral part of the theory – the reader should refer back to section 8.2 or failing that read the five or so pages of Ch. 1, sect. 1 of Vol. I of Capital* (Marx 1970).
2. *There is no money in Marx* – there is: Marx distinguishes between money and money-capital; and there are long sections on these in *Capital* – see Ch. 3 of Vol. I, Chs. 1, 4, and 18 in Vol. II, and Ch. 19, and 21–36 of Vol. III. For our (necessarily brief) treatment, see parts of 8.2, 8.3 and 8.4.
3. *Marx was a monetarist* – this is the argument of those who, having discovered that Marx did treat money and money-capital at some length have gone overboard and classified Marx as a monetarist. We patiently refer the impatient reader to the references above.
4. *Marx said that labour is the source of all wealth – it obviously isn't –* Marx did *not* say that labour is the source of all wealth. In fact he criticised the draft 'Gotha' programme of the German Workers Party when it advanced this argument (labour being the source of all wealth and culture). Marx argued, in his critique, that: 'labour is *not the source* of all wealth. *Nature* is just as much the source of use values (and it is surely of such that material wealth consists!) as labour. . .' (Marx 1972a: 8; Marx's emphases).
   But although labour is not the sole source of wealth (i.e. *use value*), it *is* the sole source of *value*. The formulation of the Gotha Programme confuses the two, and Marx criticised this confusion, because only by recognising the dual nature (use value and exchange value) of the commodity, can there be a basis for an analysis of, and attack on surplus value.
5. *The abstract labour theory of value cannot deal with monopolies* – for example, '. . .the labour theory of value rests on the assumption of free competition, and very little can be said about a world of monopolies' (Howard and King 1975: 166). Of course, the whole of

the abstract labour theory can be said to be based on one particular monopoly, namely a class monopoly of the means of production, but here Howard and King are referring to monopolies in circulation. But the Marxist theory is a dialectical one in which monopolies are continually appearing and being broken down. This is why market prices are rarely equal to prices of production and why absolute ground rent and other supernormal profits exist, but precariously.

6. *There is no theory of prices in Marx* – it is true, as we have stressed, that the derivation of prices is not the prime aim of the abstract labour theory, the main objective being the analysis of the dynamic of capitalism and of price formation by viewing capitalism at two levels – at the level of appearance (prices) and at the level of social relations (values). Nevertheless to say what determines prices *is* a theory of prices.

7. *Marx forecast the immiseration of the working class – he was wrong* – He wasn't – in the context of the references to the immiseration of the working class, Marx may have been stressing the *relative* impoverishment of the working class in a material sense – that is as wages rise in terms of use values, the proportion of total social wealth controlled by capital rises at least as fast. Or he may have been stressing the relative impoverishment in a cultural sense – that is, as wages rise, again in terms of use values, the cultural conditions of the working class deteriorate relative to their expectations or relative to those of capitalists.

8. *Marx forecast that the rate of profit would fall continuously – it hasn't* – He didn't – refer back to section 8.4 for a discussion of the *tendency* of the rate of profit to fall.

9. *Marx forecast that all countries would develop – they haven't* – In saying this, the preface by Marx to the first German edition of Volume I of *Capital* is often quoted, namely: 'The country that is more developed industrially only shows, to the less developed, the image of its own future' (Marx 1970: 8, 9). This is a matter of some controversy, often taking the form of a dialogue of the deaf, since invariably the *standard* of development is not specified. The context of the above quote from Volume I was a discussion of the laws of capitalist production and the spread of the capitalist mode of production. Marx was not referring to liberal notions of equality, or welfare. Indeed in the same context of the Preface, he went on to say that the less developed countries (he was referring, among others, to Germany) 'suffer not only from the development of capitalist production, but also from the incompleteness of that development' (Marx 1970: 9).

10. *The abstract labour theory predicts that capitalism will breakdown – it hasn't* – This is not what the theory predicts – what it *does* say is that capitalism is prone to crisis, that the resolution of one crisis

leads to another, and that there is a fundamental contradiction in capitalism between the social nature of production and the private nature of appropriation.

Further reading

An obvious starting point for the study of the abstract labour theory of value is Marx's three-volume *Capital* (Marx 1970, 1970a and 1972). But the student is likely to find this hard going, and will find little consolation in Marx's caveat in a preface to Vol. I, that: 'Every beginning is difficult, holds in all sciences' (Marx 1970: 7); unfortunately the beginning of *Capital*, its first chapter, is, as Marx admits in the same preface, particularly difficult. It is difficult to recommend particular sections of *Capital* but, of the 2200 or so pages in the English Lawrence and Wishart edition, the following bits are likely to be of more interest to the newcomer to Marx:

Volume I; Chs. 1 to 8, 11, 12, 16, and 26 to 33:
Volume II; Chs. 4 and 18:
Volume III; Chs. 13 to 15, 20 and 48 to 52.

These extracts total a mere 470 pages or so! In the same preface quoted above Marx says: 'I presuppose, of course, a reader who is willing to learn something new and therefore to think for himself' (Marx 1970: 8); but the reader, (including the female seemingly excluded by this quote), may find it easier to think for him/herself by first looking at other people's presentations of the labour theory or at shorter pieces by Marx. In the latter category, Marx's address to the General Council of the First International in 1865 is likely to be easier – it is certainly shorter – than *Capital*. The address delivered two years before, but published after the first publication of Vol. I of *Capital*, is titled *Value, Price and Profit* (or *Wages, Price and Profit* – Marx 1973).

In our experience one of the best discussions of the abstract labour theory is still Paul Sweezy's *The Theory of Capitalist Development* (1968) first published in 1942. The latter was somewhat of an oasis in a barren Marxist inter-war period. After a flourishing debate around 1917 through the writings of Lenin, Luxemburg, Hilferding, Bukharin, Preobrazhensky and Trotsky, the suppression of political debate in the Soviet Union and the rise of fascism in Germany made for a sterile inter-war period as concerns writings in the Marxist mould. It was not until well after the Second World War with the end of anti-communist MacCarthyism in the USA, of Stalinist orthodoxy in the USSR, and with the rise of national liberation movements in colonies and neo-colonies that there was a revival in 'Marxist economics'. Among the recent presentations and discussions in English of the abstract labour theory of value and for references to concepts and terms which we have used, but with which the reader may struggle, we recommend Ben Fine's (1975) brief *Marx's Capital*. Fine and Harris's 1979 *Rereading Capital* deals more in detail with points of debate among Marxists and, although highly recommended, should only be read, as should Armstrong, Glyn and Harrison (1978) after a basic understanding of the abstract labour theory has been obtained. For this, apart from Sweezy (1968) and Fine (1975), you may find Harrison (1978) useful.

For a potted history of socialist economic thought, the *Manifesto of the Communist Party* by Marx and Engels (1975) is better than the longer, and somewhat disjointed book by Hardach, Karras and Fine (1978). *A Short History of Socialism* by Lichtheim (1978) places Marx and his theory in historical context, as does Marx's own, much longer, *Theories of Surplus Value* (1969).

As we suggested at the beginning of this chapter, the best biography of Marx is, we think, Nicolaievsky and Maenchen-Helfen, (1976), followed by McLellan (1976) and Blumenberg (1972).

For Marx's method and modes, look at the early sections of Marx and Engels' *German Ideology* (1974), or better still at Marx's *Contribution* (especially the Preface), (1970). Also for methods and models, useful references are Ch. 1 of Howard and King, (1975) (but avoid the other chapters), and the two excellent little books by George Thomson (1975 and 1976). The reader should then be well prepared for the Frank/Laclau debate (see Frank 1969: Ch. 1 and Laclau 1971) on capitalism and feudalism in Latin America.

For the philosophical antecedents to Marx, Chapter 3 of Riazonov (1973) is a simple introduction. For other references, see the Further Reading for Chapter 1 and Thompson (1978) which includes a passionate and amusing attack on the French marxist Althusser.

There is no good treatment of the role of money in the abstract labour theory outside of Marx and, perhaps, Rosdolsky 1977 (Part Two). Brunhoff (1976) is not helpful, but we have found Ergas and Fishman, (1975), useful after reading, say, Ch. 3, of *Capital*, Vol. I, (Marx 1970).

On the labour process, apart from Marx (1970), refer to Braverman (1974), and reviews and critiques of Braverman, especially Brighton Group (1977), and Friedman A. (1977). Also refer to *Capital and Labour* edited by Theo Nichols, (Nichols 1980).

On the transformation problem, see Baumol (1974) and compare Ch. 2 of Fine and Harris (1979) and Steedman (1977). On the tendency for the rate of profit to fall start with Ch. 8 of Fine (1975), then go on to Ch. 4 of Fine and Harris (1979) and Ch. 26 and the Appx. to Part 5 of Rosdolsky (1977). By this time you will either be fascinated or bored out of your mind with the topic. If the former, then look at the relatively advanced (and recent) debate in the *Cambridge Journal of Economics* (see especially Shaikh (1978) and (1980) and Steedman (1980). And, after these, Steedman (1975) might usefully be read.

For theories of capitalist crisis, refer Fine (1975: Ch. 8), Fine and Harris (1979: Ch. 5), and Sweezy (1968). On distribution (interest, rent and profit-as-enterprise) see Ch. 9 of Fine's *Capital* (Fine 1975). More specifically, on interest, see Harris (1976) and on rent see Murray (1977/78). For references to the state and fractions of capital, see Further Reading for Chapter 9.

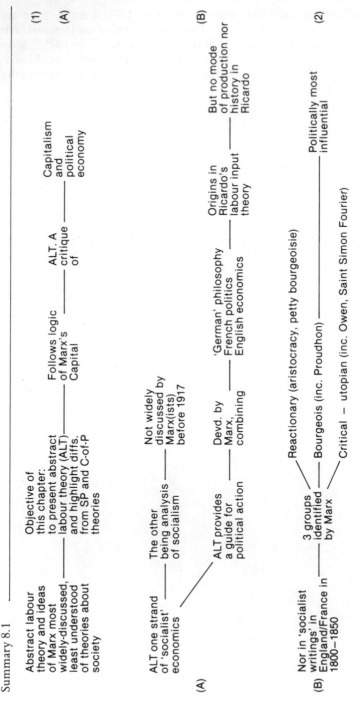

Summary 8.1

Summary 8.1 (Cont.)

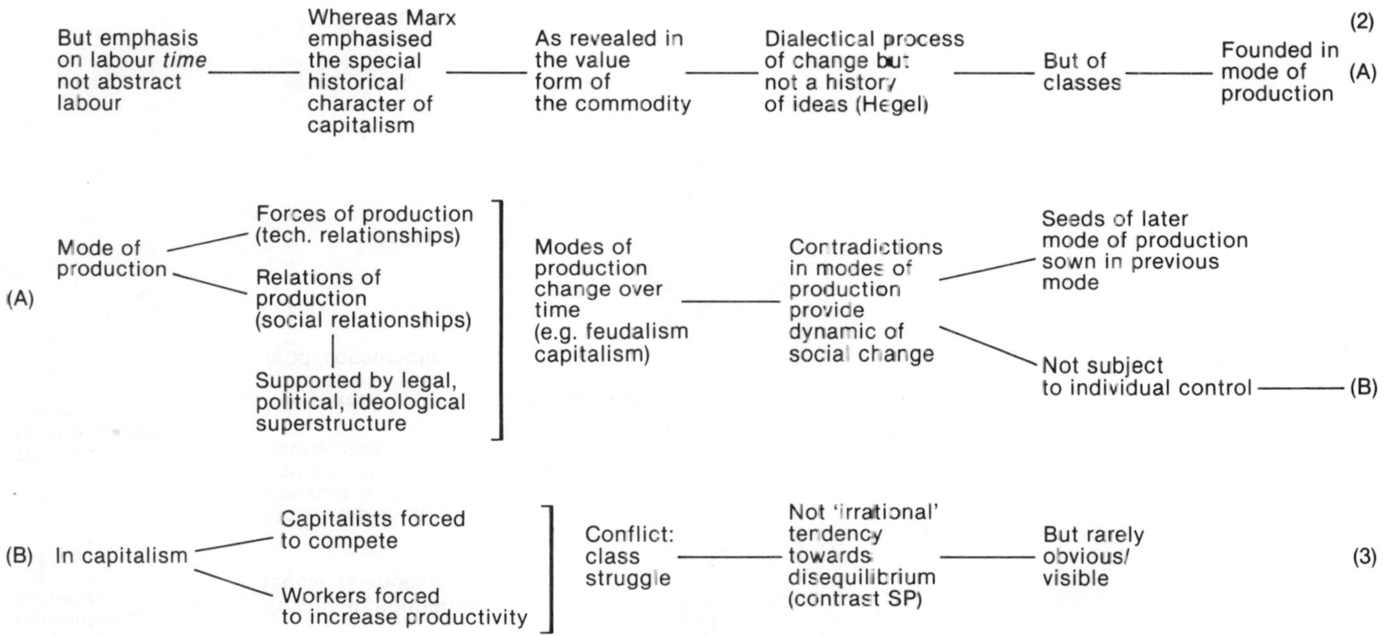

But emphasis on labour *time* not abstract labour —— Whereas Marx emphasised the special historical character of capitalism —— As revealed in the value form of the commodity —— Dialectical process of change but not a history of ideas (Hegel) —— But of classes —— Founded in mode of production (A)

(2)

(A) Mode of production

- Forces of production (tech. relationships)
- Relations of production (social relationships)
- Supported by legal, political, ideological superstructure

Modes of production change over time (e.g. feudalism capitalism) —— Contradictions in modes of production provide dynamic of social change —— Seeds of later mode of production sown in previous mode

Not subject to individual control —— (B)

(B) In capitalism

- Capitalists forced to compete
- Workers forced to increase productivity

Conflict: class struggle —— Not 'irrational' tendency towards disequilibrium (contrast SP) —— But rarely obvious/visible

(3)

Summary 8.1 (Cont.)

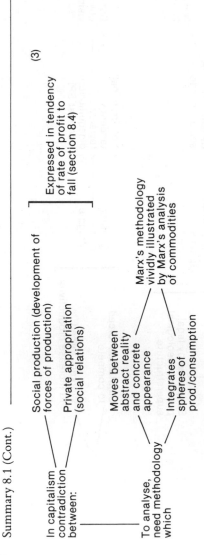

In capitalism contradiction between:

Social production (development of forces of production)

Private appropriation (social relations)

(3) Expressed in tendency of rate of profit to fall (section 8.4)

To analyse, need methodology which

Moves between abstract reality and concrete appearance

Integrates spheres of prod./consumption

Marx's methodology vividly illustrated by Marx's analysis of commodities

Summary 8.2

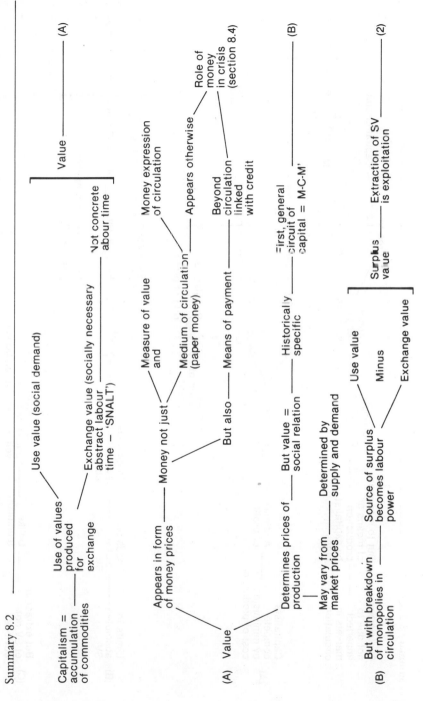

Summary 8.2 (Cont.)

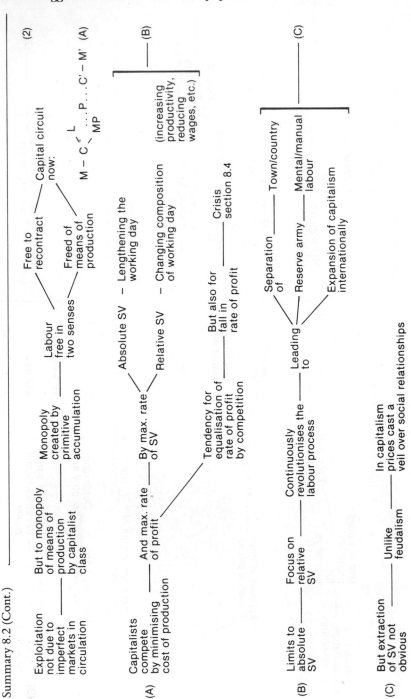

Summary 8.3

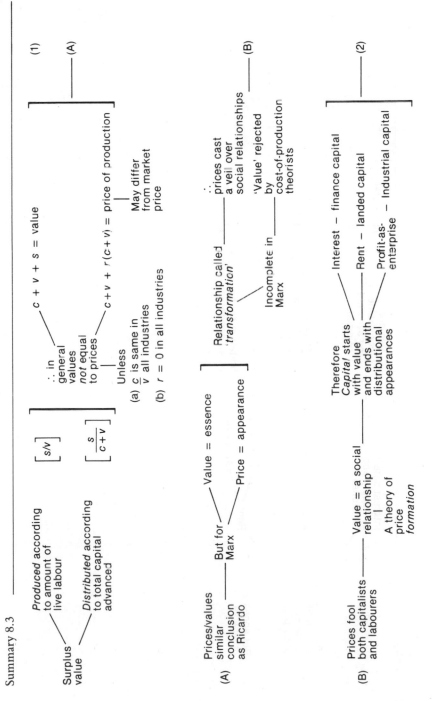

Summary 8.3 (Cont.)

(2)

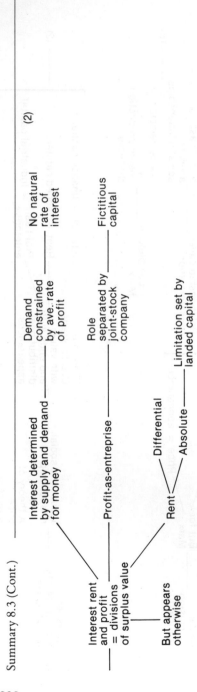

Interest determined
by supply and demand ——— Demand —— No natural
for money   constrained   rate of
                         by ave.. rate   interest
                         of profit

Profit-as-entreprise —— Role ——————— Fictitious
                       separated by   capital
                       joint-stock
                       company

Rent —— Differential

     —— Absolute —— Limitation set by
                    landed capital

Interest rent
and profit
= divisions
of surplus value

But appears
otherwise

Summary 8.4

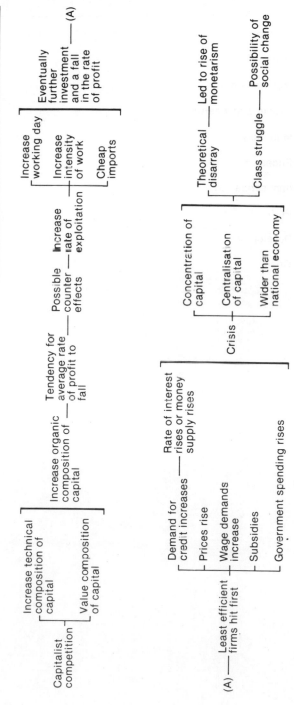

Summary 8.5 _____

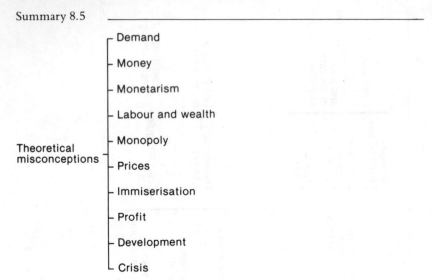

Theoretical misconceptions
- Demand
- Money
- Monetarism
- Labour and wealth
- Monopoly
- Prices
- Immiserisation
- Profit
- Development
- Crisis

Chapter 9

State power:
Policy and abstract labour theory

9.1 Communists' manifestos

Marx and Engels wrote a Communist manifesto in 1848 which looked critically at the capitalist system *and* its major adversaries. Their scorn for contemporary 'utopian socialists', who looked for the voluntary removal of poverty on moral grounds or sought to establish a new society on the basis of artisan and peasant production, stands in contrast to their respect for the dynamism of unfettered capitalism. Their manifesto was not a submission to an electorate but a cry for people in the working class to build a revolutionary movement to overthrow the existing social order and utilise its immense productive potential in their own interest. Capitalism's continuing tendency to crisis provides the conditions for overthrow and the organisation of the working class is the instrument. The resulting tension between the inevitability of crisis, suggesting that the collapse of capitalism was pre-determined, and the continuing nature of crisis, suggesting that the overthrow was a matter of voluntary working-class will, has continued for almost 150 years. If capitalism is doomed to fail economically then what is the role of revolutionary political action? If capitalism is in continuing political tension then what is the role of the abstract labour theory of value?

It is the acceptance of the tension between the beliefs that capitalism is a progressive force for gaining control over the physical world, with a continuing tendency to socio-economic crisis only finally politically resolvable by and in the interests of a working class, which distinguishes a political movement we will call communism within a wide variety of socialist positions. By no means all people in this movement will be in formally titled Communist Parties, which have had a rather special history of their own. Therefore, we will use a small 'c' to talk generally about communists in this chapter and a capital 'C' only when talking about members of official Communist Parties. The room for disagreement in the communist movement is as wide as any other despite the rather monolithic, authoritarian image that the movement has often been given by its opponents. Disagreement on how far to support nationalist movements which appear to resist the spread of capitalist relations, disagreement on suitable critical conditions for radical change, disagreement on who are in the working class and what immediate alliances will best serve their interests, are only some of the points at issue within the communist movement. Agreement does exist among communists that capitalist crises put pressure on the working class at the work place. It is in the interests of an individual capital to reduce the direct labour cost per unit of output in every possible way in order to survive. And where groups of competing capitals can find a tentative coalition then that unity can only be against their workers, since any other basis will tend to benefit some capitals at the expense of others and lead to a breakdown of the coalition. Increasing hours without increasing real wages, increasing speed of work without material compensation and little regard to safety, decreasing real wages directly, dismissing more militant and slower workers, all suit the interests of particular capitals in their struggle for survival and, in total, add up to an assault on all the people in the working class. To protect themselves against these pressures, groups of workers have formed trade unions and it is to be expected that communists would be active in such organisations. Trade unions are the first line of collective defence against the attempts of capital to reduce the relative position of workers. In the power struggle between the working class and capital in general, the trade union movement has often exercised a temporary veto on resolving crises straightforwardly in the interests of capital. But it is only the power of the veto and serves merely to deflect the crisis into new forms, such as mass unemployment, inflation, political repression, imperialism and war, rather than resolve it in the interests of working class people.

A common communist response to this failure has been to attempt to politicise the trade union movement. Under the broad strategic title of syndicalism, communists have worked in many countries to unite trade unions into one big union and push forward with a political programme with the end of setting up factory Workers' Councils, following a General Strike. The limits of syndicalism were examined in the first twenty years of the twentieth century when the difficulties of uniting the sections of the trade union movement were combined with unexpectedly ferocious propaganda and physical violence from employers and the State. The foremost writer on these limitations was Antonio Gramsci (1968) who played a prominent role in the Turin factory occupations in Italy. Nevertheless, the strike and the work-in still offer examples of working people acting directly in a way which seems more significant than in the electoral booth and the political demonstration. The official trade union leadership may constitute an obstacle but their opposition can be dismissed by communists as the self-interest of well-paid time-servers who have lost touch with their members. Thus, communists are always likely to be active in trade unions but, in trying to bend the defensive tendencies of these organisations towards revolutionary ends, they have always met considerable resistance in the workplace as well as the union headquarters. Trade unions would be weaker without communists certainly, but they are not the tools of communists. To prefer a communist shop steward for standing up to management is certainly not equivalent to wanting that communist as the manager. The relationship between communists and fellow trade unionists has had tensions which are felt in the West and in the East. Effective trade unions are an important base for communists and the defence and extension of trade unions' rights is an important policy goal, but the struggle for fundamental change has forced communists into the more formal political sphere.

For communists, the State in capitalist society is essentially little different from that in previous types of societies. The State in every society has been primarily the collective expression of the dominant class interest, providing both the legitimation and coercion necessary to maintain that dominant class as a ruling class. The capitalist State in all its forms is essentially the same, constructed with difficulty out of the competing demands of individual capitals, whose common interests are discovered in the struggle with other classes and other groups of capitals. For instance, the free operation of markets is always in the interests of more successful capitals and thus the use of alternative means of allocating resources will find opposition, unless a threat to several capitals exists by a rising working class, an entrenched aristocracy or a group of capitals which have sunk their differences sufficiently to present a united front to exclude others. In all cases the limits of conciliation are soon reached and violence results. The institutions through which such alliances of capitals carry out attempts at conciliation and violence constitute the State.

Thus, if communism is about the transfer of power from capitals to workers, the State is an obvious arena for action, involving a head-on collision between the collective violence of capital-in-general and the militant organisation of the working class. In contrast to syndicalism and its emphasis on struggle in factories, the perspective that emphasises the struggle over control of institutions other than factories can be called Statism. Two problems of this strategy are immediate. Firstly, the struggle is fought on the class enemy's own chosen ground, where the ability to exercise violence against opposition is most legitimated and concentrated. Secondly, the definition of the State is broad and includes institutions like the family and the church as well as more obvious, formidable targets like the police, military and communication systems. The major temptations of the strategy are that the means to success can be found in an alliance with social democrats and the ends of success are direct shifts in formal power.

Social democrats see an active, interventionist State as a vital instrument to the success of capitalism and emphasise the planning role of the State in providing incentives and guidance to individual capitals and redistributing consumption from the affluent to the deprived. Communists see an active, interventionist State as a vital instrument in the defeat of capitalism and emphasise the planning role of the State in directing production enterprises as the expression of a redistribution of power between classes. Thus the alliance between social democrats and communists is possible, although very tense, with communists being more aware of the necessity for violence in bringing about social change. For communists, welfare measures and planning agreements alone are as likely to be concessions to capital to ensure the reproduction of the work-force and the restructuring of industry to restore overall profitability as they are victories for the working class. This concentration on the repressive, rather than the welfare and economic rationalising, functions of the State has distinguished communists from social democrats since Marx's own time, although the precise content has changed over the years.

These limitations to trade unionism and social democracy were critically analysed early in this century by V. I. Lenin in his pamphlet *What is to be done* (Lenin 1975), in which he arrived at the conclusion that the interest of the working class would be best served by the creation of a Communist Party, which would be able to resist coercion and intimidation by being highly selective in membership (a cadre Party), and secretive in organisation (a Party organised in cells, literally in some cases). The extent of the Party would match the extent of the State in geography, propaganda and level of violence. Lenin's analysis suggested that capitalism had certainly become a world system in the early twentieth century, a consolidation marked by the First World War. However, the revolution in Russia and the failure of that revolution to spread to Germany left the Communist Party of the new USSR with the social and industrial organisation of a relatively underdeveloped capitalist country, isolated and surrounded by enemies. The development of other national Communist Parties between the two World Wars was therefore dominated in organisation by the Communist Party of the USSR and in tactics by protecting the interests of the young USSR. Only after the Second World War with the consolidation of the USSR as a major world military power, the partial split with Yugoslavia, the repudiation of some of Stalin's inheritance and the complete break with China, did disagreements among communists become public again. But during the 1960s and 1970s the debate among communists became politically highly significant. Communists played disproportionately major roles in many anti-colonial political struggles and, in several cases, appeared to achieve real power in setting up States under an explicit Marxist-Leninist banner in places as far apart as Cuba, Vietnam and Mozambique. Also world capitalism appeared economically very vulnerable in the late 1970s with no major capitalist economy looking as strong in 1980 as it had in 1970. And lastly, capitalism was again becoming noticeably more domestically repressive and internationally violent in the late 1970s without apparently succeeding in inspiring a whole-hearted moral revival on the basis of a rediscovered rugged individualism. Capitalism appeared vulnerable and, even if it was as unlikely to end in a whimper as in a very big bang, communists were active on a world scale in trade unions, political parties and communication media, albeit often prosecuted, but also often close to power.

The opportunity appeared great, but so were the divisions. The two major countries led by Communist Parties were deeply hostile to each other and in other countries communists were criticising each other as much as they were criticising social democrats and conservatives who would appear to be more basic opponents. The combination of capitalism and communism in crises has an irony which perhaps can best be understood in communist terms by looking at the history of both in their relationship with each other. To summarise these histories it is useful to recall the three general maxims of Marx in debates with his contemporary socialists. Firstly, the development of competitive capitalism is generally progressive. Secondly, capitalism develops in an international fashion unevenly, but leaving no relationship untouched. Thirdly, the working class are the leaders of the anti-capitalist struggle, but other struggles will occur within capitalism because of the enormous tensions as capitalist relations develop.

Communists can always disagree about whether the potential of capitalism has been fulfilled. Whilst no communist can stand aloof from political action it may be valid to align with competitive producing capitalists against the broad monopolistic spectrum, including feudal landowners, merchants and moneylenders, who all seek to restrict markets in their own interests, individually and collectively. The anti-colonial and subsequent anti-imperialist struggle can be viewed in this light and the prominence of communists in these struggles has owed much to this interpretation. In those countries where communists have achieved political office then the progressive nature of capitalism raises questions about the relationships with outside individual capitals and the degree to which these relationships should be market relationships. Lastly, in the countries where capitalism has developed longest without a colonial period or a period of communist rule then the question is raised about how far the progressive nature of capitalism includes political and cultural aspects. Relatively liberal politics and generally tolerant cultures have developed in several countries in which capitalism has existed longest. Are these advances for communists to build upon or the short-lived flowers of privileged decadence in societies which materially are falling behind!

Certainly for most people in the past five hundred years capitalism has been a repressive, violent experience, especially as we look at the extension of capitalism on a world scale. But the experience of capitalism has differed from place to place and the movements to resist the most violent effects of capitalism have often taken on a local form, stressing shared identity of religion, ethnicity or race rather than class interests. In the early years of this century, Lenin reconciled nationalism and communism in his pamphlet *The Rights of Nations to Self-Determination* (Lenin 1976). Lenin argued that, in a capitalist world, local struggles for autonomy should always be politically supported because they either directly advanced capitalism or advanced communism against the monopolistic tendencies of the powerful capitalist centres. This fitted with his arguments on *Imperialism* (Lenin 1969) which raised the limitations of political internationalism, even though capital tended to be totally internationally mobile. But the tension between an international political perspective and a concentration on meeting capitals on a predominantly national level leaves much room for debate in the communist movements, especially around the inter-war slogan of building 'socialism in one country'.

Lenin's model of the cadre, secretive Party as the instrument of working class political expression has also come under discussion. Those who regard it as an appropriate form for a relatively small number of factory workers in tsarist Russia may have grave doubts about its universal applicability. In its relationships with trade unions, local political initiatives and state officials the Party has often proved to be a dubious instrument for allowing effective expression to, or exerting firm control on behalf of, people whose working class background appears impeccable. On the other hand, no other form of communist political organisation has been capable of gaining power in the face of widespread, violent opposition. Opposition which still may involve a majority of the population in most countries where only a minority of people work in factories for wages. The experience of Chile in the early 1970s when a broad-based elected socialist government was violently deposed and its president and many supporters murdered will continue to condition much communist thinking on the 'parliamentary road to socialism'.

Thus in 1981 there is a great deal of debate among communists about the means needed to advance working class interests in the current capitalist crisis. At one pole are the Eurocommunists who consistently tend to argue that the existing political system in Western Europe is both desirable and robust, that nationalism is compatible with communism, and that the effective representation of working class people must rest on their political party gaining the respect and confidence of many people who are not obviously working class in their experience. At the other extreme are the Cubans who see capitalism as inherently violent in its politics, stress internationalism and solidarity in the communist movement and look to the cadres of the Communist Party for active leadership as the vanguard of the working class. To understand the essential unity of the communist position requires us to return to the abstract labour theory of value and deduce the range of political options which can be derived from that theory.

9.2 From the abstract labour theory of value to communism

The relationship between communist politics and the abstract labour theory of value is direct and explicit. Not least because most leading communist politicians have also laid claim to roles as leading theoreticians. Marx, Engels, Kautsky, Lenin, Gramsci, Trotsky, Stalin and Mao Tse-tung are all known both for their political *and* their intellectual activities. This interweaving is not coincidental but demanded by the very nature of dialectical, historical materialism as a theory of knowledge, which includes action by the knower. Rigorous materialism means accepting that our sensory and neurological systems set the limits to what we can ever truly know about human existence. Any theory of human existence which explicitly assumes the existence of a being which cannot be seen, touched, heard, smelt or tasted by all human beings is obviously anti-materialist. More subtly, a theory like the subjective preference theory of value can be considered as non-materialist in so far as it implicitly assumes a God-given human nature, with inherent competitiveness as an expression of some original sin.

In comparison, abstract labour theory and cost-of-production theory do agree on the relative malleability of human nature responsive to changing material circumstances. However, they disagree on the emphasis to be placed on physical as opposed to social relationships. In abstract labour theory, the most important aspect of human experience is the complex, inescapable structure of power relationships which enmesh everyone from cradle to grave. Power relationships which can only be understood from a historical perspective. For cost-of-production theory, technical demands of physical production are fundamental and social relationships outside those demands are amenable to enlightened rational reform from above without much regard to previous historical precedent. The difference between the schools of economic thought is completed by the concept of the dialectical method. In simple terms at the level of thought, the dialectical method predicts the inevitability of constant criticism as every knowable concept is only intelligible in terms of its negation, which suggests that thought can never be at rest even in our deepest convictions because each conviction carries the knowledge of its opposite. In a more fundamentalist exposition, the dialectical method maintains that the social reality of human existence is in constant movement through conflict after conflict in which the direction of outcomes is finally, but not in detail, predetermined. No peace, no equilibrium, no super-rational agency is the unsettling message of materialist dialectics.

Marx, as the leading dialectical, historical materialist, made little distinction between a politician and an intellectual. The intellectual who accepts that 'being determines consciousness' is forced also to accept that any ideas which appear to be original are merely extensions of particular experiences and likely to be lagging, rather than leading, new complicated experience. But, even with these limitations, all human beings still have to make history, albeit 'not in conditions of their own choosing'. Intellectuals, like everyone else, have to make decisions which involve the future. These actions have to be undertaken on the basis of current experience imperfectly illuminated by the lessons of the past. Intellectuals have an advantage if they explain the world through logical thought in such a way that this act of so-called explanation has significance for action in the context of inevitable social change. If the task of worthwhile intellectual activity is 'to change the world', the only choice is in whose interest to change it. Dialectical historical materialism is a theory of knowledge which sees the human condition as a continual, unified process of change over which human beings can only exert influence within the constraints of their physical and social experience.

Thus, the nature of intellectual activity is to generalise and abstract from experience, to seek the unifying principle which explains the complex chaos of the concrete reality perceived by the senses in terms of logical relationships which form an intelligible abstract reality in the mind. The nature of political activity is sensitively to develop that abstract reality in the mind as a guide to action in new situations, in which the chaotic appearance has been diminished by the intellect. The desirable combination of these intellectual and political activities into a single process, we can call praxis. The intellectual aspect without the political we could call contemplation, which contains the danger of concepts in the mind becoming fixed and unquestioned categories defining concrete reality. The political without the intellectual we could call pragmatism, which contains the danger of action becoming aritrary and confused because it is derived from chaos. The test of good praxis is the ability to win through against strong, inevitable, and usually violent, opposition and learn from the experience.

For abstract labour theory the essential relationship which explains human experience on a world scale in the present epoch is the commodity relationship, as we have seen in Chapter 8. No other abstract reality in the mind has offered the breadth and depth of this concept for constructing political theory and action. From the concept of commodity production can be derived logical rules of exchange, a law of value. By generalising the concept of the commodity to include the ability of people to work, i.e. the buying and selling of labour power, we can conceive in our minds of a capitalist mode of production that will exist under certain historical conditions, especially a condition of unequal distribution of power over the means of production between groups of people and individuals. From the concept of a capitalist mode of production we can logically deduce that there will be constant tension which is likely to periodically erupt into crises, taking a variety of forms. We can start making suggestions about formal politics in capitalist society by putting forward the conflicts between workers and capitals; between capital and capital; between industrialists, rentier, landowners and merchants; and between manual and mental labour as struggles requiring the exercise of formal political control in specific institutions, if capitalist relations are to be reproduced. It is this logical derivation of politics that we shall concentrate on for the rest of this section.

The conflict between workers and capitals derived from abstract labour theory is summarised in the term exploitation. Exploitation abstractly summarises the peculiar nature of labour in capitalism, in that the exchange value of labour power (the general ability to work) is only the amount of commodities necessary socially to reproduce the labour force and this is likely to be less than the total amount of commodities that the labour force is able to produce if its labour power is fully used. The threat to the reproduction of this relationship can come from two directions. Firstly, a worker may be able qualitatively to opt out of the exchange of labour power with capital if the individual can gain control over other means of production. The need for political action to restrict mass desertion has been decreasing as the more easily cultivable areas of the world have been claimed. A plot of fertile land is one of the most obvious resources which can allow a wage worker to be free from the necessity to work on terms dictated by capital. Easily available credit and high social welfare benefits relative to the average cost of a workplace or average wage also constitute threats to capital-worker relations. In so far as social institutions exist to ensure that alternatives for workers are restricted other than to sell their labour power to capital, then those institutions are part of a capitalist state.

Secondly, and more commonly today, the actions of workers do not qualitatively threaten exploitation itself, but quantitatively tend to reduce the rate of exploitation. The dynamic nature of capitalism rests on the deduction that the law of value makes all individual capitals vulnerable to economic extinction. One way to limit this vulnerability is to put pressure on the work-force to work longer, harder and faster for a less than proportionate gain in reward. Analytically, this amounts to increasing the rate of exploitation, but practically it also constitutes an erosion of previous working conditions and thus constitutes a change for the worse in workers' experience, encouraging resistance. Now relations between workers and capitals are based on equality in exchange for the commodity, labour power. Thus, direct coercion is not a legitimate method of extracting surplus value at the level of the individual capital. This confinement of violence is important to capitalist development, otherwise confidence in all voluntary contracts including those between capitals would be undermined. Thus, specialist institutions are required to reduce the ability of workers to resist increases in the rate of exploitation in the interests of capital in general, especially if workers reach beyond the boundaries of their immediate employing individual capitals and present a challenge to the power of capital to set the conditions of work. Compared with some non-capitalist societies, capitalism appears to be qualitatively restricted in the use of coercion in terms of who may legitimately exercise violence against whom. But abstract labour theory leads to the conclusion that to survive, capitalist relations must involve violence in the general interests of capital against the collective interests of workers. To that extent capitalist society is a political dictatorship of capital and the essential nature of the capitalist State is violent, as for every State before it and even after.

Paradoxically, if the process of repressing workers becomes too successful, then a new problem about the reproduction of the capital-worker relationship may result. Whilst the survival of individual capitals is untouched by the death of individual workers, there is a point at which wholesale deaths due to the failure to gain employment or the pace and conditions of work may become threatening to capital in general. The reproduction of a healthy, skilled, well-disciplined work-force is in the interests of capital in general, even though not in the interest of individual capitals. The question of how far the work-force is reproduced through in-migration of new workers or protection of existing stocks of workers through health, education and unemployment benefits, depends upon the precise historical conditions. In all cases, the need for some institutions to act in the interests of capital in general is present, though not compulsive.

The rational behaviour of individual capitals produce disturbing tendencies for workers to desert, revolt and die, all three of which require responses at the level of capital in general if capitalist relations are to be reproduced. If the pattern of such responses is inappropriate at any point in history then a political crisis results. The mixture of policies subsequently adopted cannot be simply structurally or functionally predicted but depends on understanding the actual historical situation in its own right. What can be derived from abstract labour theory is that coercion by state institutions is likely to be an important factor, welfare concessions may be made without fundamentally altering power relationships, and that the continuing reproduction of basic capitalist relations is problematic but not impossible. The struggle between capitals and workers is important to understanding the nature of the capitalist state but not crucial to explaining crisis. To explain crisis we must understand the relationship between capitals. Competition between capitals, including processes of mechanisation and monopolisation, creates a continuing tension virtually independently of the actions of workers. As we saw in Chapter 8, if a competitor mechanises then probably this will reduce the minimum unit costs and increase the volume of production. Thus, there is a downward pressure on costs for everyone and a consequent downward pressure on prices, because the volume of commodities produced tends to increase relative to demand as self-defensive mechanisation proceeds. Two responses to this challenge are to block access to new technology and old demand outlets. The search for protection from competition is perpetual. Commodity exchange, as the basic relationship of capitalism, demands that economic relations are conducted freely and anonymously and thus protection is generally a political matter. Coercion is necessary if commodity exchange is to be locally restricted in capitalism. Coercion in capitalism tends to locate itself in institutions independent of individual capitals, institutions which are at the core of the capitalist state.

However, a capitalist state can only give support to one capital at the expense of other capitals. Such a policy will only be sustainable if these other capitals can be convinced it is also to their advantage for the State to intervene or they are forcibly excluded. If the first is not the case, then the legitimacy of the State is undermined and the interest of capital in general will express itself in a political movement to overthrow that government, even if this means destroying the privileged individual capitals it has represented. Situations in which State protection may be advantageous to large numbers of individual capitals can occur but are likely to be temporary and unstable. For instance, some manufactured inputs, like energy and transport, are used by many individual capitals and certainty in supply and stable prices can be guaranteed by political regulation. Also, some large industrial plants, like those producing vehicles, are the customers for the outputs of many individual capitals and certainty in demand and stable prices may be the derived result of State intervention. Lastly, many individual capitals operating in a particular area may find it desirable to protect themselves from outside competition by restricting access to the local labour force and markets. Thus state intervention in the economy is not ruled out by abstract labour theory, though it will always be controversial and fraught with tension.

But even if every local group of capitals has acquired a protective state, then the dynamic imperative of capitalism will flow over the boundaries, bringing capitals back into economic competition and states into political confrontation. The tendency to capitalist economic expansion is like a tide which flows around political obstacles initially, and in so doing undermines and reshapes them into a new, less obstructive, form. The strength of this largely invisible expansion is chiefly seen in the highly visible growth of military power needed to preserve the position of the most significant groupings of capitals on a world scale. Increasing productive ability means increasing capacity to produce destructive forces and thus the ability, and the temptation, violently to resist or initiate expansion grows with the pressure of economic competition. Also the production of weapons is an interface between so many individual capitals and the State, that the interests of capital in general appear to be economically better served by increasing State expenditure on weapons, than has ever seemed the case with State intervention in public utilities or giant manufacturing enterprises. Simultaneously being required to look outwards to defend and extend privileges for local capitals and inwards to provide guaranteed markets for their outputs, the capitalist State will tend to be a highly armed State. In this form, it will serve the interests of many capitals and offend few within its territory. Abstract labour theory alone cannot explain the historical formation and dissolution of nation-States but it does suggest that, in a world of such States, competition between capitals will take on political, and hence military forms, and not remain at the narrowly economic level.

Within the boundaries of particular States there is one further insight that abstract labour theory can give into the broad outlines of the politics of capitalism. Even after surplus value has been exploited from the workers and the State has provided some of the general conditions for the realisation of the surplus value in monetary form there still remains a struggle over the distribution between rent, interest and profits. This distribution is primarily decided at the political level as the abstract labour theory of value provides no necessary economic rules beyond the broad conclusion that when rent or interest grows at the expense of profits, then an accumulation crisis will be precipitated which must be resolved in the interest of profits, if capitalist relations are to be reproduced. In the nineteenth century, there was a struggle which resulted in the political eclipse of the rent-receiving, landowning interest in the centres of capitalist development. In the twentieth century, some aspects of politics can be understood as a reflection of the struggle between finance and industrial capital.

Finance capitals control the flow of credit and exact interest as the price of releasing that flow in one direction rather than another. The close association of credit with money, and the fact that it is in the interests of capital in general for the control of money to be vested in the State rather than individual capitals, tends to give finance capitals a close relationship with the State. But, if this relationship dominates politics then monetary and stock market crises will appear. Industrial capitals go bankrupt in the face of increasing interest charges and dividend payments. Charges, which are unrelated to the real ability to extract surplus value in production. The contrast between the political impotence and real economic power of industrial capital compared with the political influence and economic impotence of finance capital provides abstract labour theory with some insights into some of the forms of crisis in contemporary capitalist societies.

In Marx's own vivid terms it is 'the army that beats itself up at least' which wins the struggle in capitalist society. We have already seen that the distribution of surplus value brings tensions within capitalism which can give some insights into the nature of the capitalist state as an institution for reconciling conflicts within the dominant class. The question also arises about how far the division of the working class is also a matter conducive to action by institutions which form part of a State. Divisions between craft trade unions and a stress upon individual achievement, when fostered in legal and educational systems, are obvious examples of such activities. More subtle is the deeper structural division between manual and mental labour, a split between the conception and execution of tasks. To make that division politically effective seems to require differential messages being sent to different sections of the working class through the communications and educational media.

Communists have tried to conceptualise this situation in terms of 'false consciousness', a deceived section of the working class failing to know their own best interest, and 'agents of capital', which implies a more material interest in maintaining relative privileges. Neither of these rather conspiratorial formulations carries real conviction and a more satisfactory dialectical formulation is that most members of the working class have a real individual material interest in preserving their existing conditions for survival and a collective interest in fundamental change. The proportions in this mixture will vary from group to group in the working class and institutions which encourage the individual interest and repress the collective form part of the capitalist state. The tension around this contradiction, like all the other tensions we have outlined above, give some broad, rather abstract, insights into the politics of capitalism. But to be true to the dialectical historical materialist theory of knowledge which underpins the abstract labour theory of value requires the application of these insights to action in a particular historical situation. The next two sections attempt to complete that project in a critical fashion for the leading capitalist societies in the 1980s.

9.3 The communist response to crises in the 1980s

The implications of the abstract labour theory of value for politics point towards its various conflicts. Conflicts which express the economic struggles but whose specific forms cannot be simply reduced to the economic. Abstract labour theory predicts continuing tension and crisis in capitalist relations and therefore is not a good prediction of the precise forms in which crisis appears in any particular time and place. When an open crisis erupts from the deep tensions of capitalism, all abstract labour theory can predict is that the crisis will appear in every sphere of relationships and on a world scale. The position in 1981 corresponded to such a prediction, though the different forms that crisis took require both local analysis and local action by communists. For our purposes in this section we will concentrate on the situation in the countries of North America, Western Europe, Australia and Japan. This is not to dismiss the significance of activity in other parts of the world, for instance Central America and Poland in 1980 and 1981. That communists often appear to think internationally but primarily act nationally is an appropriate, if not totally satisfactory, rationale for accepting the limitation on coverage we set here.

Governments were chosen in the late 1970s in these countries by mass electorates on the basis of manifestos which were dominated by claims offering superior economic management. Other prominent issues were law and order and the role of trade unions, reflecting wider tensions in other spheres, and we shall look at these issues in the next section. The dominant criteria for assessing economic management in 1980 were still those of the post-Keynesian debates, price inflation, registered unemployment, the balance of international trade and growth of National Income. But in 1980 the choice seemed to come down to the issue of whether price inflation or registered unemployment was the most important policy goal. The communist perspective on this apparent choice was that the working class were merely being offered a choice between methods of execution. An emphasis on reducing registered unemployment would mean accepting rises in retail prices at the expense of wages and thus restoring profitability. The reverse of emphasising the control of inflation would mean accepting higher registered unemployment and a consequent decline in the bargaining power of the remaining workers. Any attempt to tackle both unemployment and inflation simultaneously would destroy immobile local capitals and lead to the desertion of more mobile capitals to more profitable locations. The government could then face an international payments crisis compounded by a budgetary crisis if it attempted to maintain high employment through its own activities.

In practice, the efforts of any government which accepted the basic terms of capitalism would probably result in an unplanned mix of price rises and unemployment as a result of much trial and error, but a mix which would tend to restore local profitability and reincorporation of the economy in a new niche in the world capitalist system on terms relatively attractive to internationally mobile capitals. The real losers would be the working class whose aggregate material affluence and, more importantly, power to influence events would have declined in the face of restored profitability. The only alternative would then be to return to work on the terms of capital and struggle for a share in the rewards of any subsequent local economic growth. Thus governments can only choose the forms of the crisis to some degree, they do not choose whether there is a crisis or not. The problem for communists is whether that choice matters and, if it does, then what side should they support.

On one side are those communists who consider that confrontation should be forced. Let right wing political forces have the government and the communists will gain the people in the end. On the other side are those who urge that a government to the left of the centre will choose a form of crisis conducive to building a working class movement capable of taking power when the government's policies prove inadequate. This division was present in the communist movement through the inter-war period when a number of shifts in policy occurred which in retrospect can be seen as failing to produce a politically effective working class movement anywhere outside the USSR. Generally, the communist movement in the most affluent capitalist societies has accepted the desirability of working with reformist political movements recently and rejected the proposition that the immiserisation of the working class is conducive to a shift of power away from capital.

However, the question of what policies communists themselves should adopt on achieving political office is still a problem. The system of generalised commodity production with all its economic, cultural and political ramifications and more than two hundred years of history behind it cannot be dismissed by a prime ministerial declaration. Communists challenge the capitalist law of value as the determinant of human relations, but that challenge requires tactical decisions about what priority relationships should be given in the sequence of changes. The abstract labour theory of value says that the relationships of capitalism are generally market relationships in which equivalents are exchanged. For our purposes we will classify these markets into groups: financial markets where the medium of exchange is traded; investment markets where the capacity to produce on a large scale is created; international markets where commodities and labour cross borders; consumer goods markets where the mass of the population obtain the means of social survival; the market for labour power where people sell their ability to work under given conditions of speed, duration, consultation and safety. Each type of market has a claim to first priority, which we shall examine now.

In subjective preference and cost-of-production theories the central importance of money is stressed as a primary factor in economic decision-making. Money, in one or other of its forms, is present in virtually all relationships and banks, as institutions, stand at the central nodes of whole networks of transactions. Throughout the history of communist thought there has been a love-hate relationship with money. Money as a concept epitomises commodity-fetishism and the inability of people in capitalist society to see through its veil to the concealed, real human relationships. Thus, the abolition of money is a recurring slogan in communist writing. But money also is a major instrument of the massive resource mobilisation in capitalist society. Seizing control over the financial system may then be a necessary, if insufficient, condition for taking power away from capital in general. The possibility of an alliance with radical social democrats on state control over the banking system also exists. However, the fundamental disagreement on whether state control is aimed at aiding or attacking capitalism would undoubtedly emerge in policy decisions.

Closely linked to the money markets are the markets for investment and the associated direct links between capitals for obtaining produced inputs and spreading innovations. Abstract labour theory locates the primary cause of crisis close to these markets. Capitalist accumulation finds its most obvious physical expression in the increasing use of complex machinery. The imperative to develop new machinery and put it into operation comes from competition between capitals struggling against each other to survive. When the crisis deepens, the problem of a slow-down in accumulation appears as a breakdown in relationships between capitals, that is as a failure of investment markets. Bankruptcies and lack of innovation are aspects of this failure and indicate to communists the end of the progressive role of capitalism in developing human control over the physical environment. In such circumstances, communists can claim to be able to break through the stagnation by abolishing the anarchy of capitalist accumulation, replacing it by planned socialist accumulation. The practical attraction of this policy is that centralisation and concentration of manufacturing capitals has now proceeded to the point where it appears that taking direct control over the investment decisions of a few dozen capitals will give control over the whole process of accumulation.

For any local communists close to taking power, one problem of a transition period is the desertion of capitals to outside capitalist states. This desertion may take the physical form of removing existing productive capacity, or the location of new productive capacity elsewhere and simply closing down local factories, or selling factories at low prices to speculators who will simply use the equipment until it is physically rundown or economically uncompetitive, and taking the financial proceeds out in the form of foreign currency. This process, plus the risk of a boycott by individual capitals, who supply imports and will often have a threatened stake in the local economy, has led many communists to stress the need to control international markets for investment, finance and consumer goods. The model derived from the experience of the USSR, of 'socialism in one country', evoking the image of a siege economy, is less relevant now that there are Communist Parties in office in many countries. But the language of 'planned trade' has yet to completely displace the earlier model.

Under capitalism, production is for exchange not for use. This does not mean that what is produced is useless but that the dominant characteristic of a good as a commodity is its exchangeability. The conditions under which a commodity appears to be exchangeable includes the existence of guaranteed, effective demand. In so far as an individual capital gains a temporary, local monopoly then it has an incentive to restrict production to increase its price; on the other hand if competition is fierce then many capitals may find themselves accumulating inventories and working below capacity. In either case, communists can point to the ability immediately to increase production for mass consumption by putting unemployed people to work with existing machinery. A parallel with Keynesian aggregate demand stimulation is clear, but communists would stress the physical distribution of goods towards working class people on a basis of right through a system of rationing , rather than more indirect measures such as general tax reductions.

The markets for labour power are closest to what defines the working class for communists. The necessity to exchange the general ability to work for money in the terms of capital is the most striking evidence of the powerlessness of the mass of people in capitalist society. The attack on this powerlessness would seem a natural priority for communists. It would be hoped that this attack would prove even more effective than raising consumption levels in consolidating working class power throughout society. The communist concept of 'workers' control' in large-scale industry goes far beyond the proposals for dispersed shareholding and participation put forward by subjective preference theory and cost-of-production theory respectively. But the concept has to be made practical in the face of opposition from conventional trade unionists, skilled in oppositional tactics to maintain the conditions of their own members, and the need to co-ordinate and secure supplies from all productive enterprises in the general working class interest. Syndicalism failed to arrive at a convincing resolution of the tension between control at the workplace and control from the State and stressed control at the workplace. Bolshevism moved in the opposite direction, despite initial emphasis on the importance of worker soviets.

In conclusion, the problems of the communist economic revolution can be understood as deriving from the difficulty of deciding priorities between a number of areas for taking direct control. All areas of the economy have their own attractions and problems in theory or practice and no particular area can guarantee that control there automatically will bring control elsewhere. In the end, communists have to give themselves room to make mistakes and act determinedly in fast-developing emergencies. Economic rules cannot give that room on their own. Communists must be concerned with the exercise of power to secure that room for manoeuvre. And it is to this question of the exercise of power, and the consequent implications for coercion, that we shall turn in the next section.

9.4 Socialism as the transition to communism

Communists want power to abolish the control of capital over working people and move towards a more peaceful and egalitarian world order in which people give according to their abilities and receive according to their needs. The commodity relationship is fundamental to understanding capitalism as an unequal, violent world system where people give because they have needs and receive according to the profitability of their abilities. Thus, in terms of the exercise of power and the essential basis of people's relationship to each other in production, capitalism and communism seem to stand analytically at opposite poles. But between the analysis of these two opposites, in which communism is constructed in the mind as the antithesis of capitalism, lies the problem of real action in actual existing, complex and hostile historical situations. In section 9.3 we saw that a fundamental challenge to the commodity relationship as it appears in the form of markets cannot be left at the level of the economic and, in section 9.2, we saw that the State in a historically long-established capitalist society will consist of a large number of institutions well adapted to ensuring the reproduction of capitalist relations.

For all their claims to be acting finally in the universal human interest, communists have to accept that there will exist a period of transition in which at best they can claim to represent a majority interest. In communist terms, this transitional period is called socialism. Some would argue that socialism is a continuing process emerging within early capitalism and unevenly making gains and suffering losses throughout the capitalist epoch. Others, that a generally acknowledged, indeed violent, political revolution is necessary as a prerequisite for the start of the process of socialism. The advocates of peaceful transition, generally known as Eurocommunists, in the longest established capitalist societies had tended to dominate the debate in the 1970s, after the flurry of insurrectional activity in the late 1960s. In the economic sphere, they pointed to the continuing crisis as evidence to everybody, including many outside areas of conventional communist support, that capitalism was failing. Politically, Eurocommunism redefined the Leninist principle of socialism as 'the dictatorship of the proletariat' in a more benign manner, which stressed that the existing situation was also analytically a dictatorship, a dictatorship of capital, but one carried on through liberal-democratic institutions.

This redefinition, which tends to emphasise the historical part that the working-class movement has played in creating the liberal and welfare aspects of existing states, cannot deny though that what is sought is power for one group of people over others. Communists would accept that they are acting in a particular interest more willingly than conservatives and social democrats. However, they would claim that interest is a majority interest, despite their failure to achieve a majority of the seats in any national parliament following an open general election. Eurocommunists argue that the continuing, deepening crises of capitalism and the complete acceptance of the parliamentary road, demonstrated by a willingness to join coalition governments, can increase electoral support for communists substantially. Their communist critics stress that capitalist crises have regularly tended to be associated with political repression in the interests of capital in general against communists, leaving the latter greatly weakened. They argue that an exposed, electorally-oriented communist movement would be ill-prepared to resist. In both cases, either the limited exercise of State power or the organisation of resistance to hostile State power, there is the need to identify core support, as well as reliable allies. For communists, the core support is summarised in the term 'proletariat'.

The proletariat are people who work at the lower organisational levels in large factories on the terms dictated by capital, except where they have achieved limited areas of control through collective action. A proletarian works alongside many others performing complementary tasks, working with large units of machinery which demonstrates the immense productivity of large-scale industry, on a basis of immediate hire and fire at the discretion of others. This experience more than any other demonstrates the reality of interdependence, the myth of becoming self-employed, and the limitations of liberty in capitalist society. An experience which leads to, firstly, the rejection of individualism as the basis for effective social change and, secondly, the investigation of collective forms of action. But, on these strict experimental criteria, only a minority of the working population of any society can be considered truly proletarian. If socialism means the exercise of power on behalf of this minority, it is worth asking what other groups of workers can expect under communist rule.

The relationship between communists and self-employed workers, for instance small farmers, has historically been one of great suspicion. The self-employed embody the capitalist ideal of independent producers meeting in competitive markets to their mutual benefit. Communists may offer to attack the power of landlords, moneylenders and monopolies to extract resources at less than their full exchange value, but establishing the full operation of the abstract labour theory of value is establishing capitalism, not socialism. If the productive resources controlled by the self-employed are large and strategic (for instance, food supplies), then part of socialist development will be taking power over those resources by institutions representing the proletarian interests. That some take-over can be postponed though not cancelled is shown by the history of agriculture in the USSR between 1917 and 1930. However, the proposition that the take-over can stop short of full collectivisation of productive resources and still feed the proletariat is supported by the experience of China. It is worth noting that the self-employed in the major capitalist societies, though numerous, do not control large amounts of such strategic resources and thus can be treated as economically irrelevant by communists in those countries. The political significance of the self-employed in the ballot box does mean however that, at least, their fears of expropriation must be allayed by explicitly directing attacks against large capitals, especially if the targets can be labelled as foreign.

Many workers in the cultural sphere, including the mass media and education, tend to share the characteristics of the self-employed due to the relatively individualistic nature of their work and the low cost of setting up a workplace. But such workers cannot be treated as virtually irrelevant. An important part of the human experience from which people derive rules for present action are messages from other people and the specialist institutions concerned with communication. These images inform people about possible individual and collective efforts to achieve change and help them to decide whether such action is futile, worthless, dangerous or evil. The major communications institutions in capitalism are committed to capitalist values in a search for profits, are dominated by an individualistic ethos stressing creative genius, and simply suffer from the tendency for new ideas to lag behind new experience, which is implied in materialist philosophy. Thus, communists are likely to be very concerned with taking direct control over the activities of communications workers to remove these biases in favour of capitalist values. How far such control involves open repression will vary but communists generally accept censorship as an aspect of all States, pointing to the persecution of communist intellectuals, artists and writers under capitalism.

But it is not only the leading workers in communications who may lose elements of autonomy, and indeed control, over their work in socialist society. Managers, designers, engineers and many office workers have apparent privileges compared with workers on the factory floor. Communists argue that, in the vast majority of cases, these workers find the process of capitalist development eroding the small areas of control they previously possessed. The introduction of data-processing equipment is a form of de-skilling for many workers, making them subject to the requirements of machinery, performing routine tasks with little significant decision taking. But communists do not offer the restoration of individual and group privileges, instead they offer subjection to the collective demands of the whole work-force including the factory-floor workers who are at present largely excluded. A situation in which managers can be promoted or demoted by the rest of the work-force rather than vice versa is unlikely to appear attractive to the managers.

Even within the proletariat itself communists must face divisions. Women are often very limited in the work they can enter on an equal basis with men. Again communists believed that the processes within capitalism itself would diminish this discrimination. Certainly the textile industry of the UK has disproportionately used the labour of women, and this industry led the world expansion of British capitalism in the early nineteenth century. However, processes which result in women finding their main social position in wage-work rather in the home have proved very uneven in the UK and elsewhere. Certainly, the image of 'the family' in which a man does factory work and the woman does housework has always been suspect, but the collapse of 'family' has not gone as far or as fast as some communists expected. The position of all women, and many men from ethnic minorities, has not been given sufficient, explicit attention by communists to convince those who suffer from discrimination that socialist society offers them a significant improvement in control over their lives.

Thus, the broad definition of the working class as defined by abstract labour theory can be contrasted with the narrow definition of proletariat as the core of support for communist politics. Socialism as it is actually practised in self-proclaimed socialist societies reveals this tension between the claim to represent the universal interest and the fear that only a minority interest is really represented. But this is only parallel to the claims derived from the subjective preference theory of value that conservative politics are in everybody's individual interest, and cost-of-production theory that social democrats act in everybody's wider interest. In all three cases, the economic theory legitimates the political practice. There may be an economic reality to be discovered. However, current economic theories are all very convenient for substantial interests in present society, and thus cannot escape the charge that they are simply the rationalising ideologies of large groups of people seeking justification for changing society in their particular direction. It is therefore appropriate that we end this book with a chapter in which the practice of real politics is illuminated, but not dictated, by the three theories of economics.

Further reading

A vast body of writings of the great historical political figures we have associated with abstract labour theory have been made very widely available by the national presses of the USSR and China. Marx and Engels' *Manifesto of the Communist Party* (1975) is an early call to arms, whilst Marx's *Critique of the Gotha Programme* (1972) shows how unwilling Marx was to specify precisely the road to communism. Lenin's *What is to be done* (1975) sets the limits to trade unionism, parliamentarianism and regionalism as socialist tactics and, though it is not always inspiring, it does show the particular conditions in which the Bolshevik Party was formed. Lenin's *The Right of Nations to Self-Determination* (1976) shows the knots into which even the most eminent communists can get in coming to terms with the nation-State and Mao Tse-tung's rather enigmatic writing on this and many other subjects is well represented in Stuart Schram (ed.) *Mao Tse-tung Unrehearsed* (1974). Collections of readings which include more activist, but often unfashionable, writers like Trotsky and Gramsci as well as more academic commentators are becoming more common. Notable examples of this genre are Robin Blackburn (ed.) *Revolution and Class Struggle* (1977) and Tom Clarke and Laurie Clements (ed.) *Trade Unions under Capitalism* (1977). But those readers who want a reasonably accurate overview of some of the most famous Marxists after Marx, but who lack the time or inclination to go even to selections of original sources, should look at David McLellan's (1980) *Marxism after Marx*. Also, apart from journals directly associated with left political parties, it is worth mentioning Monthly Review (New York) and New Left Review (London) as important journals in their own right as well as prominent publishing outlets for socialist, if sometimes esoteric, literature. Significant, sophisticated, modern summaries of the nature of the State in socialism and capitalism from a communist viewpoint are Paul M. Sweezy and Charles Bettelheim *On the Transition to Socialism* (1971) John Holloway Sol Picciotto (ed.) *State and Capital* (1978) (see especially Ch. 1). These analyses take on lively current political form in Filo della Torre, Mortimer and Story (ed.) *Eurocommunism: Myth or Reality?* (1979), Peter Hain (ed.) *The Crisis and Future of the Left* (1980) and Miklos Haraszti *A Worker in a Worker's State* (1977), the last of which raises important questions about the nature of socialism arising from a particular experience in eastern Europe.

Summary 9.1

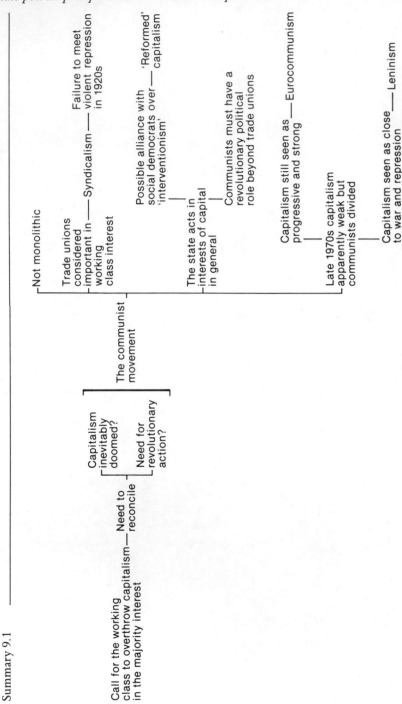

Summary 9.2

```
Materialist
theory based
on experience
    │
    ├── Denies ──┬── God-given human
    │            │   nature (subjective
    │            │   preference theory)
    │            └── Technological determinism
    │                (cost-of-production theory)
    │
    └── But ──┬── Historically
       emphasises │   defined power
                  │   relationships
                  │
                  ├── Dialectical method
                  │   (continued social change)
                  │
                  └── Thought itself
                      is historically ── Praxis
                      specific
```

```
In present epoch ── Capitalist ── Definition
commodity relation   mode of      of political
central              production   interest
    │
    ├── Worker:capital ──┬── Labour may
    │   conflict (exploitation)  opt-out
    │                    │
    │                    ├── Increasing rate
    │                    │   of exploitation
    │                    │
    │                    └── Any repression must
    │                        be compatible with
    │                        reproduction of the
    │                        labour force
    │
    ├── Capital:capital ──┬── Call for
    │   competition       │   protection
    │                     │
    │                     └── May lead to ── Arms
    │                         competition    expenditure
    │                         between states
    │
    ├── Industrialist:rentier: ──┬── C19th struggle between
    │   landowner:merchant       │   landowners and industrialists
    │   competition              │
    │                            └── C20th struggle ── The forms of
    │                                between         economic crisis
    │                                rentiers and
    │                                industrialists
    │
    └── Mental labour:manual ── Conflict of self interest
        labour competition      vs. class interest
```

Summary 9.3 _____ _____

| Economic theory and political practice | Theory of crisis not time and place specific | In 1980 main form of crisis either unemployment or inflation | Communist policy towards different markets |

Effectively
working class
asked to choose

Summary 9.4 _____ _____

| Communist goal of people giving according to ability and receiving according to need | The transition to such an epoch called socialism | Eurocommunism follows parliamentary route |

Peaceful
transition
or not?

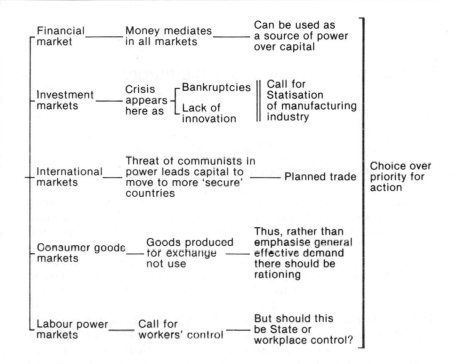

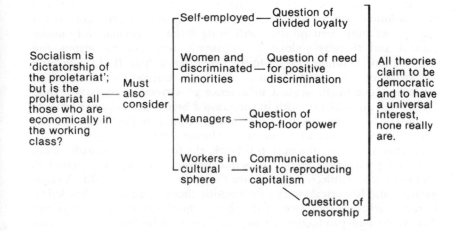

Chapter 10

Political practice and economic theory

10.1 Economics and politics

The purpose of this chapter is to show how the theoretical principles and broad policies discussed in previous chapters are reflected in current political argument. Economic theory is not independent of political philosophy. In Chapter 1 we noted Keynes's observation that, 'Practical men [or politicians]...are usually the slaves of some defunct economist' (Keynes 1973: 383), and provided an alternative interpretation: 'defunct economists are usually slaving to bring themselves to the attention of practical men'. The point is, that economic theory does not lead to political issues or practice, rather, the causation goes the other way. Politicians look to economic theory to provide rationalisations for policy proposals. True, the implications of a particular policy may be spelt out by theory, leading to ancillary policies to reinforce the original intention, but the initial choice of direction is not a theoretical issue. It is not open to verification or refutation by empirical evidence alone. This point is illustrated by the signed statement sent by 364 university economists, 76 of them professors, to the Prime Minister and Chancellor of the United Kingdom on 30 March 1981, condemning the government's economic policy. The statement said, 'There is no basis in economic theory or supporting evidence for the Government's belief that by deflating demand they will bring inflation permanently under control and thereby induce an automatic recovery in output and employment' (Huhne 1981). On the other hand, Alan Budd, a leading supporter of the Government's economic strategy and himself an academic economist, argued in defence of Government policy that, 'The long run evidence both in the United States and here has broadly supported both the link between money supply and inflation and the self-stabilising nature of economies' (Huhne 1981).

In terms of the argument of this book, the first quote is broadly from a cost-of-production theory of value perspective and the second in keeping with a subjective preference theory view of the world. A comparative and historical study of economic theory and policy has led us to the conclusion that each of the three schools, subjective preference theory, cost-of-production theory and abstract labour theory, represents the interests of a major group in society. It is no accident that these approaches emerged towards the end of the nineteenth century, at the same time as the joint-stock company became the dominant form of economic organisation. The three interests which became explicit were that of the *owners* of the means of production, that of the *managers* or organisers of the production process, and that of the direct *producers*. There does not have to be an explicit link between a particular interest and its rationalisation in the form of a theory about the operation of the economy. People do not consciously have to justify or excuse their behaviour by reference to a theory about how societies work, whether that theory be called sociological, philosophical, historical, psychological or economic. Rather their understanding of society and social processes reflects their experience and becomes what to them is 'common sense'. Hence the constant reference in economic writings to 'economic reality', as if that reality is common to everyone. To use Marx's dictum, 'It is not the consciousness of men that determines their being . . . it is their social being that determines their consciousness' (Marx 1970: 21).

This is most aptly covered by the concept of *ideology*, the idea that the experience of a particular group is presented as being common to all. This does not have to imply a conspiracy. We are sure that most people are quite sincere in their views, even economists! Rather it appears to be a 'natural' occurence and explains the congruence of views across a whole spectrum. Those who are 'left wing' in their views on the economy, also tend to hold 'left wing' views on politics, philosophy, history, etc. And similar distinctions to those outlined for economic theory in this book could be made for each of the other 'social sciences'. This points to an undervaluing of the study of ideology in social studies in general (see Eccleshall 1980).

The relationship between economic theory and political action has never been a wholly comfortable one: economic thought is characterised by logic and deduction, and political action by flair and experience. For much of the last 200 years the changes in economic thought have seemed relatively autonomous of more general political changes. Universities and Parliaments have asserted their independence from each other and claimed that independence as a virtue which allowed economics to be 'objective' and 'scientific', or politics to be 'realistic' and 'pragmatic', depending on whether an economist or politician was speaking. But the space between economics and politics can contract rapidly when a crisis situation is generally recognised and accepted in both spheres. The 1970s was such a 'crisis' decade. The UK started the decade with an economy performing badly in comparison with her neighbours in terms of economic growth, inflation (the general rate of price increase), registered unemployment and balance of trade deficits. And the media saw the series of coal miners' strikes against the policies of a Conservative government committed to increasing the role of markets and 'free enterprise' in the economy, the continuing poor performance of the British economy, and the ongoing violence in Northern Ireland, as symptomatic of the increasing 'ungovernability' of British society. In 1974 a Labour government took office and to tackle economic problems enforced a rigid incomes policy in the public sector and was forced to adopt restrictions on government spending in order to ensure continuing international credit from the IMF to cover the continuing balance of payments deficits. In the spring of 1979, after the media-entitled 'winter of discontent', the Labour Party was resoundingly defeated by a revitalised Conservative Party openly demanding a radical shift towards a free market economy.

During 1980 unemployment rose swiftly, along with some moderation in the rate of inflation, a balance of trade surplus primarily due to the domestic production of oil, and a negative growth rate with falling manufacturing output being the major component. In politics there was some debate about the costs of reducing inflation in terms of employment, but in 1981 one simple, widely held interpretation of UK politics was that it had become economically doctrinaire, subordinated to the dogmas of an elderly, American, money-obsessed economist, Milton Friedman, and a dead, German, class-obsessed economist, Karl Marx. The Conservative Government elected in 1979 brought one variant of economic theory to the centre of the political stage. Popularly called monetarism, this policy fundamentally expressed the principles underlying subjective preference theory and emphasised 'free', individual, exchange. By the end of 1979 the self-proclaimed 'left' of the Labour Party responded to the challenge and resurrected an Alternative Economic Strategy, stressing nationalisation of major companies, planned international trade (including withdrawal from the Common Market), increased government expenditure, and a bigger role for trade unions in planning. Such a strategy was labelled as 'Marxist' and parallels quickly drawn with Eastern Europe.

But a large number of people were unable to accept either of the strategies on offer and the search for a third position resulted in the formation of the Social Democratic Party which dominated the British political scene in 1981. At first sight this position appears as 'undogmatic' and 'pragmatic', which is how the social democrats portrayed themselves, but in practice their position is an expression of cost-of-production principles.

In the following sections we consider alternative diagnoses of the economic ills of Britain and the cures prescribed by each of the three schools of thought as embodied in different political programmes. For subjective preference theory/Conservatism we primarily consider the Conservative Party's manifesto for economic policy, *The Right Approach to the Economy* (Maude 1977) published in late 1977. For cost-of-production theory/Social Democracy we look at a book by David Owen, a leading member of the new Social Democratic Party, *Face the Future* (Owen 1981). And for abstract labour theory/Socialism we look at the recent work of another ex-minister of a Labour Government,

Tony Benn, and his *Arguments for Socialism* (Benn 1980). We also take a brief look at the issue of international development from each of the three perspectives.

The texts that we have chosen do not necessarily put forward the political principles of each of the three schools in an *unblemished* way. Each of the three schools of economic thought has been presented in this book in its most logically consistent form. This is not the same thing – and we cannot emphasise this too strongly – as saying that *every* economist can be neatly pigeonholed into one of the three schools. In the same way as a person's place in the social structure does not uniquely determine his or her consciousness, so a person's place does not necessarily express itself unambiguously in a particular set of wholly consistent economic ideas. But even if it does, the economic theory may not reflect precisely the political programme which it purports to support. The links between

- a person's relationship to the means of production
- his or her identification with a class or interest group
- the economic theory with which the person identifies
- the political programme which is supported

all may be tenuous. Thus the texts on which we focus attention in the following sections only more or less neatly coincide with the three schools of economic thought. We leave the reader to judge which are more, which less imperfect reflections of each school.

10.2 Subjective preference theory/Conservatism

'In everything we seek to do we must recognise the unique importance of each individual in the scheme of things. That is our instinctive outlook and it comes from the roots of Conservative belief. We shall look to people, not corporate bodies and institutions, to individual flair and drive, not to committed analyses and sector plans, to provide the spearhead of industrial and commercial recovery.' (Maude 1977: 5; unless otherwise stated all subsequent references in this section are from the same source). This statement is central to the economic manifesto of the Conservative Party, *The Right Approach to the Economy*. At the heart of their economic strategy lies individual tastes and talents, individual exchange and thus the 'free' market, and the emphasis is put on individual talents as the way to increase output. Again, to use their own words, 'All our ideas and proposals are designed to reinforce responsibility at work, not to undermine it. To this end the next Conservative Government will put into effect a realistic philosophy for earnings, incentives and ownership in order to encourage industry and enterprise.' (Maude 1977: 5). And they do not accept that there is an alternative interpretation of social life, using such phrase as '...the Labour Government has been forced to face *reality*', and '...the British people are now ready to turn back to *common sense.'* (pp. 4, 24; emphasis added).

They basically follow three policy proposals, as well as a general point, in order to try and make their view of a highly individualistic basis of social life more acceptable to those who apparently stand to benefit little from the action of free markets. 'For us a free society is a society in which property in all its forms is held by as many people as possible...We would like to see the habit of personal capital cumulation...much more ingrained in our society.' (p. 34). Thus their schemes to encourage the private ownership of local council-owned houses and their proposal that tax relief be introduced to encourage share ownership by employees.

Their three main lines of policy proposal, apart from this general theme of 'individualising' the economy are anti-inflation policy closely linked to government spending restraint, the reduction of taxation and the limitation of government involvement in employer-trade union negotiation with the aim of producing 'responsible' collective bargaining for wages through free market forces.

There is little specific analysis of inflation, but we are told that inflation is a greater destroyer of '...jobs, living standards and a stable order...' (p. 3) and there is no discussion about the precise links between the money supply and a generalised increase in the price level. Instead the general assertion is made that: 'Monetary targets openly proclaimed and explained, can have a crucial effect in reducing inflationary expectations.' (p. 9). In order to reduce the rate of growth of the money supply, and hence reduce inflation and increase individual freedom of choice over consumption, government expenditure has to be cut, 'Our intention is to allow State spending...a significantly smaller percentage slice of the nation's annual output...each year. The reduction will thus be progressive...We shall be looking for major savings in the cancellation of Socialist programmes...; in an end to nationalisation; in the reduction of indiscriminate subsidies; and in housing.... We shall also press for a major increase in the efficiency of administration in local government...' (pp. 10, 11). For what is left, progressively lower 'cash limits' will be applied to government departments. This policy has the added advantage in subjective preference terms of increasing the scope for competitive private enterprise, which will be more subject to 'consumer sovereignty' than subsidised, nationalised, monopolies.

'Lower taxation on earnings, capital and savings, to increase the rewards of skill and enterprise...' (p. 7) is the second major theme of Conservative economic strategy. It is assumed that reducing the taxation of people's incomes will induce them to work harder. With regard to personal income, they find it essential '...to restore a reasonable differential between those at work and those who are not' (p. 35) and allege that, 'More and more people, who receive almost as much in tax-free social benefits when out of work as they can earn in post-tax income from employment, are asking themselves the question: why work?' (pp. 25, 26). And to pay for these tax cuts it may be necessary to increase indirect taxes, to switch away from 'pay-as-you-earn' taxes, like income tax, and move more towards 'pay-as-you-spend' taxes like VAT.

In addition to providing incentives to work harder it is alleged that lower taxes would divert people's attention away from tax avoidance, 'moonlighting' and trying to pursue second jobs, which detracts from their ability to do '...the basic regular work that needs doing in a healthy economy.' (p. 25). As a general rule, the taxation system should not be used to redistribute income and wealth or indulge in what they call '...social engineering...' (p. 23), as a '...*bad tax* system creates feelings of injustice and discourages effort. It destroys some businesses and acts as a blight on others – as is clearly reflected in the stagnation of British industry over the past four years.' (p. 29; emphasis added).Broadly a 'bad' tax system is identified as one with high rates of marginal taxation on large incomes.

In addition to promoting incentive by reducing taxation, they seek to encourage productive enterprise by reducing legal restrictions on economic behaviour, intending '...to review the full range of health, safety and other regulations' (p. 48). With regard to regional policy, the aim of which has been to encourage industry to invest in depressed areas to provide employment opportunities by subsidies, the Conservative manifesto considers that there has been too much attention paid in the past to 'problem areas', and not enough attention paid to the general 'climate' for enterprise. And in keeping with their theory of production, that production is an expression of innate individual talents, they pay particular emphasis to encouraging small firms, believing that there is enough 'skill and entrepreneurial ability' in the 'depressed' regions to solve their unemployment problems as long as these talents are given sufficient opportunity to flower in an atmosphere of free enterprise.

That atmosphere would be considerably improved if the government, as far as possible, kept out of trade union – management negotiations. This is the third strand of their policy package and is particularly aimed at the incomes policy of all Labour Governments and some former Conservative Governments. The government should put no limitations on trade unions except to ensure that the unions are legally controlled in line with the principles of individual freedom, which for the Conservatives is interpreted as freedom for *individuals* to *exchange*. Except for the public sector unions which must negotiate within the monetary targets of the government and their cash limits on public expenditure, there should be no restrictions on bargaining for wages. Private sector unions should be well informed about government policy rather than consulted, allowing negotiations to be 'realistic' in terms of a trade-off between real wages and unemployment. And it may be necessary to have 'aversion therapy'. Any failure to learn the lessons of the subjective preference theory view of the 'real' world will lead to unemployment. As the Conservatives say, 'It is crucial that this reality should not be obscured by the Government stepping in between an excessive wage settlement and the consequence in loss of jobs, whether by relaxing its money supply targets, by increasing cash limits or subsidies, allowing funds intended for capital investment to be spent on meeting current pay claims, or by rescuing private sector companies crippled by excessive unit labour costs' (p. 15). But it may be that such lessons take time to be learnt. Unions may be politically manipulated, '…the moderate majority of trade unionists have become increasingly uneasy about the activities of politically motivated militants…and have recognised that a perversion of the deeply held sense of union solidarity can be brought by violent men to constitute a real threat to the rule of law and a stable society' (p. 21). And to prevent 'politics' from clouding the air they propose a voluntary code of practice on bargaining procedures. To ensure that trade unions know their place in society they are also against the 'closed shop' and the Bullock report into industrial democracy. The 'closed shop', where all employees have to belong to a particular union, they see as an infringement of the principle of individual choice, and the Bullock report, which proposed trade union appointed directors in private companies, as an unjustifiable infringement of the rights of ownership of investors derived from previous sacrifices of consumption.

At the heart of their policy lies individual motivation, the incentive to take risks and compete in 'free' markets:

'Britain's industrial weakness is not an accident. Nor is it due to any lack of managerial, technical or craft skills. It is our own creation. It is due to a combination of government errors, political prejudices, union attitudes and misguided social (masquerading as 'industrial') policies…Restrictive practices and over-manning all too often preserved by the threat of strike action, help to perpetuate this state of affairs – to the detriment of all. And with the smallest incentives in Europe (apart, perhaps, from Sweden) management is hardly well geared for the job of putting all this right' (p. 41).

Milton Friedman brings out the principles even more eloquently when he argues that economic progress is the result of '…the qualities of people, their inventiveness, thrift and responsibility' (Friedman 1980: 145) and therefore dependent upon government policies which promote competition, private enterprise and free trade, resulting in high rewards to enterprising private initiatives. To achieve this, government activity has to be held within strict limits, especially as governments have an in-built tendency to increase their involvement in the economy leading to a rise in the money supply and inflation. Firstly, in order to gain popularity, governments are anxious to spend money without necessarily taxing their constituents sufficiently or borrowing funds from the money market, which would have the effect of increasing the interest rate. Governments wish to provide '...goodies for their constituents ...' (Friedman 1980: 310). Secondly, there has been a commitment in recent years by governments to something called 'full employment'. This he thinks is essentially an illusion. In the modern dynamic economy, where technical innovation alters production methods and demand shifts between products, it is desirable to have a good deal of labour mobility. Under such circumstances, he asks, how can anyone accurately say '...what average number of persons employed corresponds to full employment?' (Friedman 1980: 311). And irresponsible governments received a rationalisation through Keynesian thought that to increase their expenditure above tax receipts and to increase demand will reduce unemployment. There is therefore a systematic bias towards running a budget deficit if the level of unemployment is taken as a primary policy target, which produces inflation, and therefore higher unemployment leading to a higher deficit. Thirdly, the monetary authorities have been 'mistakenly' more concerned with controlling the interest rate rather than controlling the money supply in an effort to 'fine tune' the economy and meet fairly precise employment targets. Friedman believes that such targets are meaningless and that the only positive way of influencing the rate of employment is to increase freedom of choice and thus individual initiative.

The result of government expenditure rising faster than taxation plus government borrowing has been an increase in the money supply. To finance the budget deficit the government indirectly allows its accounts with commercial banks to increase and the associated multiplied rise in the money supply as banks lend to individuals subject to minimum liquid asset rates, has led to inflation. And inflation, as all conservatives fear, is particularly serious. 'Unless we can achieve both a reasonably stable economy in the short run and a reasonably stable price level in the long run, our free enterprise economy is unlikely to be permitted to survive' (Friedman 1959: 136). Relative prices, for subjective preference theory, fulfill a crucial function in coordinating different individual economic decisions, in providing the raw data for choice. But people are not able to hear the signals given by *relative* prices because of the background noise given off by variations in the *absolute* price level. Inflation effectively introduces 'static' into the flow of information (see Friedman 1980: 36). And because economic progress depends upon individual motivation and if the government dominates economic activity and fails to provide a suitable environment in which individual motivation can flourish, the result will be thwarted expectations, a failure to cooperate economically, conflict between individuals and eventually a totalitarian government presiding over a stagnant economy by 'command' means rather than an open society where power is dispensed by free market forces among all of us as consumers according to our purchasing power.

According to Friedman, for three quarters of a century in Britain and almost half a century in the United States, Fabian socialism and New Deal liberalism has held sway. But now the tide is turning. Certainly in Western Europe in the 1970s there was a shift to the 'right' in the balance of power, and the rise in subjective preference theory in general and monetarism in particular is part of this trend. For them, control of the money supply is indistinguishable from a reduction in government intervention in the economy and the 'individualisation' of the economy is indistinguishable from a drift away from 'totalitarianism' and 'dictatorship'. Friedman applies this same logic in his analysis of international economic relations and the development of the less developed countries. He accepts the humanitarian ideals of increasing economic development, but interprets these ideals in a particular way: 'our fundamental objective is a world in which free men can peaceably use their capacities, abilities, and resources as effectively as possible to satisfy their aspirations' (Friedman 1958: 63). Again he sees economic activity as the result of individual decision making and government involvement in the economy as a disincentive to individual initiative. 'Free' enterprise is therefore a foreign policy objective. 'The aim should be to promote free markets throughout the world and maximum reliance by all countries on free enterprise in an environment favourable to competition and to individual initiative' (Friedman 1958: 73–74). And this environment is not helped by governments receiving economic aid, which far from helping in the drive towards economic development and the well-being of the mass of the people only serves to speed up the 'Communization' of the Third World.

Economic aid, which he distinguishes from military aid, is normally given in the form of loans and some grants, or personnel and materials for specified projects, to the governments of recipient countries. 'It has thereby tended to strengthen the role of the government sector in general economic activity relative to the private sector' (Friedman 1958: 66). Contrary to the popular opinion, that less developed countries suffer from a lack of capital for investment purposes, he asserts that where the 'other' conditions for economic development are present '...capital will be readily available' (Friedman 1958: 69). The 'other' conditions include incentives for individual initiative. He argues that the current developed countries became developed due to *private* enterprise. There was not a development policy as such:

'What is required in the underdeveloped countries is the release of the energies of millions of able, active and vigorous people who have been chained by ignorance, custom and tradition... These people require only a favourable environment to transform the face of their countries...what is required is rather an atmosphere of freedom, of maximum opportunity for individuals to experiment and of incentive for them to do so in an environment in which there are objective tests of success and failure – in short, a vigorous, free capitalistic market' (Friedman 1958: 71).

To this end, the United States in particular and Western countries in general should not give economic aid to less developed countries, but should set an example in their pursuance of free market policies. In particular, in the sphere of international economic relations, they should remove barriers which seek to protect domestic industries and allow the less developed countries to compete in these markets.

10.3 Cost-of-production theory/Social Democracy

The political concern of cost-of-production theorists is not so much creating the right environment for individual choice but more the active management of the economy to take advantage of opportunities offered by technical progress. We have argued in Chapter 7 that at the political level such economic interpretations are expressed by the social democrats. Here we consider a work by a self-proclaimed social democratic politician. The book, *Face the Future*, is by David Owen (1981) and was published at a time when the formation of a social democratic political party was being put forward as one answer to the economic problems of the United Kingdom. In our opinion the concept of a cost-of-production theory of value is essential to understand the economic strategy which arises from these apparently 'novel' social democratic policies.

Owen starts by facing the future with an assessment of the past, an assessment which regards the current situation of one of 'crisis'. 'Adversary politics continue to fan the embers of class divisions. Our standard of living...is falling behind that of our neighbours in Europe. The present economic decline is deepseated and shows every sign of continuing against a mood of despair and disillusionment. Except for a few short periods of reasonably successful management...the record overall is one of failure' (Owen 1981: 3; unless otherwise stated all subsequent references in this section are from the same source). In our cost-of-production language the description reads that 'politicians in the UK have failed to rise above the defence of particular distributional interests and thus the technological advance and rising output experienced in other countries has been blocked. This effect has become cumulative in the passive mass psychology and has been only slightly relieved during periods of relatively clear Keynesian policies'. And though concerned with the political representation of particular distributional interests in general, he is particularly concerned about the relationship of the Labour Party to the trade union movement. 'It is essential that a socialist party that hopes to win the support of all sections of society should have a measure of financial independence so that it is never wholly dependent on trade union support. It is no part of socialism to identify itself only with the interests of the trade union movement' (p. 69). According to Owen, the Labour Party should not be so dependent on trade union support if it is to put forward viable policies for utilising technological change. Such narrow support can only lead to undue attention being paid to distributional struggles which are likely to obstruct the implementation of new technology.

But trade unions are not the only villains of the piece. 'Any economic strategy aiming at a revival of the British economy should be accompanied by changes in the operations of our powerful financial institutions' (p. 142), and, 'The economy is dominated by large firms able to secure finance from the banks...or to pass on cost increases' (p. 166). But the strongest statement is saved for the major oil corporations, '...they have been given more consistent consideration...than by any other oil producing country in the world...The Whitehall bureaucracy and Ministers making the final decisions are far too sensitive to the special pleading of vested interests' (p. 218). All the major villains of cost-of-production theory are present: trade unions, financial institutions, imperfectly competitive enterprises and large multinational corporations. These institutions dominate formal politics and the distribution of resources, for instance, '...decentralised bargaining by different unions representing different crafts and skills perpetuates and often increases differentials' (p. 76). But there is also a role for indirect intervention. According to Owen the problems with the UK economy since the Second World War have not been due to inadequate analysis of the economy, but due to the failure of politicians effectively to implement consistent Keynesian policies. 'The failure of our economy has not been because the analysis of what was wrong was essentially flawed...the failure in most cases was because the economic policies were applied too late and with a timidity and reluctance to initiate sustainable change against the resistance of individuals and institutions' (p. 142). This seems to require the abandonment of Keynesian 'fine-tuning' of the economy through such mechanisms as the annual budget, in favour of a longer-run 'strategic' Keynesianism. This would be assisted by a move to proportional representation in politics, as a method of moderating the representation of particular distributional interests. The national parliament would then become more consistent and representative. 'The parties...will still disagree about many aspects of economic policy – such as, for instance, the question of the distribution of wealth – but the structure of the nation's economic life cannot be switched and changed with the rapidity of the past without weakening the country's ability to compete in world markets...' (pp. 14–15). The technical management of the economy should be left to professional economists, keeping politics for distribution. But in the end it is the discipline of the world market which is seen as an important check on the ability of any particular distributional interest, or conspiracy of interests, to exploit an advantageous bargaining position. International competition is crucial to forcing large imperfectly competitive firms, including nationalised industries, to minimise the average costs of production. The relative roles of government intervention, the market, the distributional struggle, technological innovation and increasing employment are brought out succinctly in the following quote:

'It will not be enough to improve industrial relations in the conventional sense, for this will not of itself achieve the orientation of the whole work-force towards the market place or a basic understanding of the need to compete commercially. Britain also requires a greater emphasis on the application of science and technology, on good management, the encouragement of small businesses... It means economic policies aimed at steady even if modest economic growth and increasing the demand for industrial goods supported by increased industrial investment' (pp. 72–73).

This strategic statement suggests that a social democratic government would only directly intervene in industry if the introduction of new technology was clearly imperative and unlikely to be undertaken by private interests alone. Broadly, there are three situations where such intervention might be needed, and Owen investigates all three sym-pathetically, as we might expect in the light of cost-of-production the-ory's stress on the smooth introduction of technological change. Firstly, a possible widespread reduction in the technological complexity of production, Secondly, changes in the techniques used in 'basic' industries, basic in the sense that their output is an input to many other industries. Thirdly, innovative development of risky new 'leading' industries with great dynamic potential but risky in that they require a large initial investment.

He considers the demands of those who call for less emphasis on increasing technical complexity, some of whom go as far as to call for the 'deindustrialisation' of society. 'There is a very genuine and prob-ably growing opinion that Britain should adopt a low growth strat-egy...and dismantle the industrial society' (p. 15). But he rejects this strategy and sees it as a product of the mass pessimism indicated in a previous quote. He is consistent with mainstream cost-of-production thought which sees increased productivity as a result of increasing tech-nological complexity, leaving a greater surplus for distribution. And this rejection of low growth prompts him to make one of his few 'visionary' statements: 'For people...to reject such a strategy...as a counsel of despair that will itself bring more misery than happiness they must be able to relate to a future...which holds the prospect of indi-viduals coming together freely to master the system under which they all will live' (p. 15).

Owen draws on Marshallian views about 'basic' industries, which are obvious candidates for increasing returns to scale, seeing these 'nat-ural monopolies' as legitimate targets for government intervention, although the precise form of this intervention is unspecified: 'In both energy and transport...there is not a true market...and talking about beating monopoly power is irrelevant. The task of national govern-ment, and in some of these areas also the European Community, is to try to bring different strands of policy together into an integrated

whole' (p. 179). And intervention should be extended to the technologically dynamic 'leading' industries, with valuable lessons to be learnt
from past joint ventures involving public and private resources. Again,
to a large degree, the demands of technological change can override the
differences between political parties: 'State involvement with the com-
puter industry has been a successful policy, sustained across successive
governments for sixteen years ...many of the techniques and strategies...could be similarly applied to other industries and in particular
to new technologies' (pp. 220–21).

But technical change may leave many people worse off. We have
already seen in Chapter 6 that, historically, most cost-of-production
economists went beyond simply concluding that production and distribution were analytically distinct, arguing that there was no reason
for people to be vastly different in consumption levels, especially as
industrial society grew more and more productive. Modern cost-of-
production theorists have generally been better at resisting subjective
preference arguments for the 'naturalness' of inequality in distribution
and analytical reasons for equality have been found by some contemporary economists who have devised broad guidelines for the provision
of help to the deprived. Thus, where deprivation has identifiable physical characteristics, they would advocate resources being channelled
through specialist institutions to particular target groups, e.g. the dis-
abled, the sick and the old. And with regard to the unemployed and
the low paid, there should be some form of State intervention as the
'free market' is as likely to exacerbate their position as improve it.

Total welfare government expenditure is what is meant by the term
the social wage. Distribution is here decided away from the workplace
and represents the purest case of Mill's desire to separate production
from distribution. Owen puts forward this idea as part of a strategy
to defuse the struggle over distribution. Another part of the strategy
is to 'blur' the distributional categories. Workers could have a stake in
their companies, having the right to share in profits, and hopefully
disputes would be less disruptively resolved. Cooperatives are another
form of 'harmonious', industrial organisation.

Owen consistently develops his argument in a cost-of-production
direction. The evolutionary development of technology is disturbed by
distributional struggles. Some intervention by the state is required in
production, especially in cases of 'natural' monopoly or abuses of
power by large corporations. But on the whole 'managers' should control production in the context of increased worker participation and
stimulatory Keynesian aggregate policies. And some institutional
reform is required to break out of the political mould formed by the
recurrent battle between those interests that represent those who
receive interest and dividends and those who receive wages.

The devolution of some power to local authorities and the centralisation of some power in the EEC Parliament and NATO is also seen
as a positive development. The institutional structure is made more

sensitive to the changing needs of technological change, allowing some interests to have a greater say, without fundamentally attacking any particular interest. If our factory is threatened by Japanese imports we ask the EEC to institute negotiations; if we are unemployed we may be encouraged to form a local cooperative; when we are old we can be cared for in the community; if the Soviet Union invades West Germany we can ask NATO to fire nuclear weapons in our defence. Institutions should be appropriate to the stage of development of the society which in turn depends upon evolutionary technical progress.

Cost-of-production and social democratic concern over development at the international level is most aptly expressed by, using its full title, The Report of the Independent Commission on International Development Issues, under the Chairmanship of Willy Brandt. More popularly known as the Brandt Report, this was published in Britain under the title *North-South: a programme for survival*. The report starts with the promise '...to suggest ways of promoting adequate solutions to the problems involved in development and in attacking absolute poverty' (Brandt 1980: 8). And these problems are not seen to be caused by the lack of the right environment for individual choice, as Friedman assumes, but can be overcome by applying the right social policies to promote technological development.

The acquisition of technology is crucial, not only to growth, but to the capacity to grow. The planning priorities and the economic and social objectives of a developing country will both determine the choice of technology, and be determined by it; a country will only be able to benefit from additional technology if it can absorb and adapt what it has already received, and if it can provide the 'welcoming structure' which can connect up new technology to old societies (Brandt 1980: 194).

But although governments can alter their domestic policy structure to 'welcome' new technology, the main restrictions to change are powerful vested (distributional) interests, requiring a changed national and international institutional framework to remove their malign influence.

In some areas the key issue is reform of tenancy... In others it is to divide large parcels of land among those who can farm it more intensively. 'In some situations the activities of middlemen tend to result in heightened price fluctuations at the producer level...tending to transmit instability back to the producers in aggravated form'. 'Intra-firm trade within multinationals...also opens up the possibility for corporations to impose restrictive business practices within their own organisations; they can limit the export of their affiliates, allocate their markets between nations or restrict the use of their technology or that developed by their affiliates'. But the international capital market has some major shortcomings...it is easily affected by crises in confidence...it is not easily accessible to the poorer developing countries...it tends, because of its terms, to exacerbate the problem of servicing and refinancing debt...and there are growing doubts as to the continuing availability of adequate private bank financing in the future...(Brandt 1980: 95, 146, 189, 213).

281

The distributional interests identified in these quotes, in terms of cost-of-production theory are landlords, various categories of merchants, the chief executives of large corporations and financial speculators, and a number of the report's recommendations aim at institutional reform to reduce the obstacles from such vested interests.

Adequate resources should be provided...to encourage and finance effective International Commodity Agreements which would stabilise prices at remunerative levels. 'Effective national laws and international codes of conduct are needed to govern the sharing of technology, to control restrictive business practices, and to provide a framework for the activities of transnational corporations'. 'The flow of lending from commercial banks and other private financial bodies to developing countries must be strengthened...The World Bank and other international financial institutions should assist this process by co-financing, by the provision of guarantees, and by using concessional funds to improve lending terms and reduce interest rates (Brandt 1980: 286, 288, 292).

The realistic hope, according to cost-of-production economic theory, is the final irresistibility of technological advance, which can be assisted by timely reform of political institutions. And logically the hope of social democrats, both nationally and internationally, must be the creation of qualitatively new moral orders from small quantitative changes in many directions.

10.4 Abstract labour theory/Socialism

Progress for abstract labour theorists involves a tendency towards greater collective control of economic life, a tendency which they argue is historically superseding the 'individualist' way in which economic decisions are being made at present. And this development takes place through struggle. It is fundamentally a question of *class power*.

Naturally, their understanding of the current economic crisis, which is defined in the UK by the falling profitability of capitalist enterprises, is in terms of the failure of existing institutions to reconcile individuals' search for profit with social demands for consumption, a failure which requires considerable structural change in society beyond indirect Keynesian demand management. Such an assumption underlies the recent writing of Tony Benn. He points out, that over the last 50 years there has been considerable technical development and that, '...our parliamentary, political party, civil service, trade union, educational and legal systems, all of them now under stress, were developed at a time when the machine capability was infinitesimal compared with what it is today' (Benn 1980: 109; unless otherwise stated all subsequent references in this section are from the same source).

Our social institutions not only arose in response to a technological structure but reflect a specific class structure. Social questions and theory are historically specific. In Benn's words Adam Smith put forward the free market as a better '...guide to the deployment of resources than the dictates of kings and the fumbling decisions of courtiers and land-owners who then held sway...He helped release the genius of the entrepreneur in the economic sphere and matched it by demanding the political enfranchisement of the class of capitalists who were then com-ing into their own' (p. 142). But society has changed. With technical development, enterprises have become enormous and although 'These great corporations still protest their ideological commitment to Adam Smith...they increasingly resemble the...feudal trading corporations which Adam Smith worked so resolutely to destroy' (p. 143). *Laissez-faire* economics is not universal to all social interests, as subjective pref-erence theorists believe. There is what he refers to as a 'log jam' of conflicting interests between industrial 'monopolies', free trade unions and universal adult suffrage and it is the struggle to face this 'log jam' which lies at the heart of current economic questions of inflation, unemployment, etc. Put in the simplest language of abstract labour theory, the forces of production have developed, and for this devel-opment to continue the relations of production and the political-ideological superstructure must change in keeping with the new situa-tion, otherwise they will act as fetters to future development. And these basic fetters are expressed in the forms of industrial unrest, social disorder, falling profitability, inflation, unemployment and interna-tional economic and political tensions. But behind all these symptoms lies the need for a shift in power between classes.

In particular there is a need for 'open' government and industrial 'democracy'. He argues that two trends have to be reconciled, the trend towards '...interdependence, complexity and centralisation requiring infinitely greater skills in the management of large systems than we have so far been able to achieve...' and the trend towards '...greater decentralisation and human independence ...' (p. 110). Or, the forces of production have developed to such a degree that there is now much greater specialisation in production with each producer serving a much larger market requiring greater cooperation *between* producers, and, at the same time, people have come to control, and expect to control, a much greater part of their own social existence. No longer are matters such as their livelihood simply to be under the control of an 'entrepre-neur' or a politician/manager.

Democracy (which in abstract labour terms means rule by the work-ing class) should therefore, be extended and he advocates a number of policies for achieving this. Firstly, the Official Secrets Act needs to be changed to allow greater disclosure of information thereby allowing greater participation in the decision making process by citizens. Sec-ondly, public records should not be kept secret for the 30 year period required by current legislation, we must be able to learn from any mistaken decisions taken by politicians. Thirdly, all ministers are required to take the Privy Councillors Oath, by which they are required to keep the processes of government and the Cabinet secret and this oath should be abandoned. Fourthly, the convention of Collective Cabinet Responsibility, by which any dissension by cabinet ministers over decisions taken is glossed over, should be abolished. Fifthly, the Prime Minister should be made more accountable to the electorate. At the moment he or she has a power of patronage and can appoint ministers (cabinet, state, and junior), peers who sit in the House of Lords, chairmen of nationalised industries, chairmen of Royal Commissions who meet to consider various issues, top appointments in the Civil Service and is also able to determine the Honours List, by which people are honoured for their contribution to society. 'For not one of these appointments is a Prime Minister constitutionally required to consult Cabinet, Parliament, public or party...No medieval monarch in the whole of British history ever had such power as every modern British Prime Minister has in his or her hands' (p. 126).

And other established institutions have to change. The House of Lords, the second chamber in the British Parliamentary system, approves laws without any democratic mandate from the electorate. Its members either inherit the right to sit in the House or are appointed for life by a Prime Minister. In his opinion the House of Lords should be abolished. And his opposition to Britain's entry into the European Economic Community is not over any particular economic benefits or losses from joining, though he thinks we have in fact 'lost', but over the issue of democracy. 'In short, the power of the electors of Britain, through their direct representatives in Parliament, to make laws, levy taxes, change laws which the courts must uphold, and control the conduct of public affairs, has been substantially ceded to the European Community whose Council of Ministers and Commission are neither collectively elected nor collectively dismissed by the British people, nor even by the peoples of all the Community countries put together' (p. 97).

The other constituent part of the reconciliation between the trends towards interdependence and decentralisation is industrial democracy, by which he means the collective working class control of economic activity, the direct producers controlling investment and social expenditure with reference to political priorities, not the market. Effectively, in this sense, industrial democracy means common ownership, and here Benn cites Clause 4 of the British Labour Party constitution, which commits the party 'To secure for the workers by hand or by brain the full fruits of their industry and the most equitable distribution thereof that may be possible upon the basis of the common ownership of the means of production, distribution and exchange...'(pp. 39–40). But he argues that this principle has never been effectively implemented since its adoption at the 1918 Conference of the Labour Party because the party itself is insufficiently democratically controlled. The economy has to be controlled by working people, not paternalistically managed in their interest. Like Friedman, he accepts that the half-hearted attempt at economic management since the Second World War can be held accountable for the current economic 'crisis', however it is defined. But this is because there has been too much compromise with the pre-existing power structure. The attempts politically to manage the economy should not be abandoned, but extended. And it is over the form of management that his differences with the social democrats (or in our terminology, cost-of-production theorists) are most clear. The extension of the management of the economy means increased public ownership of enterprises, but not the public ownership of the past, hierarchical bureaucratic administration, and a management controlling the workforce in its economic activity but only vaguely answerable politically. In an attempt to sustain the principle that fundamentally there are no differences of interest between people, that production and the organisation of the economy is essentially a technical problem about how to achieve the maximum output from given resources, cost-of-production theorists and social democratic politicians have argued that the management of enterprises should be in the hands of those who are best 'qualified'. The only possible source of conflict here is over the distribution of the output. Thus Galbraith argues with regard to the current coincidence of inflation and unemployment, that because trade unions have the power to increase their members' money wages and corporations have the power to raise the price of the final good, that there is as a result of this countervailing power a wage-price spiral. Governments, to try and curb the rise in prices using 'Keynesian' techniques, cut back on government expenditure and try to reduce private spending by increasing the rate of interest. This fall in aggregate demand reduces the demand for output and therefore increases unemployment but leaves untouched the 'institutional' determination of prices by trade unions and corporation managements. Thus we have both unemployment *and* inflation, the only remedy being the 'technical' solution of incomes policy (see Galbraith and Salinger 1981 Ch. 3).

In contrast Benn does not see any 'technical' solutions to the current economic ills. Policies are not apolitical and there is a fundamental difference in interest and power between classes. Economic rationality and therefore action is determined by these interests and he takes sides. Nationalisation must be linked to institutional change, allowing 'real' industrial democracy. Workers' self-management from the working membership of the trade unions, not a token worker on the board of directors. Consumer representation must also be effective and profitability cannot be the only criterion in business decisions. Further, nationalised industries must be accountable to the communities in which they operate, to their supply industries which depend upon them for their orders and to the plans of other nationalised industries. In short, there must be a *shift in power between classes*, not a *dispersal* of power (subjective preference theory) nor a *concentration* of power in favour of managers' interest (cost-of-production theory), nor any mixture of the two which still leaves the capitalist class in the 'driving seat'.

These proposals form part of a wider industrial strategy, with private firms coming under government 'management' through a system of planning agreements. Financial aid or orders from the government or nationalised industries would be contingent upon the firm fitting in with national economic priorities. But as part of this strategy trade unions themselves will have to change, and accept new responsibilities. Wage militancy is not enough, '…we must move towards free collective bargaining about wages, prices, investment, products, exports, manpower forecasting and product development' (p. 155).

The initiative must pass from directors to workers as with the industrial cooperatives that were set up in the early 1970s. Upper Clyde Shipbuilders, the Triumph factory at Meriden, the Fisher Bendix plant at Kirkby near Liverpool, the Scottish Daily News, all effectively chose themselves as candidates for cooperatives. The respective work-forces had a belief in their ability to organise themselves and a determination to protect their livelihoods. Unfortunately these cooperatives were set up in very unfavourable circumstances and because of the hostile environment into which they were born such enterprises need government help, and as yet the appropriate government machinery does not exist.

At the heart of Benn's argument is the proposition that 'knowledge is power' and therefore democracy is at the centre of the struggle for workers' power. The whole drift of 'left-wing' politics is towards démocracy and not as the 'right' would have it towards dictatorship. Benn argues, 'When the history of this period comes to be studied in greater depth it may well be that Britain's present problems will be seen to stem from too little democracy and not from too much' (p. 136). The process of social change is seen as a process of privileges becoming rights. At Runnymede in 1215 the barons won feudal rights from the king, in 1649 in the revolution the gentry and merchant capitalists won rights from the feudal state and in the 1832 Reform Act the middle class gained the vote, and this process is continuing.

The socialist movement has grown out of experience. Action has led ideas, or in Marx's words 'being determines consciousness'. But unlike the other schools of thought, he accepts that there are alternative interpretations of current economic problems and that the choice between them is not merely a question of empirical evidence. It is a political struggle between opposing interest groups and it is a struggle in which economic theory *per se* has little role to play, except as an *ex post facto* rationalisation and justification of action. He notes that there are three solutions to the current crisis mooted: monetarism, corporatism and democratic socialism. Or in the terminology of this book, he comes closest to recognising the schools of subjective preference theory, cost-of-production theory and abstract labour theory, with a strong preference for abstract labour theory.

Monetarism he sees as a return to full-blooded *laissez-faire* capitalism which can only resolve the present crisis by threatening working class institutions, and as such it must be seen as essentially violent and reactionary. Corporatism would attempt to work by the imposition of centralised controls from the top without changing the power structure and would be unworkable in present conditions. Democratic socialism, combining direct public investment in industry with self-management and expanded public expenditure with greater democratic control is seen as the only effective answer in the working class interest.

Essentially Benn is talking about the *development* of the British economy and thus he stresses the importance of the *social* relations of production, as power relations, being revolutionised to take full advantage of new *technical* relations of production. But, arguably, he deviates from mainstream abstract labour theory, by not stressing the historical specificity of capitalism as a mode of production and by treating the British economy in isolation from the world economy. Further, there is perhaps insufficient emphasis on the 'transitional' problems of moving towards a society based on production for 'use' rather than production for 'profit'. But this theme, of economic or technical development being inextricably linked to social processes of change, through 'revolutions' in power structures, is central to the work of Bill Warren, who has written extensively on 'underdevelopment'. His arguments have received their fullest treatment in *Imperialism: Pioneer of Capitalism* (Warren 1980)

He begins his argument by restating Marx's and Engles' position: 'Since Marx and Engels considered the role of capitalism in pre-capitalist societies progressive, it was entirely logical that they should have welcomed the extension of capitalism to non-European societies', (Warren 1980: 39). And the reason they could see capitalism in general as progressive is that their view of progress in the human condition could see great advantages in capitalist culture, '...if both the ability to make more effective choices and the option constantly to explore new worlds are regarded as desirable, then the fundamentally progressive moral and cultural character of capitalism cannot be doubted' (Warren 1980: 22). But capitalism is not only progressive because the social relations are compatible with more productive technical relations, but also because it provides a necessary stepping stone to a 'socialist' organisation of society. Thus the progressive policy is not to impede capitalist development but to supersede the capitalist organisation of society by making it 'redundant'. 'In respect not only of Russia, but also of the West, our Narodniks are incapable of understanding how one can fight capitalism by speeding up its development, and not by 'holding it up', not by pulling it back, but by pushing it forward, not in reactionary but in progressive fashion' (Lenin, quoted Warren 1980: 37).

For most of the post-war period it has been fashionable in 'left wing' circles to see capitalism and imperialism as the *cause* of the poverty of the 'Third World' not as part of the solution. But, as Warren points out in the spirit of rigourous abstract labour theory, '...anti-capitalist

287

ideology is not the same as socialist ideology' (Warren 1980: 20). These 'revisionist' theories all categorise capitalism in terms of *exchange* and not in terms of a *system of production* and conceptualise the supposed relations of domination between the rich countries and the poor countries in terms of one, or more, of the following: 'core-periphery' relations, 'metropolis-satellite' relations, unequal exchange and dependency. These theories do not see the root cause of the 'imperialist' problem as direct political domination through a colonial administration. Rather, market relations of exchange are somehow 'distorted' to the disadvantage of the 'underdeveloped' countries and to the advantage of the 'developed' countries. In contrast, Warren sees the main obstacle to development in the less developed countries as the difficulty of transforming rural social relations to *commodity* relations. 'One of the main reasons for the relative failure of agriculture is that it is much easier to erect a modern industrial structure on a backward rural base than to transform the rural base itself' (Warren 1980: 237). It is a problem of the internal dynamics of power structures in society, not external domination which perpetuates relative backwardness.

Warren is optimistic about the future of such societies: '...a gradual social revolution in agriculture has been under way, which is steadily creating a social framework within which the already advanced technical revolution can realise its potential' (Warren 1980: 237). This revolution is going hand in hand with the consolidation of the position of the 'industrial bourgeoisie' in many countries in Asia, Africa and Latin America, and thus the extension of commodity relations, or production for exchange, and the greater social interdependence and rising physical productivity of such societies. And he asserts that, 'There is no evidence that any process of underdevelopment has occurred in modern times...definitions of underdevelopment...almost invariably emphasise such features as mass unemployment, chronic underemployment, shanty towns, gross overcrowding, pressure on land, and so on. All these evils, however, stem from population growth...which is the most fundamental indicator of *improvement* in living standards...' (Warren 1980: 113).

Because of an improvement in their material position, more adults live longer than before and fewer babies die before the age of five. He argues that the long-term effects and benefits of population growth are going to be in the form of beneficial modifications to the social organisation of production leading to higher productivity in physical terms. 'Indeed, future historians will likely consider the population explosion one of the crucial causes of the unprecedented advance in human welfare achieved during the twentieth century, its effects in stimulating the reorganisation of human society (especially backward societies) so as to produce an ever greater volume of output far outweighing any initial per capita stagnation or decline' (Warren 1980: 131).

Warren's optimism about current capitalist development is unfashionable, but it does follow the rigorous conclusions of the abstract labour theory of value and also finds an echo in Benn's analysis of the current situation. 'The debate about democratic socialism which is now in progress in Britain is also taking place all over the world and its appeal is so great that it will prevail over both capitalism and communism' (Benn 1980: 141). Our aim in this book has not been to stifle or preclude such theoretical debates but to provide a framework in which all the vital discussions of today can be understood and that many more people can actively participate in them. A greater understanding of one's own implied basic principles and those of opponents is crucial to such participation.

Bibliography

(Where applicable, the details of publication in the United States are put in brackets after each reference.)

Ackley, G. (1967) *Macroeconomic Theory* (Macmillan, New York)

Anderson, P. (1974) *Lineages of the Absolutist State*, New Left Books, London, (Schocken, New York, 1979)

Archibald, G. C. (ed.) (1971) *The Theory of the Firm*, Penguin, Harmondsworth

Armstrong, P., Glyn, A. and Harrison, J. (1978) 'In defence of value', *Capital and Class*, No. 5

Arrighi, G. (1978) 'The roots of the present recession', *New Left Review*, No. 11

Atkinson, A. B. (1975) *The Economics of Inequality*, Oxford University Press, Oxford and New York

Atkinson, A. B. (1973) *Wealth, Income and Inequality*, Penguin, Harmondsworth

Ball, R. J. and Doyle, P. (eds) (1969) *Inflation*, Penguin, Harmondsworth

Balogh, T. (1970) *Labour and Inflation*, Fabian Tract 403, Fabian Society, London

Baran, P. A. and Sweezy, P. M. (1968) *Monopoly Capital*, Penguin, Harmondsworth, (1968, Monthly Review Press, New York)

Baran, P. (1968) *The Political Economy of Growth*, Monthly Review Press, New York

Barber, W. J. (1967) *A History of Economic Thought*, Penguin, Harmondsworth (1977, Penguin, Baltimore)

Bator, F. J. (1957) 'The simple analytics of welfare maximization', *American Economic Review*, No. 47. Also in Kamerschen, D.R. (ed.) (1969)

Bauer, P. T. (1976) *Dissent on Development*, Weidenfeld and Nicolson, London (1972, Harvard University Press, Cambridge, Mass.)

Baumol, W. J. (1962) 'On the theory of expansion of the firm' *American Economic Review*, Vol. 5, No. 52. Also in Archibald, G. C. (1971)

Baumol, W. J. (1974) 'The transformation of values: what Marx "really" meant', *Journal of Economic Literature*, Vol. 1, No. 12

Beer, M. (1939) *An Enquiry into Physiocracy*. Allen and Unwin, London (1966, Russell, New York)

Benn, T. (1980) *Arguments for Socialism*, Penguin, Harmondsworth

Benton, T. (1977) *Philosophical Foundations of the Three Sociologies*, Routledge and Kegan Paul, London

Bernal, J. D. (1969) *Science in History Vol. 4: The Social Sciences: A Conclusion*, Penguin, Harmondsworth (M.I.T. Press, Cambridge, Mass.)

290

Bhagwati, J. and Eckaus, R. D. (eds) (1970) *Foreign Aid*, Penguin, Harmondsworth

Blackburn, R. (ed.) (1972) *Ideology in Social Science*, Fontana, London

Blackburn, R. (ed.) (1977) *Revolution and Class Struggle*, Fontana, London (1978, Harvard University Press, New York)

Blaug, M. (1975) 'Kuhn versus Lakatos, or paradigms versus research programmes in the history of economics', *History of Political Economy*, Vol. 4, No. 7

Blaug, M. (1958) *Ricardian Economics: A Historical Study*, Yale University Press, New Haven, Conn.

Blaug, M. (1964) *Economic Theory in Retrospect*, Heinemann, London (1978, Cambridge University Press, New York)

Blaug, M. (1975) *The Cambridge Revolution: Success or Failure?*, Institute of Economic Affairs, London (1975, Transatlantic, New York)

Blumenberg, W. (1972) *Karl Marx*, New Left Books, London

Brandt, W. *et al.* (1980) *North-South: A Programme for Survival*, Pan, London (1980, M.I.T. Press, Cambridge, Mass.)

Braverman, H. (1974) *Labour and Monopoly Capital*, Monthly Review Press, New York and London

Briggs, A. (1962) *William Morris: Selected Writings and Designs*, Penguin, Harmondsworth

Brighton Labour Process Group (1977) 'The capitalist labour process', *Capital and Class*, No. 1

Brittan, S. (1975) *Participation without Politics*, Insitute of Economic Affairs, London

Brunhoff, S. de (1976) *Marx on Money*, Urizen Books, New York

Buck, P. W. (1964) *Politics of Mercantilism*, Octagon Books, New York

Bullock, P. and Yaffe, D. (1975) 'Inflation, the crisis and the post-war boom', *Revolutionary Communist*

Burnham, J. (1945) *The Managerial Revolution*, Penguin, Harmondsworth (1960, Indiana University Press, Bloomington)

Buzan, T. (1974) *Use Your Head*, British Broadcasting Association, London

Carey, H. C. (1848) *The Past, the Present and the Future*, Carey and Hart, Philadelphia

Carr, E. H. (1975) *What is History?* Penguin, Harmondsworth (1967, Random, New York)

Chamberlin, E. H. (1933) *The Theory of Monopolistic Competition, a Reorientation of the Theory of Value*, Harvard University Press, Cambridge, Mass.

Clarke, T. and Clements, L. (eds) (1977) *Trade Unions under Capitalism*, Fontana, London (1978, Humanities Press, New York)

Clower, R. W. (ed.) (1969) *Monetary Theory*, Penguin, Harmondsworth

Coleman, D. C. (ed.) (1969) *Revisions in Mercantilism*, Methuen, London (1969, Barnes and Noble, New York)

Deane, P. (1978) *The Evolution of Economic Ideas*, Cambridge University Press, Cambridge and New York

Dobb, M. (1963) *Studies in the Development of Capitalism*, Routledge and Kegan Paul, London (1964, International Publishers Co., New York)

Dobb, M. (1973) *Theories of Value and Distribution since Adam Smith*, Cambridge University Press, Cambridge and New York

Donaldson, P. (1973) *Economics of the Real World*, Penguin, Harmondsworth

Dow, J. C. R. (1965) *The Management of the British Economy 1945–60*, Cambridge University Press, Cambridge and New York

Eagly, R. V. (ed.) (1968) *Events, Ideology and Economic Theory*, Wayne State University Press, Detroit

Eccleshall, R. (1980) Ideology as Commonsense, *Radical Philosophy*, No. 25

Emmanuel, A. (1972) *Unequal Exchange*, Monthly Review Press, New York

Engels, F. (1959) *Anti-Dühring*, Foreign Languages Pub., Moscow (1966, International Publishers Co., New York)

Ergas, H. and Fishman, D. (1975) 'The Marxian theory of money and the crisis of capital', *Bulletin of the Conference of Socialist Economists*, Vol. 4, No. 2

Filo della Torre, P., Mortimer, E. and Story, J. (eds) (1979) *Eurocommunism: Myth or Reality?* Penguin, Harmondsworth

Fine, B. (1975) *Marx's Capital*, Macmillan, London, (1975, Humanities Press, New York)

Fine, B. and Harris, L. (1979) *Rereading Capital*, Macmillan, London (1979, Columbia University Press, New York)

Frank, A. G. (1969) *Capitalism and Underdevelopment in Latin America*, Monthly Review Press, London and New York

Friedman, M. (1980) *Free to Choose*, Penguin, Harmondsworth (1980, Harcourt Brace Jovanovitch, New York City)

Friedman, M. (1958) 'Foreign economic aid: means and objectives' in *Bhagwati J. and Eckaus R. S. (1970)*

Friedman, M. (1959) 'Monetary theory and policy' in *Ball R. J. and Doyle P. (1969)*

Friedman, M. (1953) *Essays in Positive Economics*, Chicago University Press, Chicago

Friedman, M. (ed.) (1956) *Studies in the Quantity Theory of Money*, University of Chicago Press, Chicago

Friedman, M. (1956a) 'The quantity theory of money – A restatement' in *Friedman, M. (ed.) (1956)* Also in Clower, R. W. (1969)

Friedman, M. (1977) *Inflation and Unemployment: The New Dimension of Politics*, Institute of Economic Affairs, London.

Friedman, M. (1970) *The Counter-Revolution in Monetary Theory*, Institute of Economic Affairs, London, (1972, Tranatlantic, New York)

Friedman, M. and Heller, W. M. (1969) *Monetary vs. Fiscal Policy: A Dialogue*, Norton and Co., New York

Galbraith, J. K. (1970) *The Affluent Society*, Penguin, Harmondsworth (1969, Houghton Mifflin, Boston, Mass.)

Galbraith, J.K. (1974) *The New Industrial State*, Penguin, Harmondsworth (1972, Houghton Mifflin, Boston Mass.)

Galbraith, J. K. and Salinger, N. (1981) *Almost Everyone's Guide to Economics*, Penguin, Harmondsworth, (1978, Houghton Mifflin, Boston Mass.)

Godelier, M. (1972) *Rationality and Irrationality in Economics*, New Left Books, London (1975, Monthly Review Press, New York)

Gramsci, A. (1968) 'The Turin workers' council', *New Left Review*

Green, F. and Nore, P. (eds) (1977) *Economics – An Anti-Text*, Macmillan, London (1977, Humanities Press, New York)

Hain, P. (ed.) (1980) *The Crisis and Future of the Left*, Pluto Press, London

Haraszti, M. (1977) *A Worker in a Worker's State*, Penguin, Harmondsworth (1978, Universe Books, New York)

Harcourt, G. C. (1972) *Some Cambridge Controversies in the Theory of Capital*, Cambridge University Press Cambridge and New York

Hardach, G., Karras, D. and Fine, B. (1978) *A Short History of Socialist Economic Thought*, Edward Arnold Ltd., London (1979, St. Martins Press, New York)

Harris, L. (1976) 'On interest, credit and capital', *Economy and Society*, Vol. 5, No. 2

Harrison, J. (1978) *Marxist Economics for Socialists: A Critique of Reformism*, Pluto Press, London

Heckscher, E. F. (1919) 'Urikeshandelns verkan på inkomsfördelningen', *Ekonomisk Tidskrift* (reprinted in English translation in *Readings in the Theory of International Trade*, 1950 Irwin, Illinois)

Hicks, J. R. (1937) 'Mr. Keynes and the 'classics'; a suggested interpretation', *Econometrica*, Vol. 5.

Hicks, J. R. (1946) *Value and Capital*, Oxford University Press, Oxford and New York

Hill, C. (1969) *Reformation to Industrial Revolution*, Penguin, Hardmondsworth and Baltimore

Hilton, R. (ed.) (1976) *The Transition from Feudalism to Capitalism*, New Left Books, London (1977, Schocken Books, New York)

Hobbes, T. (1968) *Leviathan*, Penguin, Harmondsworth and Baltimore

Hobsbawm, E. and Rude, G. (1973) *Capital Swing*, Penguin, Harmondsworth (1975, Norton and Co., New York)

Hobsbawm, E. (1968) *Industry and Empire*, Weidenfeld and Nicholson, London (1970, Penguin, Baltimore)

Hollis, M. and Nell, E. (1975) *Rational Economic Man*, Cambridge University Press, Cambridge and New York

Holloway, J. and Picciotto, S. (eds) (1978) *State and Capital*, Edward Arnold, London (1979, University of Texas Press, Austin, Texas)

Howard, M. C. (1979) *Modern Theories of Income Distribution*, Macmillan, London (1979, St. Martin's Press, New York)

Howard, M. C. and King, J. E. (1975) *The Political Economy of Marx*, Longman, Harlow

Huhne, C. (1981) 'Economists lay mass censure at Howe's door', *The Guardian*, 3 March 1981

Illich, I. D. (1973) *Tools for Conviviality*, Calder and Boyars, London (1980, Harper and Row, New York)

Johnson, H. G. (1975) *On Economics and Society*, University of Chicago Press, Chicago

Kaldor, N. (1960) *Essays on Value and Distribution*, Duckworth, London (1960, Free Press, New York)

Kaldor, N. (1935) Market imperfection and excess capacity, *Economica*, Vol. 2, No. 5

Kamerschen, D. R. (ed.) (1969) *Readings in Microeconomics*, John Wiley, New York and London

Keynes, J. M. (1936) *The General Theory of Employment, Interest and Money*, Macmillan, London (1965, Harcourt Brace Jovanovich, New York)

Kuhn, T. S. (1962) *The Structures of Scientific Revolution*, Chicago University Press, Chicago

Kuznets, S. (1965) *Economic Growth and Structure*, Heinemann, London (1965, Norton, New York)

Laclau, E. (1971) 'Feudalism and capitalism in Latin America', *New Left Review*, No. 67

Laidler, D. E. W. (1969) *The Demand for Money: Theories and Evidence*, International Textbook Company, Scranton, Pennsylvania

Lakatos, I. and Musgrave, A. (eds) (1970) *Criticism and the Growth of Knowledge*, Cambridge University Press, Cambridge and New York

Lancaster, K. (1974) *Introduction to Modern Microeconomics*, Rand-McNally, Chicago

Leijonhufvud, A. (1968) *On Keynesian Economics and the Economics of Keynes*, Oxford University Press, London and New York

Lenin, V. I. (1969) *Imperialism, the Highest State of Capitalism*, Foreign Languages Press, Peking (1969, International Publishers' Co., New York)

Lenin, V. I. (1976) *The Right of Nations to Self-Determination* Progress Publishers, Moscow (1977, Greenwood Press, Westport, CT)

Lenin, V. I. (1975) *What is to be done?*, Foreign Languages Press, Peking (1973, China Books, San Francisco)

Lenin, V. I. (1972) *Materialism and Empirio-Criticism*, Foreign Languages Press, Peking (1970, China Books, San Francisco)

Lichtheim, G. (1978) *A Short History of Socialism*, Fontana/Collins, Glasgow

Lindauer, J. (ed.) (1968) *Macroeconomic Readings*, The Free Press, Toronto and New York

Lipsey, R. G. (1971) *An Introduction to Positive Economics*, Weidenfeld and Nicholson, London

Luxembourg, R. (1963) *The Accumulation of Capital*, Routledge and Kegan Paul, London, (1964, Monthly Review Press, New York)

McClellan, D. S. (1976) *Karl Marx*, Paladin, St. Albans. (1976, Penguin, Baltimore)

McClellan, D. S. (1980) *Marxism after Marx*, Macmillan, London

Magee, B. (1973) *Popper*, Fontana, London (1973, Viking Press, New York)

Marcuse, H. (1964) *One Dimensional Man*, Routledge and Kegan Paul, London (1964, Beacon Press, Boston, Mass.)

Marshall, A. (1947) *Principles of Economics*, Macmillan, London (1980, Porcupine Press, Philadelphia PA)

Marx, K. (1969) *Theories of Surplus Value*, Lawrence and Wishart, London (1970, Breekman Publications, New York)

Marx, K. (1970) *Capital, Volume One*, Lawrence and Wishart, London (1967, International Publishers Co., New York)

Marx, K. (1970)a *Capital, Volume Two*, Lawrence and Wishart, London (1967, International Publishers Co., New York)

Marx, K. (1970)b *A Contribution to the Critique of Political Economy*, Progress Publishers, Moscow (1971, International Publishers' Co., New York)

Marx, K. (1972) *Capital, Volume Three*, Lawrence and Wishart London (1967, International Publishers' Co., New York)

Marx, K. (1972)a *Critique of the Gotha Programme*, Foreign Languages Press, Peking (1938, International Publishers' Co., New York)

Marx, K. (1973) *Wages, Price and Profit*, Foreign Languages Press, Peking (1965, China Books, San Francisco)

Marx, K. (1973)a *Grundrisse*, Penguin, London (1972, Harper and Row, New York)

Marx, K. and Engels, F. (1975) *Manifesto of the Communist Party*, Foreign Languages Press, Peking (1965, China Books, San Francisco)

Marx, K. and Engels, F. (1974) *The German Ideology*, Lawrence and Wishart London, (1976, Progress Publishers, Moscow)

Maude, A. (ed.) (1977) *The Right Approach to the Economy*, Conservative Party, London

Meek, R. L. (1962) *The Economics of Physiocracy*, Allen and Unwin, London (1963, Harvard University Press, Cambridge, Mass.)

Meek, R. L. (1968) 'Ideas, events and environment: the case of the French Physiocrats' in *Eagly R.V. (ed.)* (1968)

Mepham, J. and Ruben, D H. (eds) (1979) *Issues in Marxist Philosophy Vol. 3: Epistemology Science and Ideology*, Harvester Press Ltd., Suffolk (1979, Humanities Press, New York)

Mesarovic, M. and Pestel, E. (1975) *Mankind at the Turning Point*, Hutchinson, London (1974, Dutton and Co., New York)

Mill, J. S. (1852) *Principles of Political Economy with some of their Applications to Social Philosophy*, J. W. Parker and Co., London (1965, University of Toronto Press, Toronto)

Mishan, E. J. (1967) *The Costs of Economic Growth*, Staples Press, London

Mogridge, D. E. (1976) *Keynes*, Fontana/Collins, London (1976 Penguin, New York)

Moore, Barrington, Jnr. (1969) *Social Origins of Dictatorship and Democracy*, Penguin, Harmondsworth (1966, Beacon Press, Boston, Mass.)

More, T. (1965) *Utopia*, Penguin, Harmondsworth and Baltimore

Murray, R. (1977/78) 'Value and theory of rent': Part 1: *Capital and Class*, No. 3 Part 2: *Capital and Class* No. 4

Myrdal, G. (1953) *The Political Element in the Development of Economic Theory*, Routledge and Kegan Paul, London (1969, Touchstone Books, Louisville KY)

Nichols, T. (ed.) (1980) *Capital and Labour*, Fontana, London

Nicolaievsky, B. I. and Maenchen-Helfen, O. (1976) *Karl Marx: Man and Fighter*, Penguin, Harmondsworth

Ohlin, B. (1933) *Interregional aand International Trade*, Harvard University Press, Cambridge, Mass.

Okishio, N. (1961) Technical change and the rate of profit, *Klobe University Economic Review*, Japan

Owen, D. (1981) *Face the Future*, Jonathan Cape, London

Popper, K. R. (1969) *The Poverty of Historicism*, Routledge and Kegan Paul, London (1977, Harper and Row, New York)

Riazanov, D. (1973) *Marx/Engels*, Monthly Review Press, London and New York

Ricardo, D. (1971) *On the Principles of Political Economy and Taxation* edited by R. M. Harthell, Penguin, Harmondsworth (1972, Dutton and Co., New York)

Robbins, L. C. R. (1932) *An Essay on the Nature and Significance of Economic Science*, Macmillan, London (1969, St. Martin's Press, New York)

295

Bibliography

Robinson, J. (1962) *Economic Philosophy*, Watts, London
Robinson, J. (1933) *The Economics of Imperfect Competition*, Macmillan, London, (1969, St. Martins Press, New York)
Robinson, J. and Eatwell, J. (1973) *An Introduction to Modern Economics*, McGraw-Hill, London and New York
Roll, E. (1973) *A History of Economic Thought*, Faber and Faber Ltd. London (1974, Irwin, Homewood II)
Rosdolsky, R. (1977) *The Making of Marx's Capital*, Pluto Press, (1977, Humanities Press, New York)
Routh, G. (1975) *The Origin of Economic Ideas*, Macmillan, London (1977, Random House, New York)
Rowthorn, R. (1974) 'Neo-Classicism, Neo-Ricardianism and Marxism', *New Left Review*, No. 86
Sampson, A. (1977) *The Arms Bazaar*, Hodder and Stoughton, London (1978, Bantam Books, New York)
Sampson, A. (1975) *The Seven Sisters*, Hodder and Stoughton, London (1976, Bantam Books, New York)
Samuelson, P. A. (1967) *Economics*, McGraw-Hill, London and New York
Schram, S. (ed.) (1974) *Mao-Tse-tung Unrehearsed*, Penguin, Harmondsworth
Schumacher, E. F. (1974) *Small is Beautiful*, Sphere, London (1975, Harper and Row, New York)
Schumpeter, J. A. (1954) *History of Economic Analysis*, Oxford University Press, Oxford and New York
Shackle, G. L. S. (1967) *The Years of High Theory*, Cambridge University Press, Cambridge and New York
Shaikh, A. (1978) 'Political economy and capitalism: notes on Dobbs's theory of crisis', *Cambridge Journal of Economics*, No. 2
Shaikh, A. (1980) 'Marxian competition versus perfect competition: further comments on the so-called choice of technique', *Cambridge Journal of Economics*, No. 4
Simpson, D. (1975) *General Equilibrium Analysis*, Basil Blackwell, Oxford (1975, Halsted Press, New York)
Smith, A. (1974) *The Wealth of Nations*, Penguin, Harmondsworth and New York
Sraffa, P. (1960) *Production of Commodities by Means of Commodities*, Cambridge University Press, Cambridge and New York
Sraffa, P. (ed.) (1962) *Works and Correspondence of David Ricardo*, Cambridge University Press, Cambridge and New York
Stark, W. (1944) *A History of Economics in its Relation to Social Development*, Routledge and Kegan Paul, London
Steedman, I. (1977) *Marx after Sraffa*, New Left Books, London (1978, Schocken Books, New York)
Steedman, I. (1980) 'A note on the "choice of technique" under Capitalism,' *Cambridge Journal of Economics*, No. 4
Steedman, I. (1975) 'Value, price and profit', *New Left Review* No. 90
Stewart, M. (1972) *Keynes and After*, Penguin, Harmondsworth and Baltimore
Stigler, G. J. (1965) *Essays in the History of Economics*, University of Chicago Press, Chicago
Stigler, G. J. and Boulding, K. E. (eds) (1953) *Readings in Price Theory*, George Allan and Unwin, London (1952, Irwin, Homewood IL)

Sweezy, P. M. and Bettelheim, C. (1971) *On the Transition to Socialism*, Monthly Review Press, New York and London

Sweezy, P. M. (1939) 'Demand under conditions of oligopoly' *Journal of Political Economy*, No. 47. Also in Stigler, G. J. and Boulding, K. E. (1953)

Sweezy, P. M. (1968) *The Theory of Capitalist Development*, Monthly Review Press, New York

Therborn, G. (1976) *Science, Class and Society*, New Left Books, London (1976, Schocken Books, New York)

Thompson, E. P. (1968) *The Making of the English Working Class*, Penguin, Harmondsworth (1966, Random, New York)

Thompson, E. P. (1978) *The Poverty of Theory and Other Essays*, Merlin Press, London (1979, Monthly Review Press, New York)

Thomson, G. (1975) *From Marx to Mao Tse-tung*, China Policy Study Group, London

Thomson, G. (1976) *Capitalism and After*, China Policy Study Group, London

Veblen, T. B. (1932) *The Theory of Business Enterprise*, Scribner, New York

Veblen, T. B. (1957) *The Theory of the Leisure Class*, Allen and Unwin, London (1959, New American Library, New York)

Warren, B. (1980) *Imperialism: Pioneer of Capitalism*, New Left Books, London

Weintraub, E. R. (1974) *General Equilibrium Theory*, Macmillan, London

Williams, S. (1981) *Politics is for People*, Penguin, Harmondsworth

Williamson, J. H. (1966) 'Profit, growth and sales maximisation', *Economica*, Vol. 33, No. 129. Also in Archibald, G. C. (1971)

Winch, P. (1958) *The Idea of a Social Science and its Relation to Philosophy*, Routledge and Kegan Paul, London (1970, Humanities Press, New York)

Index

Index

Index